kitchen garden
month by month

LONDON, NEW YORK, MUNICH, MELBOURNE, DELHI

Project Editor Anna Kruger
Project Art Editor Alison Gardner
Senior Editor Helen Fewster
Managing Art Editor Alison Donovan
Design Assistance Francesca Gormley
Pearson Image Library Emma Shepherd
Picture Researcher Myriam Mégharbi
Production Editor Luca Frassinetti
Production Controller Bethan Blase
Editorial Consultant Jo Wittingham

US Editor Jill Hamilton

First American Edition, 2010

Published in the United States by
DK Publishing, 375 Hudson Street
New York, New York 10014

10 11 12 10 9 8 7 6 5 4 3 2 1

A catalog record for this book is available from the
Library of Congress.

ISBN 978 0 7566 5014 8

DK books are available at special discounts when purchased
in bulk for sales promotions, premiums, fund-raising, or
educational use. For details, contact: DK Publishing Special
Markets, 375 Hudson Street, New York, New York 10014
or SpecialSales@dk.com.

Printed and bound in Singapore by Tien Wah Press

Discover more at
www.dk.com

kitchen garden
month by month

ALAN BUCKINGHAM

CONTENTS

316 **Troubleshooter**
The place to turn to when things don't
grow quite as planned. How to diagnose
problems and avoid them in the future.

Introduction

Homegrown fruit and vegetables are enjoying a huge renaissance. Today, growing your own food is more popular than it has been for decades. Not since the days of our parents and grandparents has there been such a demand for kitchen gardens. Much of this rebirth of interest comes from our desire to live as healthily as possible—and the recognition that what we eat plays a vital part in that. It comes, too, from increasing concern about the industrialization of commercial food production.

Grow it yourself: fresh, seasonal, local

"Fresh, seasonal, local" has become something of a mantra for a new generation of consumers who care about the quality and provenance of what they eat. Fresh, because what could be better than your own homegrown food, dug straight out of the earth, or picked and eaten right off the vine, bush, or tree? Seasonal, because not only do foods taste better at their peak of ripeness or maturity, but eating them also puts us back in touch with the rhythms of nature and the passing of the seasons. And local, because crops we grow ourselves have been raised close to home, not flown in from faraway countries on the other side of the globe.

Eat homegrown food all year round

What do you need to know to begin growing your own fruit and vegetables? Probably not as much as you think. The important thing is to start with the basics. Dig over a patch of land, sow a few seeds and—unless you completely neglect your growing plants—you're almost certain to end up with something you can eat. But with a little knowledge, a bit of advance planning, and

(above left) **Eat** soft fruits as soon after you've harvested them as possible. It's true that blueberries can be frozen —but they taste so much better when fresh.

(left) **Pick and store** late-cropping apple varieties with care and they will keep for several months. Early-season apples, on the other hand, should be eaten soon after harvesting.

(right) **Growing too much** of one thing is a common mistake. Who needs two whole rows of kohlrabi? Far better to grow a wide variety of different vegetables, in modest quantities, as shown here.

(left, top to bottom) **Raspberries** need to be inspected and picked every few days if you want to catch each berry when it is perfectly ripe. **Companion planting**, in which flowers are grown alongside vegetables and fruit, creates a diverse habitat. Marigolds are well known for attracting aphid-eating hoverflies. **Leeks** are very hardy and provide a valuable winter crop.

some regular care and maintenance, there's no reason why you shouldn't be harvesting crops to feed you and your family throughout the year.

Of course, certain months of the year are more plentiful than others. In summer and autumn you're likely to be harvesting more than you can possibly eat. No problem—simply store it, freeze it, or give it away to friends and neighbors. In winter, crops become scarcer and for fresh food you'll be relying on hardy vegetables such as cabbages, kale, brussels sprouts, leeks, and roots such as carrots, parsnips, and rutabagas. But the leanest period of all— traditionally known as "the hungry gap"—unexpectedly comes in April and May. These are the months when all of last year's crops are over but this year's are not yet ready to pick.

Getting the timing right

Ask any kitchen gardener and he or she will tell you that the questions beginners most commonly ask are not about *how*. They are about *when*. Is it time to plant my seed potatoes? When shall I sow runner bean seeds? What's the best time to prune my apple tree? Should I cut down those raspberry canes now? Can I plant out these pumpkin seedlings yet?

In short, knowing what to do when is the thing that new gardeners grapple with most. That's why the largest part of this book is taken up with the "kitchen garden calendar." It takes you through the entire year, and tells you, season by season, exactly what you should be sowing and planting, what crops are ready for harvesting, what jobs need doing, and which pests and diseases to watch out for. Armed with this advice, you'll be well on your way to bumper crops of delicious, healthy, homegrown vegetables and fruit all year round.

(above) **Every square yard** of this small plot has been pressed into service for intensive growing of both vegetables and flowers: rhubarb, tomatoes, swiss chard, carrots, beets, globe artichokes, and sunflowers. Planting this densely helps keep down annual weeds, too.

(right) **Reusing and recycling** and never throwing anything away is an inextricable part of kitchen garden culture. Everything is saved to be somehow reused or recycled. Here, cut-off plastic water bottles protect tender runner bean seedlings.

(far right) **Conserve all your water** during hot summers—every drop is valuable. Water butts collect rainwater from the roofs of sheds, greenhouses, and other outbuildings. Use them to fill watering cans so that you can transport water to the plants that need it the most.

Kitchen garden know-how

Part of the fun of growing your own fruit and vegetables is the fact that you're always learning. There are new techniques to try, new crops and new varieties to grow, and new challenges to grapple with. And, of course, one year is never the same as the next. A spell of bad weather at the wrong time, or a long, hot, midsummer drought, can change everything.

Bear in mind that, however fazed you are by the complexities of soil pH values and trace-element mineral deficiencies, or by the mysterious techniques of tip-layering and spur-pruning, none of it is as hard as it looks. The general guidance in this chapter should put you on the right course. And, if you're still struggling, ask your friends and neighbors for advice. Most will be more than happy to share the fruits of their wisdom...

These stunning 'Firetongue' borlotti beans put ordinary, everyday, green French beans somewhat in the shade—yet they are just as easy to grow, and require no special know-how.

Assess your site

If you're starting a kitchen garden for the first time, you'll want to begin by getting some initial sense of its potential. What condition is it in? Has the plot been cared for or has it been neglected? If it is completely overgrown, can you deduce anything at all about how it was once cultivated? If you're lucky and the previous owner has cultivated it carefully, what sort of things were grown? How is the plot laid out? Do you wish to retain any existing features—fruit trees or bushes, compost bins, a shed, for example—or do you want to start fresh?

Taking a longterm view

Whatever sort of kitchen garden you have inherited, it's best not to rush into decisions too quickly. Unless the plot is evidently a jungle of brambles and weeds and you therefore need to make an immediate start by clearing it, take your time. Perhaps experiment with a few crops, and try to develop a sense of what to grow and where. Most importantly, look around at what your

(below left) **Clearing annual weeds** can usually be done by hoeing, but perennials and those with deeper roots will need digging up (see p.110).

(below) **Established fruit trees** are always a bit of a mystery when you start a new garden. You may have to wait until they fruit before you can be sure of what you've inherited.

A productive rhubarb patch is a great asset on a newly started kitchen garden. It's definitely something that you would want to keep—unlike the wheelbarrowloads of weeds, grasses, and brambles that you may have to remove in order to clear the rest of the plot.

neighbors are growing. If they're having success with certain crops but struggling to grow others, the chances are that you will too.

Aspect and situation

What is the overall site like? Is it exposed or sheltered? Is it on high or low ground? Is it set on a slope? If so, is your garden at the top or at the bottom of the slope? In which direction does the site face? Where does the sun rise and set, and how does it track across the sky —both in winter and in summer? All these things affect the growing conditions that you'll be able to offer your plants.

Soil and climate

Horticulturally, soil and climate are probably the most important single factors to consider. Cultivating fruit and vegetables is more demanding than growing ornamental garden plants. You are, after all, grooming the crops for just one thing: the production of a bumper harvest. So the plants need rich, fertile soil and optimum levels of water, warmth, and sunshine.

Early on, you'll want to establish what kind of soil you have. In terms of its structure, is it a heavy, sticky clay or light, sandy, and free-draining? Most likely, it is somewhere in-between. In terms of its chemistry, is it acid, alkaline, or neutral?

You'll find advice on how to assess your soil type on p.47, and details of how to improve it, if necessary, on pp.20–21. The effects of weather and climate are dealt with on p.14.

THE PERFECT KITCHEN GARDEN
What you do want:

- An open site that receives daylong light and sunshine.
- A sheltered plot protected from strong, prevailing winds.
- Well-drained, fertile soil that is rich in organic matter —ideally with a slightly acid pH value (below pH 7).
- A suntrap, perhaps tucked in against a south-facing wall or fence, for growing tender fruit and vegetables.
- Easy access to faucets or hand pumps for watering.

What you don't want:

- Tall, overhanging trees that block the light and shield your crops from both rainfall and sunshine.
- An exposed site that receives the full blast of strong winds.
- Poorly drained, boggy soil that is prone to being waterlogged.
- Soil so light that water and nutrients wash right out of it.
- Excessively acid or alkaline soils that make many crops hard to grow.
- Frost pockets that trap cold air and damage or kill off tender plants.

Weather, seasons, and microclimates

The general climate of the region in which you live is pretty much a given, and there's really not much you can do about it. In cool, temperate climates, you're going to have trouble growing heat-loving fruit like peaches, nectarines, and melons, as well as vegetables such as eggplants, cucumbers, and okra. In hot regions, you're likely to struggle with cool-climate black currants, cauliflowers, raspberries, and spinach. It'll certainly make your life easier if you appreciate your local climate and focus on fruit and vegetable varieties best suited to it.

Seasonal weather variations

From one year to the next, variations in weather are played out against the general background of your climate. They can be extreme—more so, perhaps, with the advent of global warming and climate change. A bitterly cold winter, an early spring, a series of late frosts, a midsummer heatwave, a prolonged Indian summer—all these are unpredictable and can play havoc with plant growth.

Temperature and rainfall

Of all climatic variables, temperature and rainfall are the most important. Temperature affects plant processes such as germination, root growth, photosynthesis, and the efficiency with which nutrients are absorbed from soil. In sheltered, sunny spots the air temperature is higher than in exposed areas, enabling tender fruits such as melons to ripen, but they may not succeed elsewhere. If you cover the soil with plastic sheets in winter and early spring, it will warm up more quickly and then provide temperatures suitable for seed germination earlier than it otherwise would.

Water is vital to plant growth. Much of the moisture that plants need falls as rain, soaks into the soil, and is absorbed through the roots. More crucial than total rainfall is the regularity with which it falls. More than any other plants,

vegetables and fruit require an uninterrupted, steady supply of water. A torrential downpour followed by a drought is no good to them at all. That's why regular watering is vital (see p.130).

Frost

Frost is extremely destructive. When the temperature falls below freezing point, the sap within plant cells expands and ruptures the cell walls. The effect is worsened if the damaged plants then thaw rapidly—in morning sunshine, for example. Fruit buds and blossoms, and the leaves of tender seedlings, are most at risk. Frost pockets—caused by heavy, cold air collecting in dips in the ground or at the base of walls and fences—are particularly dangerous.

Microclimates

Even in an average-sized garden, surprising variations in conditions can occur from one part to another. These are microclimates—a sheltered suntrap, an area protected by a windbreak, or a cool, dry spot shaded by a tree. And, of course, polytunnels, greenhouses, cold frames, and cloches are all microclimates that we deliberately create and control.

Midwinter is an unforgiving time. If hardy crops such as leeks and Swiss chard can withstand it in your area, then you should be able to grow pretty much anything.

Plot layouts and bed systems

The layout of your plot is important. Since it's an area in which you are going to spend a good deal of time, you want it to be as easy and efficient to "work" as possible. You want it to provide all your crops with the best growing conditions. You want a certain amount of builtin flexibility so that you are able to rotate the crops from one year to the next. And of course, you may also have requirements that aren't strictly concerned with horticulture—a kitchen garden may also provide a kids' play area, a place for a barbecue, or simply a spot where you can sit and relax on warm summer evenings.

Perfect, straight rows of vegetables are traditional. For the tidy-minded, there's a great satisfaction in imposing such order, but the soil will become compacted as you walk on it.

Raised beds keep you off the soil. If they are not too wide, you can do everything from sowing to harvesting from the paths, so you never stand on the soil and compact it under your weight.

Designing your plot

Find a pencil and paper, measure the overall dimensions of your plot, and sketch it out. Now block in the features that are going to stay in one place, at least for the foreseeable future: boundaries and paths, sheds and compost bins, fruit trees and fruit cages, and longterm perennial crops such as asparagus beds or rhubarb patches. Are they in the right place, or do you want to move them?

The next thing is to decide is whether you want rows or beds. Traditionally, kitchen

Grass paths dividing up beds undoubtedly look good, but they need mowing and edging regularly to stop the grasses from self-seeding and to keep the paths neat.

gardens were planted in neat, parallel rows or patchwork squares interspersed by trodden paths. It's an efficient use of space and because nothing is permanent it is completely flexible. However, constantly walking up and down over soil compacts it, which is bad for its structure.

The bed system

Laying out a permanent pattern of beds and paths will keep you off the areas that you are cultivating. The beds are solely for growing crops, not for walking on, and should be small enough for you never to have to stand on them. Likewise, the paths are always paths—so you can grass them or lay down paving slabs, gravel, or bark chips, if you wish.

If you regularly add organic material to your beds, the soil level will in time become higher than that of the paths. For this reason, raised beds are edged with boards, bricks, concrete blocks, or even tiles and slates to retain the soil (see pp.170–71). Deep beds are the same as raised beds, but without the edging.

THE "NO-DIG" SYSTEM

As its name suggests, this approach does away with the need for digging—at least it does once it's up and running. The aim is to create beds full of well-structured soil that are "topped up" each year with a surface layer of fertilizer and organic material. This layer controls weeds and is incorporated into the soil by earthworms and other organisms, rather than by digging it in. For the system to succeed:

- Begin by thoroughly digging the bed to open up the soil and improve drainage.
- Carefully remove all perennial weeds.
- Each year spread a surface mulch of well-rotted compost or manure.
- Disturb the soil as little as possible at harvesting.
- Use a sheet mulch if necessary to suppress any persistent weeds.

Crop rotation

With the exception of one or two perennials that occupy a permanent position (artichokes, asparagus, or rhubarb, for example), vegetables are sown or planted afresh each year. It's smart to grow them in different places from one year to the next. That way, you will prevent your soil from becoming exhausted by the same crop continually taking the same nutrients out of it. You'll also reduce the risk of pests and diseases establishing and becoming difficult to eradicate. There are numerous crop-rotation systems, which all group together crops belonging to the same family or sharing the same needs.

FIVE-YEAR CROP ROTATION

Most kitchen gardens are large enough to be divided into numerous, different-sized beds or planting areas. If so, you might like to try this longer-term rotation plan, which means that it will be five years before any one crop is grown again in the same place.

- Year 1: brassicas
- Year 2: peas and beans
- Year 3: potatoes and fruiting vegetables
- Year 4: the onion family
- Year 5: root and stem vegetables

It's not as critical to rotate vegetables such as zucchinis and squashes, or leaves such as lettuce, spinach, and other salads; they may be included in any rotation group.

THREE-YEAR CROP ROTATION

YEAR 1: peas, beans, and fruiting vegetables

Peas and beans are all legumes and share an important characteristic. They absorb nitrogen from the air and store, or "fix," it with the help of bacteria in small nodules on their roots. If you leave those roots in the soil after harvesting, the crops that you grow there next year can benefit from the nitrogen left behind. Along with brassicas, this group includes fruiting vegetables like eggplants, cucumbers, peppers, corn, and tomatoes.

YEAR 2: brassicas

This rotation group includes related crops such as broccoli, brussels sprouts, cabbages, cauliflowers, kale, and Oriental greens—as well as the lesser-known brassicas such as kohlrabi, radishes, rutabagas, and turnips. Moving them around a plot from one year to the next is particularly important because they are all susceptible to the soil-borne fungal disease clubroot (see p.324). Brassicas are all nitrogen-hungry, so grow them in the section in which last year's peas and beans were grown.

YEAR 3: roots, onions, and leaves

Root crops—for example beets, carrots, and parsnips, and tubers, such as Jerusalem artichokes, potatoes, and sweet potatoes—don't have a particularly high requirement for nitrogen. They are therefore ideal for following on in an area after brassicas, where the nitrogen levels in the soil will have been depleted. This rotation group may also include crops from the onion family, such as garlic, leeks, and shallots, and salads and leafy vegetables, for example lettuce, spinach, and Swiss chard.

(left to right) **Year 1 vegetables** could include eggplants, green beans, tomatoes, soybeans, sweet peppers, and broad beans. You could also grow peas, snow peas, and snap peas, lima beans, chilies, okra, and corn, as well as cucumbers, pumpkins, and squashes.

(left to right) **Year 2 vegetables** could include cauliflowers, cabbages, brussels sprouts, kale, radishes, and rutabagas—both summer and winter varieties. You could also grow calabrese, sprouting broccoli, kohlrabi, and turnips, as well as oriental brassicas such as Chinese cabbage, choy sum, mustard greens, and bok choy.

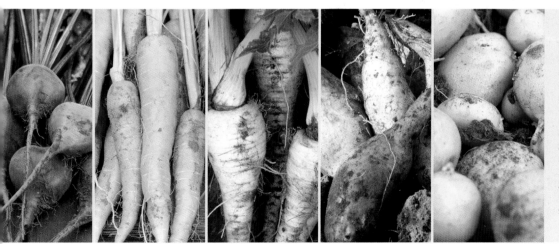

(left to right) **Year 3 vegetables** could include onions, beets, carrots, parsnips, potatoes, and sweet potatoes. You could also grow garlic, shallots, spring onions, celery, Florence fennel, Jerusalem artichokes, leaf beet, spinach, and Swiss chard, as well as chicory, endive, lettuce, and other salad leaves.

Composts, manures, and fertilizers

Growing fruit and vegetables makes greater demands on a plot of land than growing ornamental garden plants. Guaranteeing healthy growth and the production of generous crops, fruit, and vegetables depends on being able to extract a lot of nutrients from the soil. And of course, the more you grow, the more is taken out. It will come as no surprise, then, that all soils need some of that goodness to be put back. The way to feed your soil is twofold: first, by the addition of bulky organic material, such as composts and manures, and, second, by the use of fertilizers—either organic or inorganic, as you choose.

Manures and composts

These are organic materials that are composed of rotted plant matter and animal waste. They may vary in fertility. Some materials may be rich in nutrients, others may not. Some may be high in nitrogen, others high in potassium. The important thing is that, because they are all formed from bulky organic matter, when added to the soil they significantly improve its structure. They break up compacted masses, improve drainage in heavy soils, and increase water retentiveness in light soils. Well-rotted manure and compost can be dug or forked into the soil, or spread over the soil surface as a mulch and left for the earthworms to carry it underground and mix it with the soil.

Farmyard and stable manure

If you can find a good source, manure is among the most highly prized of all soil improvers. It is usually a mixture of straw and animal dung, although it sometimes contains wood shavings or sawdust too. It must be well rotted before you add it to your soil.

Garden and household compost

Compost is decayed and decomposed plant matter that has been broken down by microorganisms into a rich, fertile material that itself looks much like a dark, crumbly soil. See p.156 for directions to make your own.

Leafmold

Fallen leaves rot very slowly, so it's best not to add them in large quantities to compost heaps. Instead, pile them in wire cages or store them mixed with a little soil in plastic bin liners punctured with small holes. Leafmold is particularly good for aerating heavy clay soils.

Mushroom compost

Spent mushroom compost is the medium in which mushrooms have been grown commercially. It is usually still fairly high in nutrients, but can be alkaline so is not always best for limy soils.

Organic and inorganic fertilizers

Commercial fertilizers provide nutrients in a more concentrated form than composts and manures. Organic fertilizers are derived entirely from plant or animal material and rely on soil microorganisms to break them down so their nutrients can be taken up by plants. They include: bone meal; dried blood; hoof and horn; fish meal; blood, fish, and bone meal; and seaweed extracts. Inorganic fertilizers come from minerals or are produced by large-scale chemical processes. They are absorbed in solution, not via soil bacteria. Most important soil nutrients are nitrates (N), phosphates (P), and potassium (K). Others include trace elements such as boron, magnesium, manganese, and molybdenum. Most fertilizers include some or all, in differing amounts.

(left) **Compost everything** from your kitchen garden except diseased plant material, perennial weeds, and annual weeds that have gone to seed.

(right, top to bottom) **Manure and composts**: farmyard or stable manure, garden compost, leafmold, spent mushroom compost.

Must-have tools and equipment

It's surprising how few tools you really need. Of course if, like me, you are a tool junkie, you have far, far too many: our sheds are full of them.

If you're prepared to listen to any advice at all, here it is. Buy fewer tools. Buy the very best-quality ones you can afford. And look after them. That way, they will be a pleasure to use for years and years.

1 Fork
Most standard-sized forks have four prongs or "tines," each about 12 in (30 cm) long. They are usually square in section, although special potato forks have flat tines, sometimes with rounded tips. The handle grips may be D-, Y-, or T-shaped. Forks are also available in border, or—somewhat disparagingly termed—"ladies," sizes that are narrower and lighter to use, whatever your gender.

2 Spade
The rectangular metal blade on a standard spade usually measures 8 in (20 cm) wide and 11 in (28 cm) deep. It's invaluable for heavy digging. However, border spades are lighter and much easier to use; they usually measure 6 x 9 in (15 x 23 cm).

3 Clippers
There's a certain amount of snobbery about clippers, but it's worth investing in a good-quality pair since you'll use them almost constantly—for cutting, trimming, pruning, and even harvesting. Keep the clippers clean and sharp so that you make neat, tidy cuts and don't spread diseases.

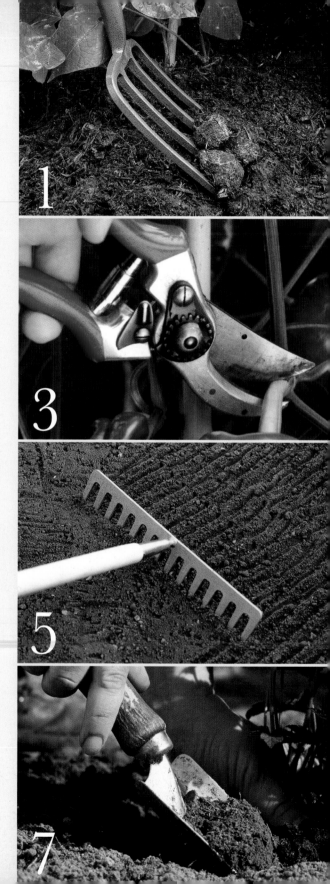

4 Draw hoe

With its flat blade attached to the handle by a curved, or swan, neck, the draw hoe is used to cut through weeds with a sort of chopping action. It's also useful for earthing up (potatoes, for example) and for marking out seed drills. The onion hoe is a small, hand-held version.

5 Rake

Most standard rakes have metal heads that are 12–15 in (30–38 cm) wide with 12–16 short teeth, or prongs. To be comfortable, the handle should be at least 5 ft (1.5 m) long. Rakes are most often used for leveling soil and breaking it down into a fine "tilth," ready for sowing or planting. There are also wider, wooden, plastic, or wire rakes that are useful for clearing up fallen leaves.

6 Dutch hoe

Also known as push or scuffle hoes, these are probably the most useful of the different types of hoe. They each have an angled, flat blade that can be pushed and pulled backward and forward, to slice off weeds just below the surface of the soil.

7 Trowels and hand fork

Although somewhat all-purpose, trowels are most often used for digging small holes and for planting out. They may have either wide or narrow blades. Hand forks are used to loosen the soil when weeding or lifting crops. Long-handled versions of both are available.

8 Loppers and pruning saw

Long-handled loppers and pruning saws take over when clippers are not strong enough. Most loppers will cut through branches up to about 1½ in (4 cm) in thickness. Any thicker than that and a pruning saw should be used instead. Grecian saws have curved blades and will cut only when pulled, not when pushed.

9 Ridger

A ridger is similar to a draw hoe, but instead of a flat blade it has one shaped like a reverse-plow. When using it, walk backward while dragging it toward you, in order to dig a furrow in the ground for planting or to earth up soil into a ridge.

10 Gloves

Good, strong gardening gloves are essential—both to keep you warm in winter and to protect your hands, particularly when pruning. Go for suede or leather in winter and for a lighter pair, made of cotton or a similar fabric, in summer.

11 Netting

Medium-gauge netting will keep birds off crops such as brassicas and fruit bushes, but you'll need a finer mesh to prevent insects such as cabbage moths and butterflies from laying their eggs.

12 Dibber

A dibber is just about the simplest tool you can imagine. It's little more than a stick used to make holes in the soil, for sowing seeds and transplanting seedlings. However, smart ones may have pointed ends and measurements marked on their shafts to indicate how deep the hole is.

13 Watering can

The best watering cans feel well balanced and comfortable to carry when full. If it's a long walk from your garden to the nearest water faucet, choose lightweight plastic cans. A long-necked can with a fine rose is useful for watering delicate seedlings; turning the rose upward creates a finer spray.

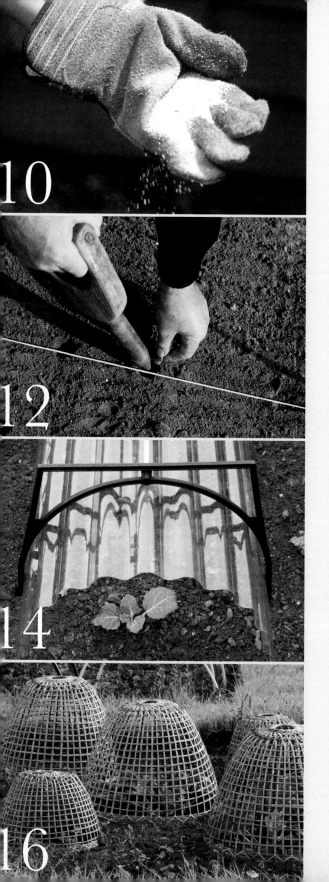

14 Tunnel cloches

Long cloches in the form of a tunnel are designed to cover a row of plants. They may be made of clear, rigid plastic or from plastic wrap that is stretched over wire hoops. They may be closed at either end to retain warmth or left with the ends opened to allow ventilation.

15 Cloches

Cloches are designed to keep plants warm, either to protect them from overnight frosts or to raise the temperature to the point where seeds will germinate and seedlings will grow. They are made of glass or plastic, come in the shape of domes, bells, barns, tents, or lanterns, and may be moved from place to place as required.

16 Bamboo cloches

Despite their open weave, bamboo cloches are surprisingly good at maintaining a microclimate in which plants are protected from wind and light frosts. They also keep birds such as pigeons away from young pea, brassica, and other seedlings.

YOU WILL ALSO NEED:

Sprayers
Pressurized sprayers that have a pump-action compression system are useful for liquid fertilizers, weedkillers, and pesticides. You'll need three: one clearly marked for each type of spray.

Wheelbarrow
For anything but the smallest kitchen garden, it's worth investing in a builder's barrow, which has an inflatable tire, a good-sized metal bin, and is tough enough to carry any load you may subject it to.

Cultivators
Three- or five-pronged cultivators are used for breaking up freshly dug earth, for loosening weeds, and for mixing in fertilizer or compost that has been spread over the surface of the soil. Long- and short-handled versions are available.

The kitchen garden calendar

Cultivating a successful, productive kitchen garden depends more than anything else on knowing what to do and when. Sow at the wrong time, plant at the wrong time, prune at the wrong time—and, however hard you try to straighten things out, you're unlikely to end up with a bumper harvest. In this section, you will find a guide to what to sow or plant and when, what to harvest, what jobs you should be tackling, and what pests and diseases you should be on the alert for.

Bear in mind, however, that the advice given here is inevitably generalized. The climate of the United States ranges widely, so precise timings will vary according to where you live, the microclimate in which your crops grow, and the seasonal fluctuations in the weather from one year to another. In mild regions, when blessed with a warm spring or a hot summer, you may be ahead; in cold regions, after a late spring or a persistently cloudy, rain-sodden summer, you could equally well be behind.

At the height of summer, in July and August, so many different crops may be ripening and maturing that you could well be harvesting something fresh from your kitchen garden every day.

January

Winter conditions vary widely across the country—cool and rainy if you live in the Southeast, Southwest, and along the West Coast, cold and snowy or dry if you garden in the Midwest and East. Only the mildest of days are likely to draw you out to the garden in January. That may not matter, because attempting to dig and work soil that is waterlogged will only compact it. Stay indoors, order the seeds you want for the year, and perhaps start a few by sowing them in a heated propagator. Obtain your seed potatoes and lay them out to sprout in a cool, light room. Buy shallot and onions sets ready for planting in February and March. And sketch out a planting plan for what you're aiming to grow and where you're going to grow it during the coming year.

Hardy winter cabbages are tough plants that can withstand even the coldest temperatures. They can stay in the ground, even when rimed with frost, until you are ready to pick them.

Top tasks for January

■ **Harvest** hardy winter varieties of cabbages, cauliflowers, and other brassicas, plus leeks, celeriac, and roots such as parsnips, rutabagas, and winter radishes. Rhubarb can be forced in milder areas.

■ **Spread** well-rotted manure or compost over empty vegetable beds.

■ **Warm up** areas of your seedbeds by covering them with sheets of plastic sheeting, carpet, or cardboard.

■ **Buy** and start to sprout seed potatoes.

■ **Winter-prune** established apple and pear trees.

■ **Check** fruit cages for damage after heavy snowfalls.

■ **Devise** your sowing and planting plan for the year.

Vegetables and salads

1 **Winter cabbages**
A welcome source of fresh greens in midwinter, winter cabbages can be left in the ground until needed—as long they are netted against pigeons.

2 **Rutabaga**
Lift any rutabagas still remaining in the ground before they grow too large and turn woody in texture. They can be stored (see pp.190–91).

3 **Celeriac**
Harvest celeriac as you need it. Or, if the winter is very cold, spread a protective layer of straw around the roots and leave them in the ground for another month or two.

4 **Parsnips**
In all but the very coldest regions, parsnips should survive the winter. In fact, they are said to taste sweeter after they have been exposed to frost.

5 **Leeks**
Harvest leeks just before you need them because they don't store well once lifted. Trim, then wash carefully to remove any soil trapped in between the leaves.

6 **Endive**
Both hardy, broad-leaved endive (shown here) and curly-leaved varieties will withstand the winter if covered with frames or cloches to protect them from the worst of the weather.

7 **Brussels sprouts**
By now, you should be working your way up the stems in order to harvest the sprouts as they mature. Pick and eat them before they grow too large.

8 **Kale**
All kale should be winter-hardy and can be harvested right through the winter months. Varieties such as 'Red Russian' (shown here) with its pink-colored ribs can look very dramatic on an otherwise empty plot.

9 Winter radishes
As long as there have not been any really hard frosts, you may still be able to harvest the last of your winter radishes. Eat them raw in salads or cooked, like turnips.

10 Jerusalem artichokes
Don't dig up artichokes until shortly before you want to use them. Unlike potatoes, they won't keep for long once they've been lifted. Scrub them clean, then boil or roast them.

11 Sprouting broccoli
Hardy varieties of purple sprouting broccoli sown the preceding summer should produce a long-lasting harvest that continues from winter well into the spring.

12 Winter cauliflowers
January should bring the first of your winter cauliflowers, the ones you planted out toward the end of last summer. The heads should have survived any hard frosts if you remembered to tie a few outer leaves over them.

ALSO HARVEST

Winter salad leaves
Corn salad (see p.252), land cress and winter purslane (see p.256) are among the few salads that can be grown outdoors for a winter harvest—although they will need to be covered during the colder months.

Chicory
If you lifted your Belgian or Witloof chicory roots last autumn and replanted them under lightproof covers in order to force new shoots, you may have your first, blanched "chicons" to enjoy at this time (see p.183).

Broad bean seeds that you ordered or even saved and dried yourself from last year's crop can be sown in pots now. Plant one seed to each 3½ in (9 cm) pot about 2 in (5 cm) deep and keep indoors until early to mid-spring, when seedlings can be planted out.

VEGETABLE SEEDS TO SOW INDOORS
- Broad beans
- Cauliflower (early summer)
- Leeks
- Onions
- Peas
- Radish
- Salad leaves
- Spinach

Sow or plant in January

Anywhere other than the mildest regions will be too cold and wet or snowy to sow seeds outdoors this month. They'll either rot or simply fail to germinate. Broad bean seeds sown under cloches or in cold frames are perhaps the only exception. Otherwise, it's best to wait for a month or two. Indoors is a different matter, however. Germinating seeds, in a propagator or in a heated greenhouse, will enable you to get a head start on the year.

Broad beans
If you didn't sow broad beans outdoors at the end of last year, it may be possible now—as long as the ground is not frozen. Otherwise, sow them in pots and keep them under cover, or wait until spring when it's warmer.

Fruit trees and bushes
Plant new, bare-root trees and bushes during the winter months, when they are dormant. Prepare the ground in advance by clearing all weeds and digging in plenty of well-rotted manure or compost. If conditions are too cold or too wet, keep the plants in a sheltered, frost-protected spot such as a shed, and wait until next month.

Garlic
Plant only in mild areas and only if the soil is not frozen or waterlogged. Otherwise, wait until February or March.

Onions and leeks
To give onions and leeks the longest possible growing season, sow seeds in modules filled with fresh seed or potting soil and keep them indoors at a temperature of at least 50°F (10°C). Transplant them outdoors in March or April.

Multi-sown onions
Sow seeds undercover in modules, with five seeds to each cell so the seedlings form a clump and can be planted out as a group.

Peas

For a very early crop of peas—as early as May, if you are lucky—sow seeds in pots, modules, or guttering and keep them indoors until you can harden them off and plant them outdoors in March or April.

Radishes

Radishes germinate and grow quickly, and can give you an early spring crop if you sow seeds in pots or modules indoors, or under cover somewhere where the temperature at night won't fall below about 40°F (5°C).

Rhubarb

Plant new sets or divide and replant old crowns at any time during the winter. Rhubarb will happily tolerate the cold but doesn't like being waterlogged.

Winter salad leaves

It's possible to harvest baby salad leaves all year round if you raise plants from seed under cover, in a brightly lit, well-ventilated spot such as a conservatory, greenhouse, or cold frame. For containers, use plastic mushroom or polystyrene fish boxes, or adapt wooden crates

Baby salad leaf seedlings that have been planted undercover in lined wooden crates or recycled wine cases (above) will now be showing their first true leaves. Thin them out at this stage to give the strongest plenty of space to grow.

by lining them with plastic sheeting. Drill drainage holes, fill them with multipurpose soil, and sow seeds generously. Try lettuces, rocket, spinach, kale, chard, Oriental leaves, and even a few herbs. You should have leaves large enough to harvest within about a month, and if you treat them as cut-and-come-again crops they should keep producing for three or four months.

Multi-sown onions are, as the name suggests, deliberately sown in groups of four or five seeds to a pot. When the seedlings are large enough, transplant the whole clump. They will grow together to form a tight cluster of bulbs.

SOW OR PLANT OUTDOORS

- Broad beans
- Fruit trees and bushes
- Garlic
- Rhubarb sets

Pruning apple and pear trees

Pruning can seem daunting. To many, it is a dark art, a mysterious, specialist skill. Really, it's not. If you follow this simple advice you'll find that in fact it's no more difficult than any other routine task.

Always prune established, freestanding apple and pear trees in the late autumn or in winter, when they are dormant. Before you make your initial cut, bear in mind what you're trying to achieve. Your first aim is to cut out any dead, damaged, or diseased wood. Your second is to remove any overlapping and overcrowded branches. And your third is to stimulate the growth of new fruit buds for the coming year.

Note that trees grown as columns and cordons or trained into espalier and fan shapes are treated slightly differently.

1

4

(left) **Use steel wool** to remove any dried sap from clippers and to keep the blades from sticking together. (right) **Rub lubricating oil** on your pruning saw to protect the blade.

"To many, pruning is a dark art, a mysterious, skill. Really, it's not."

1 **Remove branches** growing in toward the middle of the tree. Use a pruning saw to cut them back to the "collar" where they join a main stem. Aim to open up the center of the tree so that air can circulate freely.

2 **Shorten by a half** or a third any branches that have grown too long. Cut them back to a side branch (a "lateral") that faces outward, not inward. Make two saw cuts: the first from underneath, halfway through; and a second from above to join the first.

3 **Cuts should be made at an angle** so that the face of the wound slopes gently downward, allowing rain to drain off and reducing the risk of rot.

4 **Make your cuts as clean** as you can, and trim any torn or ragged edges. In winter, when the tree is dormant, wounds should heal without becoming infected.

5 **Remove old, tired branches** and thin out some of the recent, new growth by cutting back to shorter, outward-facing stems or short spurs. This should clear any overcrowding and create space for fresh growth.

6 **Cut out any new shoots** and stems that have sprouted from around the wounds of previous pruning cuts. They are unlikely ever to fruit.

PRUNING TIPS

■ **Use clean, sharp clippers**, loppers, and saws; otherwise, you run the risk of damaging the tree and spreading disease.

■ **Carefully clean the blades** of your clippers with steel wool to remove any dried sap.

■ **After cleaning your saw blade**, wipe it with a little lubricating oil to prevent it from rusting.

■ **Wear gloves** to protect your hands.

■ **Look for any branches** that are rubbing against one another. Remove the weaker one.

■ **If you're pruning heavy branches** that are likely to tear, get a friend to help support their weight, or cut them back in stages.

■ **Pause frequently**, step back, and review what you're doing. Ensure that you're maintaining the overall shape of the tree.

■ **If in doubt, don't**. If you prune the tree too hard, it will tend to put more of its energy into producing new foliage than fruit.

Jobs for January

Frankly, there's not much going on in January. It's largely a matter of finishing off routine tasks that you perhaps didn't complete before the end of last year—digging over your plot and adding organic material to feed the soil, winter-pruning fruit trees and bushes, and so on. If the weather is very bad, stay indoors and map out a plan for the year ahead and a wish list of what you want to grow.

Continue digging over your plot

As long as the ground is not frozen or waterlogged, complete your winter digging of any empty areas of your plot. Digging aerates the soil and encourages it to break down into smaller particles. Heavy clay soils may be too wet to work, however. If the soil sticks to your boots when you walk on it, keep off— and leave the digging to next month.

Spread compost or manure

Feed your soil with compost or well-rotted stable manure. Either work it in as you dig over the ground or—in the case of deep beds—simply spread it over the surface and let it become incorporated naturally.

Start sprouting seed potatoes

Buy your seed potatoes for the year. It's worth putting out the money on good-quality tubers rather than saving and reusing your own, because commercially grown seed potatoes are fairly sure to be disease-free. When you get them home, spread them out in single layers in egg crates or seed trays and store them somewhere cool and light. Within a few weeks the eyes will begin to sprout and form new shoots, or sprouts.

(left, top to bottom) **Sprouts** or tiny new shoots quickly form on seed potatoes. **Chicons** produced by forcing Witloof chicory indoors are a welcome addition to winter salads. **Tie cauliflower** leaves over the "curds" (heads) to protect them from frost.

(right) **Add well-rotted manure** to your soil to give it a good feeding and improve the structure. If you simply fork it over the surface, earthworms will gradually incorporate it into the soil beneath.

Continue to force chicory

Belgian or Witloof chicory roots dug up, trimmed, replanted, and then covered with pots to blanch new leaves can produce a valuable salad crop in midwinter (see pp.182–83).

Protect cauliflowers from frost

Throughout the coldest months, protect the heads or "curds" of overwintering cauliflowers from both frost and light by wrapping their leaves around them and tying them with string.

Winter-prune fruit trees

Unless it is very cold, January is a good time for pruning dormant fruit trees such as apples and pears (see pp.34–35) to remove older wood.

Winter-prune fruit bushes

If you haven't already done so, winter-prune gooseberry and currant bushes (see p.184).

Prune grapevines

This month may be your last chance to prune outdoor grapevines (see p.194). In many regions, by next month the sap will be rising and it will be too late; they will "bleed" if cut.

Check wires and ties

Inspect all stakes, wires, and ties on your fruit trees and bushes. Replace any that are worn or broken, and ensure that others are secure enough to provide support but not so tight that they constrict new growth.

FORCING RHUBARB

The new year is the time to start "forcing" rhubarb. By covering the crown of the plant in order to keep it in darkness, you will encourage it to produce shoots a few weeks earlier than normal.

1 Place a special forcing jar, an upturned pot, or even a pile of straw, over the crown before the first shoots appear, to block out any light.

2 When the shoots reach the top of the pot or pile of straw—after about 4 weeks—remove the cover to reveal tender, pink stems.

Clean pots and seed trays

Take advantage of the quiet month to give all your pots and seed trays a thorough washing and cleaning, using a weak solution of household bleach or detergent and a stiff brush. This will help prevent any diseases or viruses from last year carrying over to this year's batches of new seedlings.

Plastic pots and seed trays that have been thoroughly cleaned and dried are grouped by size and stacked in neat piles, ready for sowing seeds under cover.

"Keep your pots and trays clean and you'll be rewarded with strong, healthy seedlings."

January pests & diseases

Vegetables

■ **Slugs** can still be a problem in all but the very coldest of winters. Check for them in the outer leaves of cabbages and cauliflowers.

■ **Check nets** on winter cabbages, cauliflowers, and broccoli. You'll need to keep them in place all winter to keep off pigeons and other birds. Repair any holes and refasten any nets that have become loose, particularly after heavy snowfalls.

■ **Remove dead leaves** from brussels sprouts and cabbages. If they start to rot while still in place, they can spread mold and downy mildew.

■ **Check stored vegetables** such as potatoes, rutabagas, squashes, onions, shallots, and garlic for signs of rot. Watch for any signs of mice or rats.

Fruit

■ **Check for aphids** on cherries, plums, currants, and gooseberries. In a mild winter, their new leaves may start to unfurl toward the end of the month and are a seductive target for early attack. Deal with infestations as soon as you spot them, before they get out of hand.

■ **Spray fruit trees and bushes** with a plant-oil based winter wash to help control aphids, mites, scale insects, and winter moths. Spray once, then again a couple of weeks later.

■ **Check apple and pear trees** for signs of canker. Cut out any diseased wood.

■ **Renew grease bands** on the trunks of fruit trees if necessary.

■ **Net gooseberries** to protect the buds from waxwings.

■ **Spray peaches and nectarines** with copper fungicide. It may help protect them against the fungal disease known as peach leaf curl. Try to spray as the buds begin to swell but not once they start to open. Erecting a rain-proof cover can shelter them from rain spreading the spores that carry the disease.

■ **Check stored fruit** such as apples and pears for signs of rot. Discard any damaged or diseased fruit.

(top to bottom) **Slugs** are, unfortunately, still a threat to overwintering brassicas. **Netting winter cabbages** will deter pigeons. **Remove diseased** branches from fruit trees. **Take off dead lower leaves** from brussels sprouts to prevent the spread of disease.

February

February can swing from one extreme to another. Although the days are longer than in January, in some parts of the country, including the Northeast, February is the coldest month of the year. Gray, heavily overcast days with persistent rain, sleet, or snow can make winter feel never-ending. Then a sudden stretch of bright, sunny days can signal that the season is turning. Whatever the climate, there is a limit to how much you can do in the kitchen garden—don't be tempted by a few warm days because even in the South the heavy rains of February can wash away tender seedlings. If the ground is not frozen or too wet to work, complete your winter digging, improving the structure and composition of your soil by incorporating as much rotted-down manure and compost as you can. Warm up seedbeds in preparation for sowing and planting by covering them with sheets of plastic, old carpet, or cardboard.

Swelling buds and splashes of bright green, as the first leaves unfurl on fruit bushes and trees, are sure signs that spring is on its way.

Top tasks for February

- **Harvest** cabbages, cauliflowers, brussels sprouts, and kale, along with leeks, celeriac, parsnips, and rutabagas for warming winter stews.
- **Sow** seeds indoors to raise seedlings for planting out in the spring. Few seeds will germinate if sown outdoors now.
- **Plant** shallots and garlic.
- **Chit** seed potatoes.
- **Dig** over your plot and add plenty of well-rotted organic material.
- **Cover** seedbeds with plastic sheeting, carpet, or cardboard to warm up the soil.
- **Force** rhubarb and Belgian or Witloof chicory.

Vegetables and salads

1 Winter salad leaves
A wide range of salads can be grown outdoors for a winter harvest if they are protected with cloches or frames in cold weather. They include baby-leaf kale and Oriental brassicas such as mizuna (shown here).

2 Kale
All kales are tough and hardy, and are capable of withstanding most winters. Harvest the leaves and boil, steam, or stir-fry them, or add them to hearty winter soups and stews.

3 Chicory
Forced "chicons" of Belgian or Witloof chicory are a valuable salad crop this month. Grow them as new shoots from roots lifted and replanted last autumn, and blanch them under lightproof covers (see p.183).

4 Rutabagas
This month, you should lift any rutabagas that you haven't yet harvested. Although they are fairly indestructible, they will become too coarse and woody to eat—if they haven't already.

5 Winter cauliflowers
Cauliflowers will have stopped growing by the time you pick them, and should keep for a while after harvesting, especially if you leave some of the outer leaves in place around the heads.

6 Leeks
Leeks should survive even very severe winters. Lift them only when you need them because they don't store well once they are out of the ground.

7 Brussels sprouts
Sprouts should be still available for harvesting if you planted out a late batch in June or July of the preceding summer. Pick them one by one as they mature, or uproot the whole stem and use the sprouts as you need them.

8 Sprouting broccoli

Early varieties of purple sprouting broccoli are sown the preceding summer for harvest in the following spring. Pick the spears regularly to stimulate the growth of new shoots.

9 Parsnips

If the weather turns very cold, protect parsnips by spreading a 6 in- (15 cm-) thick layer of straw or bracken around them. If you don't harvest them now, they should last until next month.

10 Endive

Cut whole heads of winter-hardy endive or pick a handful of leaves as and when you need them. If covered with frames or cloches, the plants should continue to survive all but the very lowest temperatures.

11 Winter cabbages

Either leave hardy winter cabbages in the ground until you need them or cut them and bring them indoors for storage. Hang them up in a cool place.

12 Celeriac

Lift celeriac as and when you need it. Trim, scrub, and peel it carefully, because the tangle of roots often harbors slugs. Once cleaned up, celeriac is delicious boiled, mashed, or roasted.

ALSO HARVEST

Jerusalem artichokes
Lift the last of your Jerusalem artichokes now. Any left in the ground after the end of this month are likely to sprout new shoots and regrow.

Sow or plant in February

February can be an extremely cold month, colder even than December and January. It can therefore present a real dilemma. Should you sow and plant early, in an attempt to get ahead, but risk your seeds failing to germinate or young plants dying because the ground is too cold or too wet? Or should you be patient and wait till the weather warms up, but resign yourself to a slightly later harvest? It's probably best to hedge your bets and do a little of each.

Broad beans
Sow direct outside if the ground is not frozen hard, and indoors in pots if it is still very cold.

Brussels sprouts, kohlrabi, and sprouting broccoli
Sow the first early varieties indoors in deep modules this month. You should be able to plant them out in April or May.

Fruit trees and bushes
New, bare-root trees and bushes are still dormant and can be planted this month provided the ground is not frozen or too wet. Prepare the site in advance by digging a hole wide enough for the roots to spread out, and check the depth. Once the plant is in position, mulch generously to keep moisture in.

SOW OR PLANT OUTDOORS
- Broad beans
- Fruit trees and bushes
- Garlic
- Grapevines
- Jerusalem artichokes
- Peas
- Rhubarb sets
- Shallot sets
- Turnips

PLANTING SHALLOT SETS
Each shallot "set" will produce up to ten separate bulbs.

1 Loosen the soil with a rake and make a shallow drill. Press the sets into the drill about 7 in (18 cm) apart so that the tips are just showing, and then water them in and keep weed-free.

2 Once the leaves have died down, around mid- to late summer, lift the shallots carefully. Allow them to dry completely, either on the ground if the weather is dry, or on wire racks.

Garlic

Plant cloves of garlic now if the soil is not frozen or waterlogged. Otherwise, wait until next month.

Globe artichokes

Sow in pots and keep in a propagator at a minimum temperature of 65°F (18°C) until they have germinated. Keep them indoors until you can harden them off, and plant them out in April or May.

Jerusalem artichokes

Plant tubers directly outside in a single row somewhere where the plants won't overshadow other crops when they reach their full height. Protect with cloches if very cold.

Lettuces

For crops that will be ready to harvest in May and June, sow seeds indoors this month in modules or biodegradable pots. Thin out seedlings and then plant out under cover next month if it's not too frigid, in cold frames or under cloches or fleece.

Onions and leeks

To grow from seed, sow in modules and keep indoors at a minimum temperature of 50°F (10°C) to give them an early start. Transplant outdoors in March or April.

Peas

In mild areas, sow a few peas outdoors under cloches as long as you have warmed up the soil in advance by covering it.

SOW SEEDS INDOORS

- Broad beans
- Brussels sprouts
- Globe artichokes
- Kohlrabi
- Leeks
- Lettuces
- Onions
- Peas
- Radishes
- Rhubarb
- Salad leaves
- Spinach
- Sprouting broccoli
- Tomatoes

Radishes

Sow seeds in pots or modules indoors, or outside under cover as long as the temperature at night remains at about 40°F (5°C).

Rhubarb

Rhubarb can be grown from seed—sown now and transplanted in May—but it's easier to buy new sets or divide and replant old crowns at any time during the winter (see p.192).

Spinach

For an early crop in April or May, sow a fast-growing variety indoors and plant out in March.

Tomatoes and cucumbers

If you're raising plants for a greenhouse or polytunnel, sow seeds indoors now. To ensure germination, use a heated propagator and maintain the temperature at a minimum of 70°F (21°C).

Turnips

Sow early varieties outside under cover.

Winter salad leaves

Continue to sow salads such as rocket, spinach, kale, chard, mustard, and various Oriental leaves under cover in a greenhouse or cold frame (see p.33).

> "Forget special seed trays, plastic guttering is ideal for sowing peas."

SOWING PEAS IN GUTTERING

Lengths of plastic guttering are ideal for sowing peas indoors until the weather warms up. With this method, root disturbance when transplanting is minimized.

1 Half-fill a length of standard plastic rain guttering with good-quality seed soil.

2 Sow seeds about 2 in (5 cm) apart in a single row, or two staggered rows. Cover with more compost, water well, and keep under cover in a light spot.

3 Once your seedlings have grown to about 3 in (8 cm), make a shallow drill outside and gently slide the entire contents of the guttering into the drill. Firm in and water.

Give your soil a health check

As long as the ground is not frozen, February is a good time to take a look at your soil and see if it needs any attention before the year begins. What sort of soil do you have? Is it heavy or light? What about its chemistry? Is it acid, alkaline, or neutral? Whatever the answer, there's plenty you can do to make it as fertile and well structured as possible.

Soil acidity and alkalinity

All soils are acid, alkaline, or, as is much more common, neutral. It is not normally an issue, since most fruit and vegetables are fairly tolerant. If anything, they tend to prefer slightly acidic conditions. Only in extreme cases does it become a problem—when soils are either very acid or very alkaline, in which case you may be attempting to grow plants in inappropriate conditions.

Acid soils are low in calcium. They can be made more alkaline by adding lime or a lime-rich material such as mushroom compost. Alkaline soils are high in calcium. They are trickier to make more acid—although you can try adding composted sawdust, pine bark, or pine needle leafmold.

Measuring the pH of your soil

Buy a soil test kit from a garden center and use soil samples from different parts of your plot. Depending on the level of acidity or alkalinity, the results will reveal your soil's rating on the pH scale.

THE pH SOIL VALUES

1–5	very acid
6	acid
6.5	slightly acid
7	neutral
7.5	slightly alkaline
8	alkaline
9–14	very alkaline

Add soil to the solution in the test tube, shake, then match the resulting color against the pH chart.

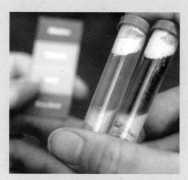

SOIL STRUCTURE

The tiny particles that make up all soils vary in size. Very small particles tend to produce a clay soil, which is heavy and sticky. Larger particles produce a light, sandy soil that is easier to work, but doesn't hold nutrients or water.

1 **Clay soil** Heavy clay soil sticks together like pastry when you squeeze it, and can be formed into a ball.

How to improve clay soils

■ Each year spread a mix of organic matter and grit over the surface and dig it in to open up the structure.
■ Avoid treading on the soil, especially when wet. Lay wooden planks to distribute your weight.
■ Consider creating raised beds.

2 **Sandy soil** Light, sandy soil feels gritty to the touch and slips more readily through your fingers.

How to improve sandy soils

■ Regularly fork in plenty of well-rotted farmyard manure, compost, or leafmold.
■ Add organic fertilizers such as seaweed extract and blood, fish, and bone meal.
■ Mulch in summer to reduce water-loss through evaporation.

Jobs for February

Much of the work for February lies in preparation for the coming year: getting your garden ready for sowing and planting by digging in lots of organic matter and warming up the soil by covering it with cloches or plastic sheets, old carpet, or even cardboard. Otherwise, probably the most important thing in warmer regions is to finish winter-pruning fruit trees and bushes. They will be starting to wake up from their winter dormancy now and next month may be too late.

Finish digging over your plot

Complete your winter digging. Turn over the soil to help aerate it and remove any weeds that have survived the winter. If the ground is still very wet, lay planks over the surface. These will spread your weight evenly, and reduce compaction of the soil.

Spread compost or manure

There's still time to feed your soil with compost or well-rotted stable manure. Work it in as you dig or simply spread it over the surface as a top dressing, to be drawn underground by worms.

Turn your compost heap

A new compost heap full of last year's old plant material will benefit from raking through with a fork in order to aerate it. Add some water if it seems dry, then cover it up again to keep it warm and ensure that everything decomposes.

Warm up seedbeds

If you covered areas of your plot with plastic sheets last autumn, it should already be dry and relatively warm, ready for your first sowing of seeds this month or next. Homemade cloches constructed from clear plastic sheeting or

MAKING A RUNNER BEAN TRENCH

Because they grow so large, runner beans are notoriously hungry plants. A specially dug bean trench filled with compost or manure is the traditional way to create a super-rich bed to supply all the nutrients they need.

1 Mark out the position of your row and dig a trench about 2 ft (60 cm) deep and 2 ft (60 cm) wide. Loosen the soil in the base with a fork.

2 Tip manure plus kitchen or garden waste into the trench, replace the soil, and scatter over pelleted poultry manure. Leave it all to rot down thoroughly.

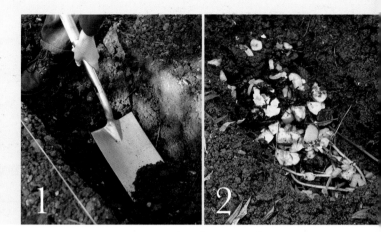

fleece stretched over wire hoops will prepare the ground still further.

Continue sprouting seed potatoes

Make sure you have bought all your seed potatoes for the year by the end of this month. And they should all be spread out in egg crates or seed trays in a cool, light room busily sprouting shoots (see p.36). If the sprouts look pale and spindly, then the room is probably too warm or too dark.

Force rhubarb and chicory

Covering rhubarb crowns should stimulate them to produce an early crop in or around March (see p.38). And planting up Belgian or

(left to right) **Fork compost** into your soil to nourish it and improve the texture so that everything you plant will get the best possible start. **Turn your compost heap** to incorporate air; this is vitally important to the microorganisms that transform your waste plant material into compost. **Warm up seedbeds** ready for planting by making a simple tunnel cloche from plastic sheeting and wire hoops. The clear plastic allows light to penetrate and traps warm air.

Witloof chicory roots and blanching new shoots can provide some welcome fresh salad leaves (see p.183).

Protect cauliflowers from frost

Continue to cover the curds of overwintering cauliflowers by tying their own leaves around them (see p.37). It helps protect them from both frost and light.

Order new asparagus crowns

New asparagus is best planted in March or April, so it's worth ordering crowns from a nursery now. Consider carefully where you're going to site a new asparagus bed, since it's likely to occupy that space for several years. Prepare the ground well in advance by digging it over and adding lots of well-rotted compost.

Finish winter-pruning of fruit trees

Any remaining winter-pruning of apples and pears should be completed by the end of this month (see pp.34–35), particularly in warmer regions of the country. The trees will be starting to come out of dormancy and if you leave it any later to prune them, they will bleed sap from anywhere you have made cuts.

Winter-prune gooseberries, currants, and blueberries

If you haven't already done so, winter-prune gooseberry and currant bushes (see p.184). Established blueberry bushes may need some pruning, too.

Prune raspberries

Summer and autumn raspberries need pruning in different ways. Summer raspberries, which you should have pruned after they finished fruiting last July or August, should need no more than a trim. Cut off the tops of any tall canes so that they are only slightly taller than their supports or bend them over and tie them in the shape of hoops.

Autumn raspberries should be cut right down to the ground now. They'll produce fruits on new canes that grow during the summer.

Inspect fruit supports

Check all stakes, wires, and ties before new growth starts. Once new foliage appears it's harder to see what needs attention. Replace any supports that are worn or broken.

Feed and mulch fruit trees and bushes

Spread a high-potash fertilizer or an organic mixture of blood, fish, and bone or seaweed around the base of your fruit bushes and trees. If possible, follow up with a covering layer of rotted-down farmyard manure or compost, to retain moisture in the soil and suppress weeds.

Protect apricots, peaches, and nectarines

Trained apricot, peach, and nectarine trees grown in a sheltered, south-facing spot should begin to come into blossom in February. Cover them to protect them from rain and frost—although, if you do so, you may have to hand-pollinate the flowers.

(left) **Prune established black currant** bushes by taking out any dead or diseased wood, and then remove weak or thin stems, because these will not produce much fruit.

(right) **Autumn raspberries** that have been left over winter should be pruned right down to ground level now. New canes will soon grow to replace those you have removed.

February pests & diseases

Vegetables

■ **Slugs** can still be a problem in late winter. Check for them in the outer leaves of cabbages and cauliflowers.

■ **Net winter cabbages**, cauliflowers, and broccoli to protect them from pigeons. There's little else for pigeons to eat at this time of year, so they'll be even more persistent.

■ **Remove dead leaves** from brussels sprouts and cabbages. If they start to rot while still in place, they can spread mold and downy mildew.

■ **Check stored vegetables** such as potatoes, rutabagas, squashes, onions, shallots, and garlic for signs of rot. Discard anything damaged or diseased.

Fruit

■ **Check for aphids** on cherries, plums, currants, and gooseberries. In a mild winter, their first new leaves may start to unfurl toward the end of the month and are a seductive target for early attack. Deal with infestations as soon as you see them, before they get out of hand.

■ **Spray fruit trees** and bushes with a plant-oil–based winter wash to help control aphids and scale insects—if you haven't already done so. This is your last chance to spray before the plants' dormant period is over.

■ **Check apple and pear trees** throughout winter for signs of canker. Cut out any diseased wood.

■ **Net gooseberries** to protect the buds from birds.

■ **Continue to check for big bud mite** on black currants by looking for abnormally rounded, swollen buds.

■ **Spray peaches and nectarines** with copper fungicide if you didn't do so last month. It may help protect them against peach leaf curl—as will a rain-proof cover to shelter them from rain spreading the spores that carry the disease. Don't spray once the buds open.

(top to bottom) **Netting** is the best way to protect your cabbage crop from pigeons. **Peach leaf curl** is a fungus that is spread by wind and rain. Affected leaves pucker and blister. **Big bud mite** prevents foliage from forming. Each swollen bud contains tiny white mites.

March

As winter begins to recede, sowing and planting outdoors can start in milder regions of the country. Seed potatoes, onion and shallot sets, Jerusalem artichoke tubers, and rhubarb sets can all go in. So, too, can a few hardy seeds that will germinate at fairly low temperatures—broad beans, broccoli, cabbages, leeks, parsnips, peas, and spinach. But most others must still be sown indoors or under the protection of cloches or cold frames. If that leaves you with time on your hands, probably the most useful thing you can do this month is to begin preparing beds for sowing and planting in April and May. March winds, although they may be bitterly cold, help dry out the soil after the storms of winter. Remove any weeds that have survived, rake the soil thoroughly, and apply some fertilizer.

Early rhubarb adds a burst of welcome color to your plot and the first, fresh stems of the year will be ready to harvest once they reach about 12 in (30 cm) in height.

Top tasks for March

■ **Harvest** your first rhubarb of the year, plus the last of any remaining brussels sprouts, celeriac, parsnips, and rutabagas.

■ **Sow** a few seeds outdoors if you've covered and warmed the soil in preparation; otherwise, sow indoors or under cloches and in cold frames.

■ **Plant** first early potatoes, shallots, and garlic by the end of the month.

■ **Bare-root** fruit trees and bushes should be planted by now. Next month, when they're no longer dormant, it will be too late.

■ **Finish** winter-pruning gooseberries, black currants, blueberries, and autumn raspberries.

■ **Apply** fertilizers to boost the nutritional content of your soil before sowing and planting begins.

Vegetables and salads

1 Swiss chard
This month you should be picking the first of the year's Swiss chard and spinach beet. It will have overwintered from seeds sown last summer.

2 Parsnips
Lift any parsnips still remaining in the ground, and eat them now. They won't last any longer.

3 Lettuces
Winter lettuces sown last September and overwintered in cold frames or under cloches should be ready to start harvesting now.

4 Sprouting broccoli
Hardy, early varieties of purple sprouting broccoli should have overwintered from sowings the preceding summer and be ready for picking now.

5 Spring cauliflowers
Provided they have survived any severe frosts or very cold weather, hardy, overwintering spring cauliflowers planted out toward the end of last summer should be ready to harvest.

6 Leeks
Although they may be starting to look a little battered after a whole winter outdoors, you should still be able to harvest leeks—both this month and next. Trim, clean, and use them as soon as you lift them.

7 Kale
One of the hardiest vegetables of all, kale will survive most winters to provide you with fresh green leaves right through to this month and next. Try shredding the leaves, steaming them, and serving them mixed with creamed horseradish.

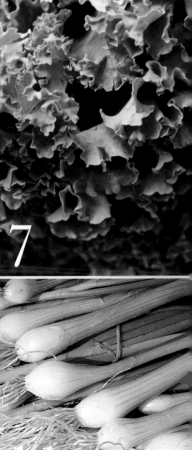

8 **Rhubarb**
March generally marks the start of the season for rhubarb—although you may have already picked some early, blanched stems if you've been forcing them under cover (see p.38).

9 **Corn salad**
Also known as lamb's lettuce, corn salad will crop throughout the year although—except in very mild climates—it does need protecting with cloches or frames in the winter months.

10 **Brussels sprouts**
Late varieties (both regular green and the more unusual purple shown here) should last until this month. Toward the end of the season, the leaves at the top of the stems —called "sprout tops"—can be cooked and eaten as spring greens.

11 **Green onions**
Your first green onions of the year should be ready for lifting now, if you sowed seeds last August or September and left the seedlings in the ground to overwinter.

12 **Spring cabbages**
March is usually the last month for winter cabbages and the first for spring cabbages. Pick spring varieties while the leaves are still loose, before they form dense heads.

13 **Chicory**
Make the most of your forced "chicons" of Belgian or Witloof chicory. This month may be your last chance to harvest them until next year.

ALSO HARVEST

Celeriac
Aim to lift the last of any remaining celeriac this month.

Endive
Finish harvesting endive you've been overwintering in frames or under cloches. You'll need the covers for this year's new plants.

Sow or plant in March

March is a big month for sowing seeds. Except in the very coldest areas, you should now be able to sow hardy crops such as leeks, parsnips, peas, spinach, and brassicas outside, although they may need to be protected under cloches. If you have space, sow seeds indoors, too. Tender crops such as eggplants, peppers, and tomatoes can be raised inside or in a heated greenhouse. This gives them time to develop before they are planted out when it is warm enough.

(top to bottom) **Asparagus** comes up year after year, so start with good-quality three- to four-year-old "crowns." Make a ridge at the base of a trench and spread the roots over it. **Eggplant** seeds sown indoors in a warm place will soon begin to germinate.

Asparagus

It's possible to grow asparagus from seed but much easier to buy ready-to-plant rootstocks known as "crowns." Plant them in preprepared trenches this month or next.

Eggplants, chilies, and peppers

These are all summer fruiting vegetables that originate in hot climates and therefore need as long as possible to ripen. Get ahead by sowing seeds indoors this month.

Broccoli, cabbages, and other brassicas

This month sow brussels sprouts indoors, and sow sprouting broccoli and summer, autumn, or red cabbages indoors, or outside if it's not too cold. Early summer cauliflowers raised from seed indoors can probably be planted out, but may still need protection under cloches.

VEGETABLE SEEDS TO SOW OUTDOORS

- Broad beans
- Cabbages (summer, autumn, and red)
- Calabrese
- Leeks
- Lettuces
- Onions
- Parsnips
- Peas
- Spinach
- Green onions
- Sprouting broccoli

Fruit trees and bushes

March is your last chance to plant new, bare-root apple and pear trees, blueberries, raspberries, blackberries, and hybrid berries, as well as gooseberry and currant bushes. By April it will be too late, and only container-grown plants will get established and fruit.

Garlic

March is almost certainly your last chance to plant garlic for harvesting this year.

Herbs

Toward the end of the month, sow seeds of herbs such as chives, coriander, dill, fennel, oregano, and parsley that can tolerate low temperatures, but cover with fleece at night if frost is forecast. In addition, begin planting out any young, ready-to-plant specimens of hardy

VEGETABLE SEEDS TO SOW OUTDOORS UNDER COVER

- Arugula
- Beets
- Carrots
- Cucumbers
- Lettuces
- Oriental leaves
- Radishes (summer)
- Salad leaves
- Summer purslane
- Turnips

herbs you've bought from garden centers or nurseries such as mint, rosemary, and thyme.

Lettuces and other salad crops

Sow lettuce seed either indoors or outdoors, and under cover if necessary. Sow green onions, radishes, salad mixes, arugula, summer purslane, and Oriental leaves under cloches or in cold frames.

SOWING CABBAGES

To give cabbages a head start, sow the seeds under cover and then plant out when all risk of frost has passed.

1 Fill a seed tray with potting soil and firm down lightly, either using another tray of the same size, or a board. Water the soil (a watering can with a fine rose is best) and allow to drain.

2 Scatter the seeds over the moist surface of the soil, distributing them evenly and sparingly so the emerging seedlings won't become overcrowded.

3 Cover the seeds with a fine layer of soil, using a garden sieve so that you don't introduce any lumps or pieces of bark, then lightly firm the soil over the seeds with your hands.

Onions and shallots

It's still possible to sow onion seeds outdoors, but both onions and shallots are better grown from commercially produced "sets." Shallot sets can be planted in February or March, onion sets in March or April.

Peas and broad beans

Sow both pea and broad bean seeds outdoors, starting them off under cloches so the soil has been warmed up before planting, especially if the weather is still cold.

Potatoes

If you started sprouting a batch of first early potatoes at the start of the year, and if the ground is not still frozen, you should be able to plant them now.

Root and stem vegetables

Carrots and turnips can be sown outdoors but will still need cloches or cold frames. Celery, celeriac, kohlrabi, and Florence fennel are not as hardy and if you sow seeds now you should keep them indoors or in a heated greenhouse.

Plant onion sets about 2–4 in (5–10 cm) apart and about 1 in (2.5 cm) deep, with the tip only just showing.

VEGETABLE SEEDS TO SOW INDOORS

- Eggplants
- Brussels sprouts
- Cabbages (summer, autumn, and red)
- Celeriac
- Celery
- Chilies and peppers
- Cucumbers
- Florence fennel
- Globe artichokes
- Kohlrabi
- Lettuces
- Sprouting broccoli
- Sweet potatoes
- Tomatoes

Seed potatoes can be planted now in well-prepared soil. Dig a shallow drill about 6 in (15 cm) deep and lay your seed potatoes in it at intervals of 12 in (30 cm). Make sure the "chits" or shoots are pointing upward.

Oriental mustards (here growing with chives and mizuna) can be sown now under cloches or in cold frames. Mustards are easy plants to grow and young leaves will be ready to harvest as a cut-and-come-again salad crop in about four to five weeks' time.

Strawberries

Plant out commercially prepared, cold-stored runners as soon as they become available; they will crop in their first year.

Tomatoes and cucumbers

Plants eventually intended for growing outdoors can be started off from seeds sown indoors at the end of the month—but no earlier or they'll get too large and become pot-bound before it's warm enough to plant them out in late May or June.

VEGETABLES TO PLANT OUTDOORS

- Asparagus
- Broad beans
- Cauliflowers (early summer)
- Chinese artichokes
- Garlic
- Jerusalem artichokes
- Onion sets
- Peas
- Potatoes
- Rhubarb sets
- Shallot sets
- Spinach

FRUIT TO PLANT OUTDOORS

- Apple and pear trees
- Blackberries
- Cranberries
- Gooseberries and currants
- Grapevines
- Raspberries
- Strawberries

Jobs for March

Except in very cold regions, sowing seeds outdoors can begin this month, so you should be busy preparing seedbeds, warming the soil under cloches or sheeting, weeding, raking, and sifting to produce the fine, crumbly "tilth" in which seeds are most likely to germinate and grow. Fruit trees and bushes will be waking up from the winter too, so finish any last-minute pruning, feed and mulch them, and do what you can to protect early blossoms from frost.

Rake seedbeds ready for sowing

Remove sheets or cloches from areas you've been preparing as seedbeds and rake over the soil, breaking down any lumps until it forms what's called a "fine tilth." This is the Holy Grail of every vegetable gardener: soil that is fine and crumbly, with no stones or large clods of earth. Perfect for sowing. If it is too dry and dusty, water it. If it sticks to your boots, wait for it to dry out a little more.

Apply fertilizers

All soils benefit from the addition of fertilizers before seeds are sown or young seedlings planted. Now is a good time to apply them. You can choose organic fertilizers, which originate from plants and animals, and include seaweed, chicken manure, and blood, fish, and bone meal. Or you can use inorganic fertilizers, which are extracted from minerals or manufactured using chemical processes.

Feed overwintering crops

Vegetables that have been in the ground throughout the winter—onions, kale, spring cabbages and cauliflowers, and hardy lettuces—may be looking a bit the worse for wear. Perk them up with a top-dressing of blood, fish, and bone meal, chicken manure, or seaweed-based organic fertilizer.

Start weeding

As days lengthen, temperatures rise, and the soil warms up, weeds will begin to germinate

and grow. Dig out perennials such as bindweed and couch grass, and hoe regularly to kill off emerging annual weeds.

Make runner bean and celery trenches

Both runner beans and trench celery need rich, fertile soil. Get ahead now by digging trenches 2–3 ft (60–90 cm) wide and 1 ft (30 cm) deep, and over the next few weeks fill them with compost. It should have all rotted down by the time you're ready to plant in May or June.

Remove rhubarb cloches

With luck, you may be able to harvest your first forced rhubarb this month.

Trim and divide herbs

Neaten up perennial herbs such as rosemary and sage by giving them a good trim. Propagate clumps of chives and mint by digging them up, dividing them, and replanting.

Cover strawberries

Place cloches over existing, overwintering plants in order to stimulate them into flowering so they produce a crop as early as possible. Once flowers form, remove the cloches on warm days to allow insects to pollinate them.

(left to right) **Lift protective sheets** that have been used to warm up your seedbeds ready for sowing. **Apply fertilizer** to give your soil a boost, but always keep to recommended quantities. **Top dress** winter brassicas by sprinkling fertilizer around the base of plants, beneath the outer leaves.

(top to bottom) **Protect strawberry** plants from the cold with clear plastic cloches, and you may get an early crop of fruit. **Prune blueberry** bushes down to a strong, healthy shoot, taking out any damaged, or diseased stems.

Finish winter-pruning gooseberries, black currants, and blueberries

If you haven't already done so, now is the time to complete your winter-pruning (see p.184). Next month will be too late.

Prune raspberries

March is your last chance to prune last year's autumn raspberry canes, if you didn't have time last month. Cut them right down to the ground (see p.50). The new canes on which this year's berries will fruit should start emerging soon.

Feed and mulch fruit trees and bushes

All fruit trees and bushes are coming out of dormancy this month and entering a growth spurt. Giving them a feed of high-potash fertilizer or an organic mixture of blood, fish, and bone meal or seaweed will get them off to a good start. Spread fertilizer around the base, water it in well, and cover with a layer of rotted-down farmyard manure or compost, which will act as a mulch.

Protect cherries, apricots, peaches, and nectarines

These trees should all be in blossom by now. If possible, cover them with fleece or polythene to protect the flowers from frost damage.

Pollinate apricots, peaches, and nectarines

In a cool spring, insects may not be around to pollinate blossom when they're needed. If so, a little human intervention may be required. Hand-pollinate your plants, using a soft paintbrush to carefully dust pollen from one flower to another.

(left to right) **Spring blossom** on a sweet cherry tree is a breathtaking sight, but the delicate flowers are vulnerable to frost. Cover with plastic, fleece, or netting at night, and uncover during the day. **Hand-pollinate** peaches with a child's paintbrush if chilly conditions have kept insects away from the blossom.

March pests & diseases

(left to right) **A netting cage** is the best method of protecting rows of cabbages and brussels sprouts from birds. **Slugs** are also fond of brassica leaves. **Brussels sprout leaves** that have started to yellow should be removed and discarded.

Vegetables

■ **Slugs and snails** can be a problem even this early in spring. Bait them and dispose of them or use slug pellets.

■ **Pigeons** must be kept well away from winter cabbages, cauliflowers, and broccoli. They quickly become blasé about scarecrows; nets are much more effective.

■ **Remove dead leaves** from brussels sprouts and cabbages. Once they turn yellow and start to rot, they can spread mold and downy mildew to other plants in the same family.

■ **Cabbage caterpillars** can appear as early as March, especially if the winter has been mild and eggs have survived from the previous autumn. Inspect outer leaves regularly and pick off any insects you find before they tunnel their way into the hearts of your cabbages.

Fruit

■ **Check for aphids** on all soft fruit bushes and deal with them as soon as you spot them, before they multiply.

■ **Start to spray apples** against scab, and pears against pear midge and scab—while they are in bud but before blossom opens.

■ **Net gooseberries** to protect them from thrushes and waxwings, and spray with a special fungicide if you've previously suffered from American gooseberry mildew.

■ **Continue to check for big bud mite** on black currants by looking for abnormally rounded, swollen buds.

■ **Cover trained peaches and nectarines** with a rain-proof sheet to protect against peach leaf curl.

■ **Don't spray** any fruit trees or bushes when they are in blossom.

April

Lengthening days and warmer temperatures throughout the country beckon the kitchen gardener. But, with the important exception of the first asparagus of the year, April is a lean month for harvesting. Indeed, in most regions the kitchen garden produces little in both April and May, and there's a real shortage of fresh vegetables and salads. Of course, supermarket produce flown in from all over the globe now conceals the issue from most of us, but if you'd like to eat as much of your own local, homegrown food as you can, you'll be relying heavily on brassicas such as cabbages, cauliflowers, broccoli, and kale at this time. Get ahead by sowing seeds indoors or outside in cold frames and under cloches, and if you've already warmed up areas of your plot by covering them, then you may be able to sow and plant certain crops directly outdoors. However, watch out if you live in the colder regions—a very cold night and sharp frost can damage fruit tree blossoms.

Delicate spring blossom on a 'Morello' cherry. Acid cherries such as 'Morello' are too sour to eat raw but bursting with flavor when cooked and used in desserts, cakes, and preserves. Grow as a fan or as a free-standing tree.

Top tasks for April

- **Harvest** the first asparagus of the year, along with spring cabbages and cauliflowers, sprouting broccoli, and any remaining leeks and kale.
- **Sow** outdoors if the soil is warm enough, otherwise indoors or under cover.
- **Plant** second early and maincrop potatoes, and the last of your onion sets this month.
- **Earth up** first early potatoes.
- **Prepare** seed beds by weeding thoroughly and raking over the soil.
- **Prune** cherries and plums now they are growing, once leaf buds have opened.

Vegetables and salads

1 Green onions
Early green onions sown in autumn last year and left to overwinter should be ready now. For salads, pick them before they grow too large and their flavor becomes too strong.

2 Salad leaves
Continue harvesting baby salad leaves grown from seed sown earlier in the year. Corn salad, arugula, and a wide variety of Oriental leaves (such as mizuna, shown here) should grow if you protect them from frost under cloches or in cold frames.

3 Spring cabbages
Certain spring cabbages develop pointed, conical heads rather than the more usual rounded ones. Either wait for the heads to form, or pick when the leaves are still slightly loose.

4 Spinach
This month you may get your first new-season spinach—provided you sowed seeds early in the year and were able to plant out last month. Tender, young leaves can be cut for salads.

5 Leeks
April may be your last chance to harvest any remaining leeks—although you may have to trim off quite a few layers of old, weather-beaten outer leaves to reach the edible white stems. Aim to lift them all by the end of the month to free up space for new crops.

6 Rhubarb
Pick rhubarb stalks by gripping them firmly around the base with one hand, then giving them a twist. You shouldn't need to cut them.

7 Asparagus
Watching the very first asparagus spears of the year pushing their way out of the ground is one of the highlights of April. Start cutting them once they are about the thickness of your index finger, or even earlier if you are unable to wait!

8 Lettuces
The small, semi-cos type shown here is a variety bred to withstand light frosts. Sown the previous autumn and given some protection during the winter, lettuces like these should be ready for harvesting now.

9 Spring cauliflowers
Overwintered cauliflowers will be coming to the end of their season by the end of the month. Cut them while the heads are still reasonably firm and before they discolor.

10 Swiss chard/Spinach beet
Chards and leaf beets come in a variety of different colors. The red-veined form shown here is sometimes called ruby or rhubarb chard. Strip the leaves from any very tough stalks and cook them like spinach.

11 Sprouting broccoli
This month may be your last opportunity to pick last year's sprouting broccoli. However, if you sowed seeds indoors early in the new year and planted them out under cover last month or this month, you shouldn't have long to wait for a new crop.

12 Arugula
Start picking arugula as soon as the young leaves are about as long as your thumb. Keep picking and they'll keep growing.

13 Kale
If you have any of last year's kale still left standing, April is likely to be its final month. Harvest and eat it now in order to make room for new crops. Don't grow kale in the same spot again—choose somewhere else instead.

Sow in April

April is a tricky month for deciding whether to sow or not. The temptation is to tear open your new seed packets and get plants off to an early start. But outdoors that's still risky. Unless you're lucky with a really mild spring, temperatures may not be high enough to guarantee that seeds germinate. In many cases, it's wiser to sow just a few advance handfuls of seeds in pots or modules kept indoors on a windowsill or in a heated greenhouse. Then you can gradually harden them off next month and safely plant them out in early June. You can always follow up with additional sowings as the weather warms up.

VEGETABLE SEEDS TO SOW INDOORS

- Cabbages (summer, autumn, winter, and red)
- Cauliflower (summer and autumn)
- Celeriac
- Celery
- Chicory (sugarloaf and radicchio)
- Chilies and peppers
- Corn
- Cucumbers
- Eggplants
- Endive
- Florence fennel
- French beans
- Gherkins
- Kale
- Kohlrabi
- Marrows
- Pumpkins and winter squashes
- Runner beans
- Sprouting broccoli
- Sweet potatoes
- Tomatoes
- Zucchinis and summer squashes

Broccoli, cabbages, and other brassicas

Brussels sprouts, calabrese, sprouting broccoli, summer and autumn cauliflowers, and cabbages of all kinds can now be sown outdoors. Either sow them in pots or modules, or in a prepared seedbed from which you can transplant them in a couple of months' time.

Carrots, beets, and other root vegetables

Most root crops can now be sown outdoors. Indeed, April may be your last chance to sow parsnips. Beets may need to be covered with cloches if the soil is cold and wet.

Celery, chicory, endive, and Florence fennel

Sow indoors to ensure that seeds germinate successfully. Harden off next month, and plant out in June.

Chilies, peppers, and cucumbers

To be safe, continue to sow indoors. Sown outdoors in April, seeds may not germinate, even under cover.

Corn

This has a long growing season so it's worth getting your crop off to an early start by sowing seeds in pots indoors.

Eggplants and tomatoes

April is probably your last chance to sow seeds indoors for transplanting out. Any later and the plants will have too short a growing season for fruits to ripen outdoors.

French and runner beans

To get ahead, sow a few seeds in pots and keep them on an indoor windowsill or in a heated greenhouse.

Herbs

Follow up on last month with further sowings. Almost all herbs can be sown or planted outdoors now.

Leaf vegetables

Spinach, Swiss chard, and Oriental leaves such as mizuna, mibuna, and komatsuna can all be sown outdoors now, although prepare to cover them if necessary. Kale is best sown in pots or modules indoors.

Leeks and onions

Sow leeks outdoors now, either direct in the ground in an area of your plot reserved as a seedbed or clustered in modules or multiblocks for transplanting later. You can sow onion seeds too, if you're not growing them from sets.

VEGETABLE SEEDS TO SOW OUTDOORS UNDER COVER

- Arugula
- Beets
- Corn salad
- Cucumbers
- Lettuces
- Oriental leaves
- Salad leaves
- Summer purslane
- Turnips

(left to right) **Cauliflower** seedlings sown in a seed tray are just beginning to show their true leaves. **Kale** seedlings sown indoors are now emerging. The first pair of "seed leaves" will be replaced by true "brassica" leaves.

(above) **Sow runner beans** in pots this month. Drop seeds into 2 in (5 cm) holes made with a pencil or dibber, and keep pots in a warm place such as a sunny windowsill.

VEGETABLE SEEDS TO SOW OUTDOORS

- Broad beans
- Brussels sprouts
- Cabbages (summer, autumn, winter, and red)
- Carrots
- Calabrese
- Cauliflowers (summer and autumn)
- Kohlrabi
- Land cress
- Leeks
- Lettuces
- Onions
- Oriental leaves
- Parsnips
- Peas
- Radishes
- Spinach
- Spring onions
- Sprouting broccoli
- Swiss chard/Spinach beet
- Turnips

Lettuces and other salad crops

Sow lettuce, arugula, land cress, summer purslane, corn salad, and other salad leaves outdoors this month. In colder regions they must be sown under cover.

Melons

Sow seeds one per pot, cover them with a plastic bag, and put them somewhere warm —a closet or propagator. When seedlings appear, move them into the light on an indoor windowsill or in a heated greenhouse.

Peas and broad beans

Continue to sow peas and broad bean seeds outdoors, protecting them with cloches if the weather is still cold.

Zucchinis, pumpkins, and other squashes

Sow seeds indoors ready for planting out next month—or when you're sure there will be no further frosts.

(right) **Lettuce seeds** can be sown outdoors in very shallow drills. Take a small pinch betwen finger and thumb and try to sow as sparingly as you can.

(far right) **Sow peas** outdoors in staggered double rows in a wide drill 1½–2 in (4–5 cm) deep and at least 2 in (5 cm) apart.

Prepare a seedbed

The term seedbed is used for the patch of soil where you sow your seeds. It's either the spot where your plants are going to germinate, grow, and spend their lives, or it may be a "nursery" bed where you raise young plants before moving them to their final positions. Whichever, the quality, structure, and composition of the soil are crucial.

Feeding the soil

The best time to add bulky organic material to the soil—either by digging it in or by spreading it over the surface—is the previous autumn. That way, it will have rotted down and been incorporated over the winter. If you were unable to do so, add compost or manure now, but only if it has completely rotted down, and dig it in thoroughly.

Warming the soil

Seeds need warmth to germinate. Covering the soil with plastic sheets during the coldest months will ensure that the soil temperature is a few degrees higher than elsewhere and will allow you to sow seeds earlier than otherwise. Using glass or plastic cloches has the same effect, with the added advantage that they can stay in place once seeds have been sown, acting like mobile greenhouses.

Raking and sieving the soil

To give seeds their best chance of germinating, the soil should be broken down into small, evenly graded particles. Stones and any bits of old, woody plant material should be removed, using a sieve if necessary. You should aim to end up with what's called a "fine tilth"—a top layer of clod-free soil with a fine, crumbly texture.

RAKING

The best time to start raking is when the soil is fairly dry. If it sticks to your shoes, it's too wet, and you need to wait until it is a little drier. If your soil is too dry, just water it.

1 **Leveling the soil** Use a rake to remove stones and break up any solid clods of earth. Level out any dips and hollows to produce a flat surface that will drain evenly.

2 **Creating a fine tilth** Push and pull your rake back and forward at a shallow angle, first one way then at ninety degrees, until the soil is broken into small, even grains.

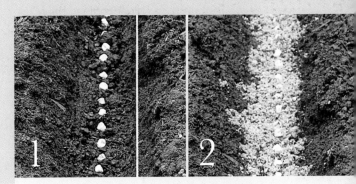

SOWING

For a straight row, pull a length of string tight over your seed bed and then, with the edge of a hoe, mark out a shallow drill of the correct depth along the length of the string.

1 **Sowing when dry** If the soil is dry, water the base of the drill generously just before you sow and cover seeds carefully with dry soil.

2 **Sowing when wet** If the soil is very wet, sprinkle a thin layer of sand along the base of the drill before you sow to prevent seeds from getting waterlogged.

Plant in April

By April, temperatures are rising and the soil on your plot should be starting to warm up, particularly if you've been preparing a few beds by covering them with plastic sheets or cloches. Seedlings raised indoors should be nearing the time for transplanting, and garden centers and nurseries will be brimming with young vegetable plants ready to take home and plant out. Don't be tempted to move too quickly, however. A hard frost can wipe out a whole bed of tender seedlings overnight.

Asparagus

Plant asparagus crowns by the end of the month. After that, it will be too late.

Fruit trees and bushes

It's too late now to plant bare-root trees and bushes, since they will no longer be dormant. However, if you've missed your chance, you can still buy and plant container-grown specimens instead.

Globe artichokes

Take offsets from established plants that you have divided and plant them out this month (see p.75).

Herbs

Most herbs can be planted outdoors now, either those you've bought or those you've raised from seed yourself. Only the most tender will need covering at night.

Jerusalem artichokes

New tubers should all be planted by the end of April.

Kohlrabi and summer radishes

Harden off and transplant young plants you've grown from seed.

Lettuces and other salad leaves

If you've been raising lettuce seedlings indoors over the last couple of months, you may be able to plant them out now—but keep them covered if there are still night frosts.

VEGETABLES TO
PLANT OUTDOORS

- Asparagus
- Broad beans
- Globe artichokes
- Corn
- Endive
- Florence fennel
- French beans
- Gherkins
- Jerusalem artichokes
- Kale
- Kohlrabi
- Lettuces
- Marrows
- Onions
- Peas
- Potatoes
- Pumpkins and winter squashes
- Radishes
- Runner beans
- Sprouting broccoli
- Sweet potatoes
- Tomatoes

Onions

April is probably your last chance for transplanting seedlings or planting onion sets.

Peas and broad beans

Harden off and plant out any seedlings you've raised indoors or under cover.

Potatoes

Plant second early and maincrop seed potatoes. You should have already "sprouted" them to give them a good head start.

FRUIT TO PLANT OUTDOORS

- Cape gooseberries (transplant)
- Cranberries
- Fruit trees (container-grown)
- Grapevines
- Strawberries

Young lettuces planted outdoors will still need protection from night frosts. Cone-shaped plastic cloches are a good fit, and are lightweight so they can be easily removed during the day.

Jobs for April

April is the lull before the storm. There's certainly plenty to do but next month, when everything bursts into life, you'll be really busy. Take advantage of any spare time you have now to finish off all your preparations—newly weeded and raked seedbeds, sturdily built pea and bean supports, and neatly pruned, fed, and mulched fruit trees and bushes. As the weather warms up, pot on young seedlings and start bringing them outside or open cloches and cold frames during the day to harden them off.

Continue preparing seedbeds

Rake over the soil, break up any large clods of earth, and weed thoroughly in preparation for sowing seeds or planting out new seedlings.

Prick out seedlings

Once young seedlings grown in trays or modules have developed a couple of true leaves, move them into individual pots or larger modules. This is called "pricking out." Use a dibber or a pencil to lever them very gently out of the soil, taking care not to damage their delicate roots. Always handle seedlings by the leaves, not the stem. Once replanted, they will develop their own root system without crowding or competition from neighbors.

Pot on growing plants

Keep an eye on the development of seedlings growing in pots. If it's still too early to plant them out, they may become "pot-bound" and their roots will be constricted. Tomatoes, in particular, are prone to outgrowing their pots. Simply replant them in larger pots until they can go out into the ground.

Harden off young plants

Plants raised indoors should be moved outside during warm days and then back in again at night in order to gradually accustom them to lower temperatures. Cold frames or cloches are good halfway houses; they can be opened during the day and closed at night.

Water and weed

Water newly planted seedlings regularly. Little and often is better than a deluge once a week. Weed thoroughly, too.

Protect against frosts

Sharp frosts can damage growing plants so cover with cloches or fleece. Peaches, apricots, and nectarines in blossom are particularly at risk so cover with fleece or plastic sheets.

Earth up new potatoes

Draw soil up in ridges or mounds around potato plants in order to ensure that the tubers remain underground. If they are exposed to light, they turn green and can become poisonous.

Put up peasticks

Peas are natural sprawlers and need supports for their tendrils to twine around in order to keep themselves off the ground. Hazel or birch peasticks are ideal, but chicken wire or plastic mesh can also be used. Whichever you choose, put them up now, before plants get established.

Build cane supports for climbing beans

It's a good idea to erect supports for beans now, while the ground is still soft enough to push in canes or stakes easily. Traditionally, supports take the form of wigwams of double rows crossed over at the top. Use strong canes and thick twine or wire to withstand winds and support the weight at the peak of the harvest.

Remove rhubarb cloches

Cloches should come off for good this month. Once you've harvested the last of the blanched stems, leave the plant to grow.

Pull up brassica stumps

Remove any roots of winter cabbages, cauliflowers, and brussels sprouts as soon as you've finished harvesting. If you leave them in the ground, you risk a buildup of disease. Burn, or pulverize with a hammer and then compost.

Take offsets of globe artichokes

Propagate artichokes by cutting "offsets"—new sideshoots or suckers with a short length of root—from the base of an established plant. Replant, trim the leaves, and water them well.

(below, left to right) **Seedlings** sown in situ need thinning once they emerge. **Rake** over seedbeds to get a fine, lump-free tilth. **Twiggy** peasticks are the most economic option for supporting young pea plants. **Trays** of vegetable seedlings must become acclimatized before being planted out. **Wigwams** can remain in place for a few months so make sure they are sturdily built. **Divide** globe artichokes to create offsets and plant out.

Propagate herbs

Dig up, divide, and replant clumps of chives, lovage, mint, and marjoram. And propagate thyme by layering—pegging long stems from the parent plant into pots until roots develop and new plants can be detached.

Cover and feed strawberries

Keep cloches in place over strawberry plants in order to stimulate them into flowering so they produce a crop as early as possible. Remove the cloches during the day to allow insects to pollinate them. Add a sprinkling of sulfate of potash or a liquid feed of tomato fertilizer.

Pick flowers off new strawberries

Remove the blossom from any new, young summer-fruiting strawberry plants you put in last autumn or this spring. You don't want them to crop in their first year.

Feed black currants and blackberries

Apply a small quantity of high-nitrogen feed plus a generous helping of a blood, fish, and bone fertilizer.

Weed raspberry and blackberry canes

Keep weeds down at this early stage. The larger they get the more they compete with the new growth and the harder they are to remove.

Prune cherry and plum trees

Once their leaf buds have opened, it should be safe to prune cherries and plums, as well as trained apricots, peaches, and nectarines. If you prune them any earlier in the year, before the trees are actively growing, wounds will be slow to heal and you risk attack by the fungus that causes silver leaf.

April pests & diseases

Vegetables

■ **Slugs and snails** can be particularly destructive this month, just as new seedlings begin to emerge.

■ **Flea beetles** leave tiny holes in the leaves of salad leaves, radishes, and brassica seedlings. Plants are disfigured but the damage doesn't usually prove fatal.

■ **Pigeons** mount a constant attack on brassicas such as cabbages, cauliflowers, and broccoli. You can try scarecrows, but nets are the only real solution.

■ **Fit brassica collars** if you are planting out early summer cauliflowers to protect them against the eggs laid by cabbage root fly.

Fruit

■ **Check for aphids** on all soft fruit bushes. Deal with them before they develop into a major infestation and cause damage.

■ **Spray apples** against scab, and pears against pear midge and scab—either before or after they come into blossom, not while they are in flower.

■ **Check cherry, peach, and nectarine trees** for blackfly, especially as the leaves start to open. Spray if necessary.

■ **Net gooseberries** to protect them from finches, and spray with a special fungicide if you've previously suffered from American gooseberry mildew.

■ **Inspect red currant, white currant, and gooseberry** bushes for caterpillar-like sawfly larvae, particularly under the leaves in the center of the bush. Pick off and destroy any you find.

■ **Continue to check for big bud mite** on black currants. Swollen buds and an absence of flowers are telltale signs.

(above) **Scarecrows** come in a range of imaginative and realistic designs, but birds soon get used to their presence and realise that they present no real threat.

(far left) **Snails** are always on the lookout for the tasty new leaves of young plants. Set traps or pick them off by hand to reduce their numbers.

(left) **Cherry blackfly** infests the leaves in early spring. They become distorted and curl up tightly. Spraying may be necessary.

May

May is a seductive month. Days are longer and temperatures higher, even in the more northern climes and higher elevations, and with luck there'll be enough warm sunshine to act as a real foretaste of summer. It's the month to begin sowing and planting outdoors in earnest. May can be deceptive, however. Even in a mild spring, too many seeds are sown in ground that is not yet warm enough. The result: they fail to germinate. Worse, a late frost can do in young seedlings or destroy a year's crop if the fruit trees are in full blossom. Young vegetable plants can be consumed in a single night by a voracious attack from slugs. And then there are the weeds... Yet, as a counterbalance to such gloom, you're likely to be harvesting your first spring crops—which makes it all worthwhile.

Asparagus spears are pushing up through the soil and should now be ready for harvesting, and, more importantly, eating. What could be more delicious than your own freshly cut asparagus?

Top tasks for May

■ **Harvest** asparagus, baby globe artichokes and turnips, fresh "green" garlic, and new-season Oriental salad leaves.

■ **Sow** outdoors if the weather is mild, and indoors or under cover if it's been a late spring.

■ **Harden off** seedlings and start planting them out once the soil becomes warm enough.

■ **Plant** the last of your seed potatoes.

■ **Protect** tender plants against sudden, late frosts. Keep an eye on the weather and be ready with cloches, fleece, and even newspapers.

■ **Weed** regularly and thoroughly, and keep young plants well watered.

■ **Net** fruit bushes to protect them from birds.

Vegetables and salads

1 Spring cauliflowers
May is a crossover month for cauliflowers. It probably marks the last of the winter and spring varieties you sowed and planted last year. But next month should see the first of the new season's early summer cauliflowers.

2 Lettuces
Nonhearting, loose-leaf lettuces like this red oakleaf variety can be either harvested whole or a few leaves at a time, as a cut-and-come-again crop.

3 Turnips
The first, baby turnips of the year should be ready now. Lift them while they're still young, small, and at their very best. Cut the leaves (or "turnip tops") too—and steam them or add them to stir-fries.

4 Chop suey greens
Actually an edible form of chrysanthemum, chop suey greens can give you a crop of young salad leaves all through the summer. Pick the leaves regularly, before the flower buds open.

5 Oriental leaves
Mizuna is just one of numerous Oriental brassicas you can harvest now for salads while their leaves are still young and tender (see p.226). You may need to keep them covered overnight if there is a risk of frost.

6 Radishes
Summer radishes are fast-growing, and if you sowed or planted out some seedlings last month they may be ready now. Pull them up and eat them before they grow too large.

7 Spinach
Pick spinach leaves as a cut-and-come-again crop. Young, tender leaves can be eaten raw in salads, while older, larger ones are best cooked.

8 **Garlic**
The first garlic of the year is a real treat. Lift a few heads while they are still green, before the leaves turn yellow, and use them right away while still "wet" and mild-tasting.

9 **Swiss chard/Spinach beet**
Yellow chard has striking, brightly colored stems. Young leaves can be eaten raw in salads. Older leaves such as these are best cooked, like spinach.

10 **Asparagus**
Harvest asparagus with a sharp knife, cutting the spears just below the surface of the soil when they are about 5–7 in (13–18 cm) long and no fatter than your thumb or forefinger. Cook and eat as soon as possible after picking.

11 **Rhubarb**
Pick rhubarb when the stalks reach about 12 in (30 cm) in height. Don't let them get much longer or they tend to become stringy.

12 **Green onions**
You may be able to harvest your first new-season green onions from seeds sown in the spring—especially if the weather has been mild or you've used cloches or a cold frame.

13 **Globe artichokes**
New-season artichokes will still be tiny and, although it's tempting to leave them to grow larger, pick some now for cooking and eating whole. They're delicious. And anyway, more will grow to take their place.

14 **Spring cabbages**
The end of this month could well mark the last of your spring cabbages. Make the most of them now—you may have to wait a month or two before the first of your summer varieties are ready.

Sow in May

Every year the first spells of warm spring sunshine draw out enthusiastic gardeners, clutching handfuls of brand-new seed packets. Sadly, not only are many of the seeds sown too early but often they are all sown at once. As a consequence, seeds either fail to germinate in soil that's still too wet or cold, or the tender young seedlings are lost in a sudden late frost. When an entire batch survives, you can find yourself with glut of produce in midsummer because everything is ready for harvesting at once. Far better to stagger the whole process. Try "succession sowing" a small batch of seeds every two or three weeks. It will maximize your chances of success and spread out your harvest.

VEGETABLE SEEDS TO SOW OUTDOORS UNDER COVER

- Beets
- Corn
- Corn salad
- Cucumbers
- French beans
- Runner beans

Cabbages, cauliflowers, brussels sprouts, and broccoli

May is probably the last month for sowing brussels sprouts if you want them ready by the end of the year. The same goes for cauliflowers and cabbages (except for next spring's early varieties). Sow them all indoors or out,

depending on the weather. Some can be sown in a temporary seedbed and transplanted later in the year when space becomes available. You can keep sowing sprouting broccoli and calabrese until July.

Chilies, peppers, and cucumbers

To be safe, continue to sow chilies and peppers indoors. Outdoors, even in May, seeds may not germinate. Cucumbers, however, can probably be sown outdoors under a cloche or in a cold frame.

Zucchini, pumpkins, and other squashes

Sow seeds indoors to guarantee that they germinate successfully. Plant out seedlings next month.

Endive and chicory

It's still advisable to sow endive and both sugarloaf and radicchio forms of chicory indoors in the warmth; they can be hardened off and planted out in June or July. However, Belgian or Witloof chicory can be sown directly outside now.

(left) **Winter cabbages**, such as these Savoy types, that you sowed in trays last month will have germinated, ready for transplanting in the next month or two.

(right, top to bottom) **Chili pepper** seedlings sown indoors should be showing strong, healthy growth.
Zucchini seedlings can be transplanted next month to their final positions.
Runner beans sown outdoors will need protection on cold nights.

VEGETABLE SEEDS TO SOW OUTDOORS

- Arugula
- Beets
- Brussels sprouts
- Cabbages (summer, autumn, winter, and red)
- Calabrese
- Carrots
- Cauliflowers
- Chicory (Belgian)

- Florence fennel
- French beans
- Green onions
- Kale
- Kohlrabi
- Land cress
- Lettuces
- Oriental leaves
- Peas
- Radishes

- Runner beans
- Rutabagas
- Salad leaves
- Spinach
- Sprouting broccoli
- Summer purslane
- Swiss chard/ Spinach beet
- Turnips

Florence fennel and kohlrabi

Sow some of each outdoors this month—fennel only when the soil is really warm enough for seeds to germinate. Reserve a few seeds for a second or even third batch later in the summer.

French and runner beans

Continue sowing seeds indoors if the weather is still cold or unpredictable; outdoors if the soil has warmed up and there are no longer any frosts. If necessary protect young seedlings with cloches or plastic bottles.

Herbs

Succession-sow further small batches of seed such as basil, cilantro, chervil, dill, lovage, parsley, and sorrel. Young plants that are tender or half-hardy, such as basil, may still need protecting with cloches or covers.

Leaf vegetables

Continue to sow kale, spinach, Swiss chard, and Oriental leaves such as mizuna, mibuna, chop suey greens, Chinese broccoli, and mustard greens. They can all be sown outdoors now, although prepare to cover them if necessary.

Lettuces and other salad crops

Sow more lettuce, arugula, land cress, summer purslane, corn salad, and other salad leaves outdoors this month to ensure a steady supply. Sow under cover in colder regions.

Melons

It may be warm enough this month to sow seeds outdoors in a cold frame or under a cloche. If not, sow indoors and position where it is warm, such as on a sunny windowsill or in a heated greenhouse.

Root vegetables

Carrots, beets, rutabagas, and turnips can now safely be sown outdoors. Beets, whose seeds can be notoriously hit-or-miss to germinate, may need covering with cloches if the spring is poor and the soil is still cold and wet.

Peas

Continue to sow maincrop peas, snow peas, and snap peas outdoors, protecting seedlings with cloches or nets if necessary.

Corn

Sow corn directly outside now. Always sow in blocks rather than rows for successful pollination. Protect young seedlings from frosts and also from attack by slugs and snails with cloches made from upturned plastic soda bottles.

VEGETABLE SEEDS TO SOW INDOORS

- Cabbages (summer, autumn, winter, and red)
- Cauliflowers (summer and autumn)
- Chicory (sugarloaf and radicchio)
- Chilies and peppers
- Endive
- French beans
- Gherkins
- Kale
- Marrows
- Pumpkins and winter squashes
- Runner beans
- Sprouting broccoli
- Zucchini and summer squashes

(left) **Runner beans** may still need protection from late frosts; use cloches to surround the stems. You can make your own very cheaply by cutting down plastic bottles.

(below left) **Chop suey greens** can be sown indoors for transplanting later. The young, aromatic leaves are used in salads.

(below right) **Carrots** sown direct outdoors last month should have produced tiny seedlings that now need careful thinning.

Maximize your growing space

Here are a number of techniques for ensuring that you get the absolute most out of your garden. Intercropping capitalizes on the fact that, because vegetables grow at different rates, it's possible to grow a combination of fast- and slow-growing crops at the same time in the same area. Catch-cropping involves making use of temporarily unoccupied ground to sow a few fast-growing crops—salads, for example—in the period between two separate plantings of slower, more long-term crops.

(top) **Intersowing radishes and parsnips** Radishes are fast, parsnips are slow. Sow the two together in the same row. The radishes will come up first, and can be carefully harvested just as the parsnips need more light and space.

(bottom) **Intercropping lettuces and leeks** Here, young leek seedlings have been planted between faster-growing lettuces. Cut the lettuces before the leeks fill out and need the space.

Intercropping

Intersowing or intercropping is a method of growing two different crops in the same row or bed—one fast-growing and the other slow. Although both may be sown or planted at the same time and then grown together, the faster of the two will have been harvested and out of the ground before the slower is ready to fill the space. Tall crops, such as corn, also leave adequate space for lettuces to grow beneath.

Fast-growing crops include Oriental salad leaves, small lettuces, corn salad, spinach, radishes, and spring-planted shallot sets. Slow-growing crops, among which the quicker ones can be sown, include corn, tomatoes, leeks, parsnips, and winter brassicas such as cabbages, cauliflowers, sprouting broccoli, and brussels sprouts.

Catch-cropping

The technique of catch-cropping means sowing and harvesting a fast-growing crop in the brief "free" period during which an area of the garden might be empty—in late spring and early summer, before planting out leeks or winter cabbages, for example. Or, perhaps, after lifting early-season broad beans or new potatoes, before the ground is used for hardy kale or autumn-sown Japanese onions.

INTERSOWING LETTUCES AND CORN

Small lettuces, particularly loose-leaf and semi-cos varieties, are fast-growing. If seed is sown between young, transplanted corn plants, the lettuces will mature and be ready to harvest before the corn grows up and completely shades the ground.

1 **Mark out a grid** of squares on the surface of the soil to create the block pattern that is best for growing corn. The sides of the squares should be about 18 in (45 cm) long.

2 **Plant out** a young corn seedling in the corner of each of the squares. Firm down the soil and water.

3 **Mix some lettuce seed** with a little fine sand and then sprinkle it sparingly in between the corn plants. Rake over the soil gently.

4 **Thin the lettuce** to about three or four plants per square. They should be ready to harvest within two or three months, whereas it will be three or four months before the corn is fully grown and ready to pick.

Plant in May

May is the month when you should be able to start planting in earnest. Only in the chilliest areas will the soil still be so cold or waterlogged that planting is impossible. However, transplant tender seedlings only when the last chance of frost has gone—or if you're sure you can cover them with cloches or fleece if you have to. Take care too, to harden off plants grown indoors or under cover before moving them outside. They won't respond well to abrupt and unfamiliar changes in growing conditions.

Eggplants, chilies, and peppers

Toward the end of the month, begin planting out young eggplant, chili, and pepper plants raised indoors. Harden them off first, and keep them under cloches on cold days and at night if temperatures are still low.

Brussels sprouts, cabbages, and cauliflowers

Except in colder regions, start planting out brussels sprouts, summer, autumn, and red cabbages, and summer and autumn cauliflowers that you've either bought from the garden center or raised indoors from seed. They all grow quite large so space them out generously and don't crowd them.

(left, top to bottom) **Fit brassica collars** around seedlings to deter cabbage root flies. **Zucchinis** need plenty of water. This membrane will keep moisture in and weeds out.

VEGETABLES TO PLANT OUTDOORS

- Brussels sprouts
- Cabbages (summer, autumn, and red)
- Cauliflowers (summer and autumn)
- Celeriac
- Celery
- Chilies and peppers
- Corn
- Cucumbers
- Eggplant
- Florence fennel
- Globe artichokes
- Kohlrabi
- Leeks
- Lettuces
- Marrows
- Peas
- Potatoes
- Pumpkins and winter squashes
- Rhubarb
- Sprouting broccoli
- Sweet potatoes
- Tomatoes
- Zucchini and summer squashes

PLANTING OUT PUMPKIN SEEDLINGS

If you want pumpkins of a reasonable size, or you'd like to try one of the giant varieties, plant them out now for impressive, Halloween-ready fruits.

1 Seedlings that have three or four true leaves are ready to plant out.

2 Dig a fair-sized hole with a trowel or bulb planter, add organic matter, then firm in the plants and mulch well to retain moisture. Pumpkins are very thirsty plants.

Celeriac, Florence fennel, and kohlrabi

Harden off and transplant seedlings raised indoors or growing outside in cold frames.

Celery

Begin planting celery this month: self-blanching types in closely spaced blocks, and trench varieties in specially prepared celery trenches. Protect from frost if necessary.

Corn

Start planting out any young corn seedlings you've bought or grown indoors or under cover. Sow them in blocks (see p.107), and if necessary protect them with improvized bottle cloches.

Cucumbers

Toward the end of the month when the soil is warm and frosts are over, harden off and then plant out outdoor or "ridge" cucumber seedlings.

Globe artichokes

This month is your last chance for propagating artichokes by dividing and taking offsets from established plants, and planting them out (see p.75).

Self-blanching celery, as the name suggests, shouldn't need earthing up. You can aid the self-blanching process by planting in blocks so that plants in the center are shielded from the light.

Herbs

Transplant container-grown herbs that you've either bought or propagated and raised yourself. Tender plants such as basil may still need covering at night.

Leeks

May is usually the first month during which you can start transplanting or "dibbing in" young leeks (see p.108).

Lettuces and other salad leaves

Continue transplanting lettuce seedlings. Homemade bottle cloches protect them from both frosts and slugs.

Peas

Continue planting out pea seedlings raised indoors or in cold frames. Provide them with supports to which they can cling, and net them to keep off birds.

Potatoes

The last of your seed potatoes should go in by the end of the month at the latest.

Rhubarb

Transplant any young rhubarb plants you've grown indoors from seed.

Sprouting broccoli

Transplant seedlings into specially prepared beds where the soil has been firmly packed down. Like all brassicas, broccoli likes firm ground. Fit brassica collars to prevent female cabbage root flies from laying their eggs.

(left) **Bottle cloches** are an effective and inexpensive way to insulate young salad leaves. Cut-down plastic soda bottles are ideal.

Strawberries
Continue planting strawberries. Alpine varieties need to be planted now if you want them to fruit this summer.

Sweet potatoes
If it has been a mild spring, it may be worth planting sweet potato "slips," burying them in special earthed-up mounds or ridges (see p.109). Otherwise, wait for warmer weather to arrive next month.

Tomatoes
In May, garden centers and nurseries are full of young tomato plants for sale. But don't be tempted until next month if there's still a risk of frost and you're unable to cover them at night. Use homemade bottle cloches if you're too impatient to wait.

Zucchini, marrows, pumpkins, and other squashes
Plant out in soil that has been enriched with plenty of organic matter. Keep vulnerable young plants well watered, free of slugs, and use cloches to protect them from lethal, late frosts.

FRUIT TO PLANT OUTDOORS
- Cape gooseberries
- Cranberries
- Strawberries

(below, left to right) **Pea seedlings** will be shooting out tendrils. Give them supports, such as peasticks, to climb up. **Corn** planted outside will benefit from the warmth provided by a plastic bottle cloche.

Jobs for May

May in the kitchen garden is as much about battling weeds and pests as it is about sowing and planting new crops. Birds, slugs, snails, aphids, flea beetles, butterflies, moths, and innumerable other forms of wildlife will regard your newly emerging seedlings and tender young plants as an irresistibly delicious free meal. And if the bugs don't get them, weeds will strangle or smother them to death. You'll need to take action—organic or otherwise—if your crops are to survive.

Harden off and plant out seedlings

Gradually acclimatize tender young plants raised indoors to conditions outside. Move them outside during the day and back inside again at night. Or, if they're in cold frames or cloches, open them during the day and close them at night. Plant them out only when there's no longer any danger of frost.

Water seeds and seedlings

Water regularly and generously. May can be a surprisingly dry month, and all growing plants need to be kept moist, especially young ones. They may not survive if you let them dry out.

Weed regularly

Controlling weeds is a continual challenge. They will be growing as vigorously as anything else on your plot this month. It's important to remove them, however, because they compete with your own plants for water and nutrients in the soil. Using a hoe is the least backbreaking way of weeding, and is best done on dry, warm days when the sun will dry out and kill uprooted weeds.

Protect plants against frosts

There's always a possibility of late frosts in May. But if you decide to take a risk and plant out tender plants regardless, it's wise to have cloches, tunnels, fleece, or even newspapers on hand to cover them at night if the weather worsens and they look as if they may be in danger.

1 Move seedlings grown under cover outdoors in the daytime to enable them to adjust to outside temperatures.

2 Water seedlings regularly, using a watering can with a fine rose. Early morning and evening are the best times.

3 Weed as often as you can—use a hand fork to remove weeds that have sprung up between crops.

4 Thin out seedlings ruthlessly. Carrots, shown here, need enough room to swell and grow.

5 Protect squash plants overnight under cloches. Take off the lids of glass types during the day, for ventilation.

6 Support broad beans with strong twine strung between canes to prevent heavily laden plants from falling over.

7 Earth up rows of potato plants so that the tubers growing underground are not exposed to the light.

8 Cover strawberry plants with cloches overnight for an early crop. Remove them during the day.

9 Reduce the number of raspberry canes in your rows. Prune out less vigorous shoots to allow in light and air.

Thin out seedlings

Seeds you sowed last month may by now have produced seedlings that need thinning. If you don't thin them, crops such as carrots, parsnips, beets, and lettuces may not have room to grow to a reasonable size. Don't throw away the thinnings—add them to green salads.

Pot on growing plants

Repot into larger containers any plants that are becoming pot-bound if you're not yet ready to transplant them outside into the ground.

Support broad beans

Stake broad beans with canes and lengths of string to help them support the increasing weight as pods start to form.

Earth up potatoes

Continue regularly drawing soil up around developing potato plants in order to prevent the tubers from breaking through the surface. If they are exposed to light, they turn green and can become poisonous.

Put up supports for peas and climbing beans

Peas need hazel or birch peasticks or supports constructed from chicken wire or plastic mesh up which to climb; otherwise, they'll sprawl on the ground and be eaten by slugs and snails. And climbing beans also need supporting canes. It's worth erecting them now, even if you have not yet sown seeds or planted seedlings.

Feed and mulch globe artichokes

Remove any old straw or bracken that you used as a protective covering for plants during the winter, and either water them with a high-potash feed or spread a rich organic mulch around them.

Cover strawberries and remove runners

In cold regions, keep cloches in place over strawberry plants so that they flower and produce a crop as early as possible. Remove the cloches during the day to allow insects to pollinate them. Cut off any unwanted runners.

Pick flowers off new strawberries

Continue to remove all blossoms from new summer-fruiting strawberry plants. You don't want them to crop in their first year.

Weed and mulch fruit bushes

Weed carefully around fruit bushes and canes. After a spell of rain, when the soil is damp, spread a layer of organic mulch over the surface to help retain moisture and suppress the growth of further weeds.

Remove unwanted raspberry canes

Raspberries tend to be over-eager in throwing out new shoots and suckers. Pull or cut some of them out, or you'll end up with a thicket of canes too dense for sunshine and air to penetrate, and your fruit may be either underdeveloped or diseased.

Thin gooseberries

Begin to thin out gooseberries as the fruits develop. Any you pick are unlikely to be ripe enough to eat raw but can be used for cooking.

Prune trained fruit trees

Prune trained cherry and plum trees, shorten leaders and side shoots on trained apples and pears, and either thin out or tie in new shoots on trained apricots, peaches, and nectarines.

May pests & diseases

Vegetables

■ **Watch for flea beetle,** especially on the leaves of radishes, rocket, and brassica seedlings such as cabbages, cauliflowers, and broccoli. Keep plants well watered so that they grow strongly and survive attack.

■ **Slugs and snails** can be deadly now. Wet weather draws them out, especially at night.

■ **Pigeons** will attack brassicas, peas, and strawberries. You can try scarecrows, but nets are the only real solution.

■ **Broad bean or black bean aphids** are attracted to tender growing shoots at the top of the plants. Pinch them out as soon as pods start to form lower down.

■ **Carrot flies** are laying their eggs this month. Protect early crops with fleece or physical barriers.

■ **Asparagus beetles** should be picked off and destroyed before they lay the eggs that hatch into hungry larvae.

■ **Fit brassica collars** around cabbages, cauliflowers, and broccoli to deter cabbage root fly.

Fruit

■ **Net strawberries** to keep off birds, and deter slugs by laying a bed of dry straw around the base of the plants.

■ **Check apples** for canker, powdery mildew, and scab.

■ **Check pears** for pear leaf blister mite, canker, and scab.

■ **Inspect gooseberries** and currants for sawflies, currant blister aphid, and American gooseberry mildew. Pick off or spray as necessary.

■ **Net soft fruit bushes** to keep birds off.

■ **Codling moths** mate this month. Hang pheromone traps in apple trees to catch the males, thus preventing the females from becoming pregnant and laying eggs.

■ **Don't spray** any fruit trees or bushes when they are covered in blossom.

(right, top to bottom) **Broad bean aphids**, also known as blackfly, eat growing shoots and can infest plants. **Straw beds** beneath strawberries help reduce slug damage. **Brassica collars** fitted around stems will deter cabbage root fly. **Pheromone traps** will lure male codling moths.

June

June is a key month—the midpoint of the year marks the end of spring and the beginning of summer. As such, while it may be your last chance to sow seeds of runner beans or maincrop carrots and peas, it's may be your first opportunity to harvest crops such as new potatoes, beets, onions, strawberries, cherries, and gooseberries. The longest day of the year—the summer solstice—is on the 21st, and the month progresses your plants will be receiving increasingly more hours of sunlight, and steadily rising temperatures. The daylength in the North may be an hour or more than in the Deep South, but spring arrives nearly a month later. Hot weather is accompanied by drought in many areas, necessitating frequent watering or irrigation. Unfortunately, insects, birds, slugs, snails, and other pests are on the attack, too. You'll need to be tirelessly vigilant to keep them down to manageable levels.

Ripening strawberries can be pampered with a bed of fresh straw. It will protect them from getting dirtied by rain splashing up from wet soil and may also help deter slugs.

Top tasks for June

- **Harvest** new-season early potatoes, peas and broad beans, onions, beets, summer salads, and fruit such as strawberries, gooseberries, and cherries.
- **Sow** seeds for vegetables, salads, and herbs that you'll pick later in the summer and autumn.
- **Plant** out tender seedlings with confidence now that the danger of frost has passed.
- **Weed** ruthlessly and water regularly to give young plants their best possible chance.
- **Net** peas, cabbages, and fruit bushes to protect them from hungry birds.
- **Keep a careful watch** for slugs, snails, blackfly, cabbage white caterpillars, carrot fly, and other harmful insects.

Vegetables

1 Potatoes
Lifting your first new potatoes of the year is always a rewarding moment. The first of the early varieties, such as 'Accent', 'Annabel', 'Red Duke of York', and 'Concorde', should be ready in June—about 100–110 days after planting, depending of course on the weather and other growing factors.

2 Swiss chard/Spinach beet
Like spinach, Swiss chard can be harvested throughout the summer—as long as it doesn't bolt. When the leaves are young they can be eaten raw as a cut-and-come-again salad; when larger they can be cooked.

3 Turnips
Many modern turnip varieties are fast-growing and will be ready to harvest just five or six weeks after sowing seeds. At that stage, the roots may be no bigger than golf balls—but they'll be at their sweetest and nuttiest.

4 Cauliflowers
Early summer cauliflowers—if planted out in March—should be ready for picking now. Catch them while the heads are firm, before they bolt.

5 Asparagus
Cut asparagus regularly, before the spears grow too thick and woody. Traditionally, harvesting is supposed to stop on June 21st, the longest day of the year, but there's no harm in continuing for a while longer if you've still got tender, tasty spears.

6 Broad beans
You should get an early crop of broad beans this month if you planted seeds the previous autumn or sowed some at the start of the new year under cover or indoors. Pick the pods when they're still small, which is when the beans are at their sweetest.

7 Garlic
Continue harvesting garlic as it becomes ready—either pulling the bulbs when they are fresh or "green" and using them right away, or waiting till the leaves turn yellow and then drying out the bulbs in preparation for storage.

8 Globe artichokes
Young, tightly budded globes can be cooked and eaten whole. Leave them to grow larger and they're best boiled or steamed then picked apart for their soft, fleshy leaves and for the heart that lies hidden at the center.

9 Beets
Harvest your first beets of the year, picking them when they are no larger than golf balls to catch them at their most tender and tastiest. You can eat the leaves in salads or stir-fries, too.

10 Onions
June is the month to start harvesting overwintered Japanese onions grown from sets you planted outdoors the previous autumn. It's also the month for "competition" onions—those lovingly raised from seeds sown indoors at the beginning of the year.

11 Spinach
Harvest spinach leaves regularly and keep plants very well watered to discourage them from bolting as summer arrives and temperatures rise.

12 Peas
The first peas of the year are always the sweetest and tastiest. Pick them while they're still young and, if you can, eat them immediately, before their sugars turn to starch.

13 Florence fennel
June is likely to be the first month of the year for fennel. Small, young bulbs can be eaten raw in salads; larger ones may be better cooked.

14 Kohlrabi
The first of the fastest growing varieties should be ready to harvest in June. To eat raw in summer salads, pick them when they are about the size of a golf ball.

Salads

1 Lettuces
Small, crisp, mini-cos lettuces like this 'Little Gem' type grow swiftly and should be ready to harvest if sown indoors in March, or under cover in April.

2 Green onions
Green onions can be harvested during most months of the year, although June may be the first month for seeds sown in the spring. For earlier crops, raise them indoors.

3 Radishes
With careful planning and successive sowing you should be able to provide a supply of radishes almost all year round. You should get a June crop from sowings in late April or early May.

4 Salad leaves
Harvest young leaves of peppery mizuna and 'Red Russian' kale and mix with other leaves, such as arugula, for a tasty and unusual summer salad.

13

16

17

15 Carrots

If you sowed an early variety in March or April, you should be able to pull your first carrots of the year this month. Small, baby carrots are wonderful in salads and need only the briefest cooking for stir-fries.

16 Rhubarb

Continue harvesting sticks of rhubarb, but bear in mind that there's not long left. Next month you should stop and let the plant grow normally, without removing any more stems or leaves.

17 Broccoli

Both calabrese and summer sprouting broccoli should be ready for harvesting this month. Cut the heads or shoots when they are firm and the flowers tightly budded.

Fruit

1

2

3

1 Strawberries

June is without doubt strawberry month. Few things signal the first day of summer more perfectly than a bowl of strawberries and cream. Check plants daily so you can pick the berries when they are perfectly ripe and at their sweetest and juiciest.

2 Gooseberries

In June pick alternate fruits as a way of thinning out the crop. Use those you pick this month for cooking because they may not yet be quite ripe. And use the ones you pick next month for eating fresh, since they'll be fully ripened and therefore sweeter.

3 Cherries

July is really the key month for cherries but if weather conditions have been favorable a few early varieties may be ready for picking in June, particularly in warmer parts of the country.

Sow in June

By June, the danger of frost should be over in all but the very coldest of areas and it should be possible to sow most seeds outside, even if some go into seed trays, modules, or pots for planting out later. If nights are still chilly, and if you're concerned that temperatures may not be high enough for germination, you can always cover seeds or bring trays and pots indoors.

Beets

Continue sowing beet seeds in June—perhaps a few at the beginning of the month and a few at the end so that in September and October you'll have some to harvest that haven't grown too large. They can be stored for the winter if necessary.

Broccoli

Sow late sprouting broccoli seeds either where you want to grow them or in a seedbed for transplanting later. Depending on the variety and your climate, you should be able to harvest them in autumn or overwinter them for picking early the following year. This late in the year, calabrese is better sown where it is going to stay as it is a crop that doesn't like being moved once the weather is warm.

Carrots

This is the last chance to sow maincrop varieties that will be ready for harvesting in September or October.

Chicory

All three types of chicory—Witloof or Belgian, sugarloaf, and radicchio—can be sown outdoors in June. The former will be ready for forcing during the winter.

Zucchini, summer squashes, and marrows

If you don't already have plants you've raised in pots, you can sow seeds directly outside now that the soil has warmed up thoroughly. Sow two seeds together and, once they've germinated, remove the weaker of the two.

VEGETABLE SEEDS TO SOW OUTSIDE

- Beets
- Broccoli (both calabrese and sprouting)
- Carrots
- Florence fennel
- French beans
- Kale
- Kohlrabi
- Marrows
- Oriental leaves
- Peas
- Pumpkins and winter squashes
- Runner beans
- Rutabagas
- Swiss chard
- Turnips
- Zucchini and summer squashes

Make sure you leave plenty of space between plants because they spread widely and need a lot of room.

Cucumbers
Outdoor cucumbers are usually started off earlier in the year in pots or under cover, but if you sow some seeds outside this month they should give you a crop in August or September.

Endive
Sow curly or broad-leaved varieties outside for a crop in autumn and early winter. Germination may be erratic in hot weather.

Florence fennel
Traditionally, the best time to sow fennel is after June 21st, the longest day of the year. It's said that the plants are then less likely to bolt. Modern varieties are more forgiving, so anytime in June should give you a crop in early autumn. Sow successively and sow more than you need in case some seeds don't germinate—or slugs gobble up your seedlings.

French beans
Sow a second wave of French beans to follow those that were sown outside last month.

French beans are ready for a second sowing this month. Sow seeds in staggered rows at a depth of about 2 in (5 cm) and at intervals of 6–9 in (15–22 cm). Keep them well-watered.

(far left) **Emerging beet seedlings** will now be showing their first true leaves. Thin out seedlings at this stage to give the strongest plenty of space to grow.

(left) **Young zucchini** are thirsty plants and need regular watering. Heap a little soil up around the stem to reduce the chance of waterlogging, and mulch to retain moisture.

SALAD SEEDS TO SOW OUTSIDE

- Chicory
- Cucumbers
- Endive
- Lettuces
- Radishes
- Salad leaves
- Scallions

Herbs

June may be your last chance to sow seeds of herbs such as coriander, basil, chervil, fennel, dill, and parsley before the weather becomes too warm for them to germinate reliably.

Kale

Sow a second batch of seeds in seedtrays, modules, or pots ready for planting out next month. Alternatively, leave them in their trays—or even in seedbeds on your kitchen garden—and pick young leaves for salads.

Kohlrabi

Continue sowing seeds where you intend the plants to grow. Thin out seedlings if necessary, keep well weeded, protect against slugs, and net to keep off birds.

Leaf vegetables

Continue sowing seeds of Swiss chard and spinach beet.

Lettuces

Sow in situ and thin out if the seedlings are too crowded. High temperatures may hinder germination—which is perhaps why folklore has it that seeds are best sown at the end of the day, when the soil is cooling down.

Oriental leaves

Sow mizuna, mibuna, mustard greens, bok choy, and other oriental leaves for salads when leaves are small, and for stir-fries when larger.

Peas

The beginning of June is probably your last chance to sow maincrop peas, snow peas, and snap peas. Toward the end of the month, switch to a fast-maturing early variety. These will be ready for harvesting in about September.

Pumpkins and winter squashes

These are usually started off earlier in the year in pots, but they can be planted straight into the ground in June. Prepare the soil by adding lots of well-rotted compost or manure.

Radishes

Sow a few salad radishes in small quantities throughout the month for a constantly replenishing crop.

Runner beans

This is your last opportunity for sowing runner beans. But with luck, seeds sown at

the end of June will provide you with a crop as late as October—as long as there is no risk of frost.

Rutabagas

Sow if you didn't do so last month. Thin out seedlings and if necessary cover with fine netting to keep off birds and cabbage root fly.

Salad leaves

Continue succession-sowing of arugala, corn salad, summer purslane, chard, kale, mizuna, and other mixed leaves to use as cut-and-come-again salads.

Scallions

Sow a couple more batches of seeds during the month to ensure you have a continuous supply through the autumn.

Turnips

Sow another batch for harvesting in August or September before the roots become too large.

Fresh, green pea seedlings are almost ready to start climbing. From this stage they are at their most vulnerable to attack from pigeons, so remember to cover them with netting.

Plant in June

June is the perfect month for planting out all the seedlings you've been raising in pots or modules. The days are now at their longest, temperatures are climbing, and the soil should be thoroughly warmed through. If you still have plants under cover, ensure that they're hardened off before transplanting. Move them outside or leave them uncovered during the day, and at night too if there is absolutely no chance of a late frost.

VEGETABLES TO PLANT OUT

- Brussels sprouts
- Cabbages (red, summer, autumn, winter)
- Cauliflowers (summer and autumn)
- Celeriac
- Chili peppers
- Corn
- Eggplants
- French beans
- Kale
- Leeks
- Marrows
- Pumpkins and winter squashes
- Runner beans
- Sprouting broccoli
- Sweet peppers
- Sweet potatoes
- Zucchini and summer squashes

Plant sweet peppers when all risk of frost has passed and choose a warm, sheltered site. Gently ease the plants out of their pots and avoid handling by the stem. It's best to space plants at least 20 in (50 cm) apart.

Brussels sprouts and cabbages

Plant out brussels sprouts, the last of your summer, autumn, and red cabbages, and the first of your winter cabbages. Fit them with brassica collars to deter cabbage root fly, and net them immediately to protect them from birds and cabbage white butterflies.

Cape gooseberries

Like melons, cape gooseberry seedlings can be planted out in a sunny, sheltered spot once the weather has thoroughly warmed up.

Cauliflowers

Cauliflower seedlings sown in spring for harvesting in summer and autumn should be planted out now.

Eggplants that have been grown in pots either indoors or under cover can be planted outside now to take advantage of warm soil and long, light days. Humidity is vital so keep plants well watered and mulched.

Celeriac

Late June is probably your last chance to plant out celeriac; it is slow-growing, and needs time to develop to a worthwhile size.

Celery

Plant in rich, fertile soil prepared with plenty of well-rotted compost or manure—in a special celery trench, or in the case of self-blanching varieties, in closely spaced blocks.

Chicory

Transplant sugarloaf chicory or radicchio seedlings raised inside or under cover, but try to disturb the roots as little as possible.

Chilies and sweet peppers

Harden off young chili and pepper plants grown under cover and, if there's no longer any chance of late frosts, plant them out.

Cucumbers

Harden off outdoor or "ridge" cucumber seedlings and plant them in low mounds of earth enriched with well-rotted compost.

"BLOCK-PLANTING" CORN

Unlike most crops, corn is not pollinated by insects or birds. It relies on pollen falling from male flowers onto female flowers. This is more likely to take place if it is planted closely in square or rectangular blocks, rather than spaced apart in long rows.

1 By June, it should be possible to transplant young corn plants, or ready-to-plant seedlings. Mark out square or rectangular blocks, and plant them about 14–18in (35–45cm) apart in each direction.

2 At the top of each plant are the "tassels" of the pollen-producing male flowers. Beneath them are the "silks" of the female flowers on which the falling pollen is caught.

"DIBBING IN" LEEKS

Leeks are planted out in deep, narrow holes made using a tool called a dibber. Burying them in the ground in this way protects the seedlings from the light and produces long, white, blanched stems.

1 Drop one leek seedling into each dibber hole with the roots sitting on the bottom of the hole and the heart tip at soil level, then water in well.

2 There is no need to backfill—after watering the soil will fall loosely back into the hole, creating a space that the swelling leek stem will grow to fill.

Eggplants

Plant out eggplants by the end of this month to give them as much time as possible to grow and ripen into good-sized fruit.

Endive

Once temperatures have really warmed up, plant out seedlings sown under cover in spring. Be patient: the colder it is, the more likely the plants are to bolt.

French beans and runner beans

Plant out dwarf bushes in rows or blocks, and climbers at the foot of canes. You may need to tie in reluctant climbers if they need a little encouragement to twine around their supports.

Herbs

Transplant container-grown herbs that you've either bought or propagated and raised.

Kale

In June you should be able to begin transplanting kale you've grown from seed. Wait until seedlings are at least 4 in (10 cm) high and disturb the roots as little as possible.

Melons

In warm regions, when temperatures have risen and there is no risk of late frosts, try planting sweet melon seedlings, either bought from a

Homemade supports for climbing beans and peas are simple and inexpensive to put together, using hazel twigs or bamboo canes. They look particularly attractive in potager-style plots.

SALADS TO PLANT OUT

- Celery
- Chicory
- Cucumbers
- Endive
- Tomatoes

FRUIT TO PLANT OUT
- Cape gooseberry
- Melons
- Strawberries

(right) **Protect zucchini** from the ravages of hungry pests by encircling young plants with cloches made from cut-down plastic soda bottles.

garden center or raised yourself from seed. They need rich, fertile soil, shelter, and lots of sunshine. A cold frame or polytunnel is more likely to give you success.

Sprouting broccoli
Plant out sprouting broccoli seedlings in a sheltered area where the soil is firmly packed down so that developing roots are able to support the weight of the growing plants.

Strawberries
Plant new, cold-stored, bare-root runners now for harvesting in about two months' time. Pot-raised plants can be planted now too—although it may be better to delay them until later.

Sweet potatoes
If you didn't plant out sweet potato "slips" in May, you should do so this month. Plant them in deep, rich soil that has been earthed-up into mounds or ridges, and sink open-ended plastic bottles into the soil alongside them so that you can water directly to their roots and growing tubers.

Tomatoes
Plant out any remaining outdoor tomatoes not already transplanted. They need warmth and sunshine, and will benefit from the extra protection of cloches or open-ended plastic bottles. Vine or cordon varieties will need stakes or strong canes for support.

Zucchini, marrows, pumpkins, and other squashes
These can all be planted out in June, whether they're for harvesting in summer or later in the autumn and early winter. Allow plenty of space, and keep them well-watered and mulched.

(above) **Sweet potatoes** need a lot of moisture; water into an open-ended plastic bottle to make sure that all the liquid goes straight down to the tubers.

Wage war on weeds

The battle against weeds is relentless. In every square yard of soil it is estimated that there may be as many as 100,000 weed seeds. Why are they such a bad thing? The simple answer is that they compete. They drink water and absorb nutrients from the soil. They crowd your crops for space, hogging the light and putting them in the shade. And they play host to all kinds of pests and diseases.

Perennial weeds

1 Bindweed
One of the most difficult of all weeds to eradicate. Dig up and destroy every piece of root, or spray leaves with systemic weedkiller.

2 Bramble
Vigorous and invasive, with painfully sharp thorns. Roots are deep and must be dug out completely.

3 Creeping buttercup
A low, spreading weed that throws out horizontal runners, producing new plants at each node. Uproot the whole lot.

4 Dock
Dig up the long taproots without letting them snap or they will regenerate.

5 Stinging nettle
Dig out the roots of stinging nettles in order to eradicate completely.

6 Creeping thistle
Its root system is so tenacious that a systemic weedkiller may be the only solution to the problem.

7 Dandelion
Remove dandelion flower heads before they fade and release their tiny, parachute-like seeds—and always dig out the entire taproot.

8 Ground elder
Dig up carefully—this determined weed will regrow from any stray bits of root left in the soil.

Annual and biennial weeds

1 **Goosegrass**
Also known as "cleavers,"
the plants have tiny, hooked
hairs that cling to supports.
Dig up by the roots.

2 **Plantain**
Uproot the whole plant
—including its entire tap
root—before it flowers and
produces seed.

3 **Annual meadowgrass**
Hoe regularly to prevent
the grass from flowering and
spreading across your plot.

4 **Ragwort**
Remove and compost
before the yellow flowers
turn to seed.

5 **Groundsel**
Dig up and remove
before the fluffy, dandelion-
like seed heads form.

6 **Common chickweed**
A low-growing weed
that spreads vigorously but
has shallow roots which are
fairly easy to pull up.

7 **Shepherd's purse**
Easy to uproot when
still young. Compost only if
the heart-shaped seed pods
have not yet formed.

8 **Hairy bittercress**
Pull up when young,
before the long, cylindrical
seed pods appear.

WEEDING TIPS

■ **Hoe regularly** so that you catch weeds
when they are young and while their roots
are still shallow.

■ **Don't let weeds flower**, or they will
generate a new crop of seeds.

■ **Hoe when it's dry** so that severed and
uprooted weeds die quickly.

■ **If the soil is damp**, collect up and
dispose of any remains to ensure that they
don't regrow.

■ **Loosen soil** thoroughly so that when you
dig up roots you leave nothing behind.

■ **Don't put perennial weeds** on your
compost heap; they may live on to fight
another day.

■ **Use lightproof membrane** mulches to
kill established weeds.

■ **Spread surface mulches** to suppress
the growth of new weeds.

■ **Use chemical systemic** weedkillers as
a last resort.

Jobs for June

June is one of the busiest months of the year. The days will be lengthening and the temperatures rising, and everything on the kitchen garden will be growing energetically—not least, the weeds. Most likely, you'll feel that the whole plot is insistently demanding your attention. June can be a surprisingly dry month, too, so there may be a lot of watering to do in order to keep your newly planted seedlings growing healthily.

Weed

Like most plants, weeds put on a growth spurt in June. Dig out any perennial weeds, such as dandelions and creeping buttercup, that you've overlooked in the preceding months. Then hoe regularly, especially on dry days, to prevent annual weeds from competing for moisture with new, young plants.

Water

Most seeds and seedlings need regular watering if they are to germinate and develop successfully. Plants are better able to take up moisture if you water little and often than if you drown them just once a week.

Mulch

Continue to spread mulches such as garden compost, mushroom compost, well-rotted manure, and bark chips. They will help suppress weeds and, if the underlying earth is damp before you apply them, they will also delay evaporation.

Check nets

Make sure peas, cabbages and other brassicas, and soft fruit are all well netted against birds.

Feed tomatoes

As soon as tomatoes being grown under cover form their first tiny fruits, they will benefit

from a weekly feed of high-potash fertilizer. Pinch out small side shoots that grow in the "V" between the leaf stems and the main stem.

Earth up potatoes

Even if you've already done this, it's worth doing again. It will help ensure that the tubers remain out of the light.

Build supports for climbing beans

Use 8 ft- (2.5 m-) long canes and strong twine to construct rows or wigwams ready for beans to climb up. Make sure they're sturdy enough to support the heavy weight of beans when they are fully grown. Protect newly sown or transplanted seedlings with makeshift cloches or collars made from empty plastic bottles.

Cut down broad beans and peas

As soon as harvesting is over, cut plants down to just above the surface of the soil and compost them. But leave the roots in the ground because they are rich in nitrogen.

Feed asparagus

Apply an all-purpose fertilizer now you're no longer picking spears—but leave the plants to grow and don't cut them down until they go brown in autumn.

Summer-prune herbs

Chop back herbs such mint, chives, sage, thyme, and lovage in order to remove tired old leaves and to stimulate the growth of fresh new ones.

(far left) **Water climbing bean** seedlings regularly once they are in their final position. Frequent watering encourages strong, healthy growth and an ability to withstand disease.

(left) **Net young brassicas** as soon as you have transplanted them to keep birds, especially pigeons, at bay. Cabbage white butterflies are eager to lay their eggs on young cabbages.

Runner beans will usually climb up bamboo canes without any encouragement. If they are slow to get started, gently twist each plant around its cane.

Pot up strawberry runners

If your strawberry plants have finished producing fruit, you can either cut off any runners, or use them to make new plants (see p.128).

Summer-prune gooseberries, red currants, and white currants

Prune bushes and cordons by cutting back to five leaves all this year's new lateral shoots —although don't touch any laterals you might want to develop into new branches next year. If summer pruning is done before harvesting it may encourage the fruit to swell.

Remove raspberry suckers

Any rogue suckers that sprout up at a distance from the base of the plants should be pulled out and composted.

Tie in blackberries and hybrid berries

Although the new canes that grow up this year will not bear fruit, they should be tied in securely during this month and next. In the autumn the canes carrying this year's fruit will be cut down, and the new ones will take their place—ready to provide you with more berries next year.

Thin out apples and pears

"June drop" usually takes place toward the end of the month. Apple trees (and to a lesser extent pears) naturally let fall a large number of tiny, embryo fruit as a way of automatically thinning out their crop. In a good year, however, you may have to thin them out still further in order to prevent overcrowding, to allow each fruit to grow to a good size, and to avoid branches breaking under the weight of too much fruit.

Twice thin plums, damsons, and gages

These stone fruit also need thinning in June. Thin once at the beginning of the month, leaving a gap of about 1 in (2.5 cm) between individual fruits, and then again at the end of the month to increase the final gap to about 3 in (8 cm).

Tie in and thin peaches, nectarines, and apricots

Tie in new shoots on wire-trained trees, and thin out fruit to about 6–8 in (15–20 cm) apart for peaches and nectarines and about 3 in (8 cm) apart for apricots.

Summer-prune figs

Prune established fig trees this month by pinching out the tips of new shoots so that they each have only five leaves left.

Grapevines

Prune side shoots, and thin outdoor fruit grown for eating so that the remaining bunches can ripen easily and grow to a reasonable size.

Nectarines, like peaches, can overproduce and heavily laden branches can break. To avoid losing some of your crop, thin fruits thoroughly—those that are touching or close together.

June pests & diseases

Vegetables

■ **Pinch out** tips on broad beans to discourage aphids.

■ **Check for blackfly** on globe artichokes, French and runner beans, and beets.

■ **Pick off** and destroy asparagus beetles and their larvae.

■ **Net cabbages** and other brassicas to protect them from pigeons.

■ **Check cabbages** for cabbage white butterfly eggs and caterpillars, and squash, pick off, or spray.

■ **Remove** and destroy any yellow leaves from cabbages, broccoli, and other brassicas. Otherwise, gray mold or brassica downy mildew may develop and spread.

■ **Check peas** for signs of pea moth. Covering the crop with fleece is the only truly reliable safeguard.

■ **Carrot fly** is still a danger in June. Protect crops with barriers or fine mesh.

■ **Protect against flea beetle** by covering crops such as radishes, rocket, Oriental salad leaves, and beets with fine-gauge mesh.

Fruit

■ **Check apples and pears** for greenfly, scab, and bitter pit, and spray if necessary. Also check that you hung up pheromone traps in apple trees for codling moths.

■ **Check plums** and cherries for aphids and slugworm (small black larvae); spray if necessary.

■ **Net cherries**, currants, and blueberries to protect from birds.

■ **Net strawberries** to keep off birds, and protect fruit from slugs.

■ **Check strawberries** for gray mold, especially in wet weather, and remove and destroy any infected fruit.

■ **Inspect raspberries** and loganberries for raspberry beetle as soon as the berries start to change color, and spray if necessary

■ **Check black currants** for "reversion," a disease carried by big bud mite.

■ **Inspect for greenfly** on currants, and spray if necessary.

■ **Check gooseberries** for gooseberry sawfly larvae and for American gooseberry mildew.

■ **Check grapes** for scale insects and mildew.

July

It's the height of summer. Days are long, temperatures are most likely at their highest and may even exceed 100°F (38°C) for days at a time in the South, Southwest, and Midwest. If all goes well, you're harvesting something delicious from your garden almost every day, and this is also the peak time for picking herbs. But, like June, July is often a dry month, too. Watering is crucial. Most crops need a steady, unbroken supply of water. Interruptions cause problems such as flowers falling, fruits failing to form, skins splitting, premature bolting, and diseases such as tomato blossom end rot. Spreading mulches helps conserve moisture from any rain you do get—and will also control weeds.

Red currants grow well in partial shade but those grown in sun will be sweeter. The beautiful, translucent berries are perfect for making summer desserts, jams, and jellies.

Top tasks for July

■ **Harvest** French and runner beans, zucchinis, carrots, beets, onions, shallots, new potatoes, and summer salads.

■ **Pick** cherries, strawberries, raspberries, currants, gooseberries, and blueberries.

■ **Sow** salad crops and the last of your beets, Florence fennel, French beans, and peas for this year.

■ **Plant** out cabbages, cauliflowers, brussels sprouts, broccoli, and kale for the autumn and winter.

■ **Water** as often as you can to keep crops growing healthily and to prevent them from bolting.

■ **Feed** tomatoes regularly and pinch out side shoots.

■ **Thin out** apples and pears if it looks like you're going to have a bumper crop.

Vegetables

1 Onions
Onions should be reaching harvestable size this month. The close-planted bulb onions shown here were multisown in modules and then planted out in clumps.

2 Oriental mustards
Harvest mixed sowings of Oriental mustard greens for baby-leaf salads, or leave them to grow larger and use them steamed or in stir-fries.

3 Peas
Your peas should be fattening up quickly now. Pick a handful every couple of days before they become too large. Eat them immediately, as soon after picking as possible.

4 Broccoli
Harvest heads of calabrese and individual spears of sprouting broccoli regularly. Both should continue to shoot to give you an ongoing harvest.

5 Beet
Continue regularly lifting beets before they grow too large. And remember that it's not too late to sow more seeds if you want a continuous crop right through to the autumn.

6 Potatoes
Second earlies should be ready to lift this month. As soon as the flowers appear, scrape away some of the soil from one of your ridges and take a look. Lift salad varieties before they become too large, and eat them right away.

7 Runner beans
The first runner beans of the year are undoubtedly the best. Don't hold back and leave them too long or they'll turn stringy. As long as there are still flowers, new beans will continue to form.

8 Florence fennel
Cut fennel bulbs with a knife, about 1 in (2.5 cm) above the level of the soil, and leave the stump in the ground. Within a few weeks, new feathery leaves should have sprouted; use them in salads or stir-fries.

9 Marrows
If you prefer vegetable marrows while they are still relatively young and small, pick them now. If size matters, leave them to grow on to giant proportions.

10 Zucchinis
This is the start of the season for zucchinis and summer squashes. They are capable of literally doubling in size during the course of a single day, so inspect them regularly and harvest them often.

11 Garlic
Continue lifting garlic as the leaves turn yellow and wilt. Spread the bulbs out in the sun to dry if you plan to store them. Otherwise, use them while they are still "wet."

12 Shallots
Your first shallots should be ready this month. They are ready for lifting when the foliage has died down. Dry them on the ground in the sun or, if the weather is wet, under cover on wire racks or wooden slats.

13 French beans
Dwarf bush varieties are likely to be ready for harvesting first. The pods grow alarmingly quickly and you'll probably find you have to pick some every day to catch them while they're still thin, tender, and at their best.

14 Globe artichokes
To catch artichokes at their best, pick the heads when plump while the scalelike leaves are still closed and before the purple flowers start to show through.

15 Carrots
Early carrot varieties are best pulled and eaten while still young, slim, and super-sweet. Eat them raw, add them to salads, or lightly steam them.

16 Turnips
Harvest close-grown, multisown turnips when the roots are still small. That's when they'll taste at their sweetest and most nutty.

17 Kohlrabi
Early varieties are fast-growing and those sown in May could well be ready now. Don't let them grow any larger than a tennis ball.

18 Leaf beet
Perpetual spinach or spinach beet (shown here) and Swiss chard can be harvested now, either when young for salads or when older to be eaten cooked.

19 Broad beans
Bean pods should be swelling rapidly now. Check them every day or two and pick them regularly, starting at the base of the plant, before the beans become mealy and their skins tough and bitter. Keep an eye out for aphids too.

ALSO HARVEST

Chilies and peppers
In temperate regions, it's still very early for chilies and peppers—unless you've grown them in a greenhouse or polytunnel.

Eggplant
Except in warm climates, July is early for eggplant, but if you sowed seeds in early spring you may get your first of the year at the very end of the month.

Spinach
Harvest and water regularly to deter spinach from bolting.

Rhubarb
This is your last chance for rhubarb. Don't pick any more now. Instead, let the plant grow on normally so that it's in good shape to withstand the winter and crop again next year.

Salads

1 Radishes
Harvest radishes from sowings made in late May or early June. Pull them while they're still small or the flavor may become too fiery.

2 Chicory
The first sugarloaf and red chicories may be ready for harvesting. 'Treviso Precoce Mesola' (shown here) is a red variety that can be picked now for baby salad leaves, or left to heart up later in the season.

3 Lettuces
Small, semi-cos lettuces are relatively fast-growing. You can start cutting them as soon as the leaves at the center begin to form a heart. 'Bubbles' (shown here) has slightly crinkly leaves.

4 Tomatoes
Unless you're growing them under cover, this will be your first month for outdoor tomatoes. However, resist temptation and leave them on the vine until they are as ripe, sweet, and juicy as possible before picking them.

5 Scallions
Continue harvesting scallions—and sow more seeds if you want a last, final crop before the end of the year.

6 Arugala
Most salad leaves, including the arugala shown here, can be harvested now. Treat them as cut-and-come-again crops: take what you want and the plant will sprout new leaves and continue growing.

7 Celery
The first crop of self-blanching or green celery should be ready to harvest this month. Watering before digging them up helps to keep them crisp for longer.

8 Cucumbers
Pick your first outdoor-grown cucumbers once they reach about 6–8 in (15–20 cm) in length. Any longer and the seeds are likely to be unpleasantly large.

Fruit

1 Plums
Early-season plums may be ready to pick late in the month. Try to catch them when they're slightly soft but not squishy.

2 White and red currants
The first white and red currants ripen this month. Snip off whole trusses or "strigs," and strip them at home.

3 Cherries
July is the month for cherries, if you succeed in picking them before the birds.

4 Black currants
Traditional varieties ripen gradually, so pick the berries at the top of the trusses or strigs first. Modern varieties ripen all at once: cut off the whole strig.

5 Blueberries
Harvest your first blueberries now. Look for the plumpest, softest berries, with the darkest blue-black color.

6 Gooseberries
By July, gooseberries are ripening properly. Some may be sweet enough to eat raw. Others still need to be cooked.

7 Strawberries
Pick strawberries regularly; remove any that are overripe, show signs of mold, or damage by slugs or birds.

8 Blackberries
The first blackberries may be ready to pick this month, as well as tayberries, loganberries, and other hybrid berries.

ALSO HARVEST

Raspberries
Pick summer-fruiting raspberries when they're fully colored and pull away easily, leaving the core or "plug" behind.

Apricots
A few early varieties may bear fruit this month, if grown in the right conditions.

Peaches and nectarines
July is the first month for early peaches and nectarines grown under cover or in very sheltered spots.

Melons
Melons grown under cover may start to ripen this month.

1

2

3

4

5

6

7

8

Grow edible flowers

The range of flowers you can eat is wider than most people think. Some you may already be familiar with: stuffed zucchini flowers, salad arugala, and herbs such as chives, dill, or coriander. Others may come as more of a surprise: nasturtiums, violas, and marigolds, for example. All will brighten up your kitchen garden, often serving to attract beneficial insects, and will add color and flavor to all kinds of dishes in the kitchen.

1 Calendula
The familiar pot marigold is usually vivid orange, but may also be yellow or cream. Sow seeds in batches between April and July. After picking the flowers, pull off the petals and sprinkle over salads.

2 Borage
Grow borage both for its flowers and for its young leaves—both taste slightly of cucumber. Borage is an annual that self-seeds easily.

3 Chives
Add chive flowers to green salads for a mild onion flavor. Sow seeds under cover in early spring.

4 Nasturtium
Nasturtiums are easy to grow and readily self-sow. Add the flowers to mixed salads—but not liberally since they taste very peppery.

5 Zucchini flower
Snip off the flowers when harvesting your zucchini and serve them either stuffed or deep fried.

6 Viola
Miniature varieties are the best for eating: the flowers have a more delicate flavor than larger pansies. Add to salads, or use to decorate cakes and desserts.

7 Lavender
Propagate lavender from softwood cuttings and harvest the flowers to make a soothing tea, or mix with sugar when making cookies.

8 French marigold
A familiar bedding plant, the French marigold is not related to *Calendula*, but its flowers add a spicy tang and a wonderful color to salads and rice dishes.

Sow or plant in July

It's now getting late in the year for sowing and planting, but there is still time for lettuces, chicory, endives, and other salad leaves as well as for fast-growing varieties of peas, beets, and carrots. If you've now harvested all your broad beans, garlic, onions, and shallots, there may be enough space to transplant any Brussels sprouts, cabbages, and cauliflowers raised from seed in pots.

VEGETABLE
SEEDS TO SOW
- Beets
- Cabbages (spring)
- Calabrese
- Carrots
- Florence fennel
- French beans
- Kale
- Kohlrabi
- Oriental leaves
- Peas
- Radishes (winter)
- Sprouting broccoli
- Swiss chard/Spinach beet
- Turnips

SALAD
SEEDS TO SOW
- Arugula
- Chicory (sugarloaf and red)
- Endive
- Lettuces
- Radishes
- Salad leaves
- Scallions

Brussels sprouts, cabbages, and cauliflowers

July is the time to sow cabbages for next spring, if you choose the right variety. If space is tight, sow them in a temporary seedbed and transplant them later in the year. Now is your last chance to plant out any brussels sprouts, winter cabbages, and autumn cauliflowers that you've been growing from seed.

Broccoli

It's late for sowing or planting broccoli now, although certain cultivars may still give you an autumn crop.

Endive and chicory

Continue sowing both sugarloaf and radicchio forms of chicory. It's probably your last chance to sow or plant out endive.

Florence fennel and kohlrabi

Sow a few more fennel seeds this month for a crop in the autumn, before the first hard frosts. And some more kohlrabi, too—they should then last you through Christmas.

Net brussels sprouts raised in pots (right) and planted in their final positions to keep off birds (far right).

Peas and French beans

This is your last chance for sowing or planting out peas and beans. Any later and the pods are unlikely to develop before the onset of frosts.

Leaf vegetables

Continue to sow kale, Swiss chard, and Oriental leaves such as mizuna, mibuna, chop suey greens, Chinese broccoli, and mustard greens. They are hardy enough to last well into autumn.

Leeks

Finish transplanting or "dibbing in" leeks raised in pots, modules, or temporary seedbeds (see p.108). They should all be in their final growing position this month.

Lettuces and other salad crops

Succession sow more lettuce, arugula, land cress, corn salad, and other salad leaves for an ongoing supply in the autumn.

Root vegetables

Sow your last batch of beets now. Late varieties of carrots and turnips can still go in next month.

(right) **Mibuna** is an easy salad crop to grow from seed and germinates reliably. Thin seedlings to 4 in (10 cm) and harvest tender young leaves as a cut-and-come again crop.

Jobs for July

"Weed, water, mulch" should remain as much of a mantra as it was in June. All three are still high on the list of the most important tasks of the month. Regular watering, in particular, is vital for the successful growth of crops. It also reduces the risk of bolting and helps prevent diseases such as blossom end rot on tomatoes. July is the month for summer-pruning certain fruit trees and bushes as or just after they finish cropping—cherries, currants, gooseberries, and summer-fruiting raspberries.

Weed regularly

Don't ease up on hoeing. Weeds will be growing as vigorously as everything else on your plot. One consolation, however, is that some plants—those that produce lots of foliage such as potatoes, zucchini, and squashes—may keep weeds at bay by covering the ground and depriving them of sunlight.

Water to prevent bolting

Certain vegetables have a natural tendency to flower and run to seed as days lengthen and temperatures rise. Lettuces, rocket, spinach, cauliflowers, and Florence fennel are particularly prone. Watering regularly can help delay or even prevent bolting.

Mulch to conserve moisture

As soon as possible after rain, spread mulches such as garden compost, well-rotted manure, and even grass cuttings to retain moisture in the soil and keep it damp.

Net against birds

Continue to ensure that peas, brassicas, and soft fruit are all securely netted to keep off scavenging birds.

Dry out garlic, onions, and shallots

A few days before you harvest them, loosen the soil around the roots. Choose a dry spell of weather, lift the bulbs, and lay them on the

ground in the sun. The more thoroughly you dry them, the longer they will keep.

Pinch out tops of climbing beans

Climbing beans don't really know when to stop. Pinch out the growing tips when they reach the top of your canes or they will quickly become tangled and top-heavy.

Spray runner beans

It's said that spraying flowers with water deters them from falling and encourages the formation of bean pods; regular watering at the base of the plants may be just as effective.

Pinch out tomato shoots

Nip off the side shoots that appear in the "V" between leaf stems and the main stems of vine tomatoes. And pinch out the growing tip at the top of the plant once four or five trusses have formed. If you allow any more than that, the tomatoes are unlikely to ripen.

Feed tomatoes and peppers

Start regularly watering tomatoes and peppers with a liquid feeding as soon as you see that the first fruits have formed. Feeding encourages both flowers and fruits.

Cover heads of cauliflowers

Protect white heads from turning yellow in the sun by pulling outside leaves over them and tying them in place.

Blanch celery and endives

Earth up trench celery to keep the stems out of the light, and place plates over curly endives to blanch the leaves.

Earth up brassicas and potatoes

Pull earth up around the stalks of brussels sprouts and other brassicas if they seem unsteady, and give them a top-dressing of nitrogenous fertilizer or an organic liquid feed. Keep an eye on potatoes and if necessary continue to earth them up.

Take cuttings of herbs

Propagate perennial and shrubby herbs such as rosemary, sage, and thyme by taking semiripe, softwood, or stem cuttings.

(below left to right) **Lettuces bolt** when they are short of water, usually in very hot weather. **Naturally dried garlic** bulbs can be stored for several months. **Spray runner bean** flowers but water well, too. **Side shoots** on tomato plants should be pinched out regularly. **Earth up** potatoes as they grow. **Rosemary cuttings** that have rooted can now be potted on.

Tidy up summer strawberries

Once your summer-fruiting strawberries have finished, you can neaten old foliage, remove straw, and either cut off and discard any runners or use them to make new plants.

Summer-prune gooseberries, red currants, and white currants

Cut back to five leaves all this year's new side shoots, except any you might want to develop into new branches next year. Removing foliage lets in light and air, helping any remaining fruit ripen and reducing the risk of disease.

Summer-prune black currants

Lightly prune black currants just before or just after picking the fruit. Prune again in winter.

Prune raspberries

As soon as you've finished picking summer raspberries, cut all the canes that have borne fruit down to the ground. Tie in this year's new, green canes in their place.

Tie in blackberries and hybrid berries

Continue to tie in new canes—those that are growing up this year without bearing fruit.

During the autumn, when harvesting is finished, you'll remove the old currant and berry canes, so that you will be ready for the new ones to take their place and produce a crop of berries next year.

Thin apples and pears

If your trees look overcrowded, even after last month's "June drop," thin them out still further in order to allow each fruit to grow to a reasonable size.

Prune cherries and plums

Summer-prune cherries and plum trees once you've harvested the fruit. Both are pruned in summer, not winter.

Check all wire-trained trees

Inspect all espalier, cordon, and fan-trained trees to ensure that all ties are secure but not too tight. Tie in or summer-prune new growth.

Grapevines

Keep on pruning side shoots and, if necessary, continue to thin fruit. Also, remove some of the foliage to increase exposure to the sun and speed up ripening.

PROPAGATING STRAWBERRIES

Strawberries do not reproduce reliably from seed, and are much easier to propagate from runners.

1 When runners that have formed from the parent plant are making strong new growth, loosen with a hand fork and lift gently, taking care not to damage the roots.

2 Pot up new runners separately and plant them at soil level, pegging down well. Keep plants well watered while their roots establish and new leaves develop.

July pests & diseases

Vegetables

■ **Check for blackfly** on globe artichokes, beets, and broad, French, and runner beans.

■ **Inspect cabbage leaves** for the eggs or caterpillars of cabbage white butterflies. Pick them off and squash them by hand, or spray.

■ **Spray potatoes** against blight. If plants are growing poorly, dig one up to check for potato cyst eelworm on the roots.

■ **Spray tomatoes** against blight, and water regularly to prevent the fruits from splitting and guard against blossom end rot.

■ **Slugs and snails** are as hungry and as destructive as ever. Deploy your chosen method of dealing with them.

■ **Birds** will devour brassicas, peas, and strawberries. Keep them off with nets.

■ **Cover peas** with fleece or spray to protect against pea moths, which lay their eggs in June and July. Pheromone traps are also useful.

■ **Asparagus beetles** and their gray, caterpillar-like larvae should be picked off and destroyed.

■ **Leek moth caterpillars** feed on the leaves of leeks, leaving telltale holes. They will also burrow into the stems. Spray or pick them off.

Fruit

■ **Net strawberries** to keep off birds, and deter slugs by laying a bed of dry straw around the base of the plants. Check for gray mold and destroy any affected leaves and fruits immediately.

■ **Check apples** for canker, powdery mildew, and scab. Also spray if necessary for greenfly, codling moth, bitter pit, and woolly aphids.

■ **Check pears** for pear leaf blister mite, pear rust, canker, and scab.

■ **Inspect gooseberries and currants** for greenflies, sawflies, and currant blister aphids. Pick off or spray as necessary.

■ **Check raspberries**, blackberries, and hybrid berries for the small, yellow-brown larvae of raspberry beetles.

■ **Prune** any diseased wood from cherry and plum trees.

■ **Net soft-fruit** bushes and peach and nectarine trees to keep birds off.

■ **Check grapes** for scale insects and mildews, and spray if necessary.

Survive a summer drought

It is horribly ironic that the months when plants most need water are usually the months when rainfall is at its lowest. July and August, at the height of summer, can be very dry indeed, yet this is the time when fruits should be swelling and ripening, and vegetables should be fattening up ready to harvest. A regular supply of water is essential to this process. Worse, droughts can throw plants into a panic: thinking they may be about to die, they bolt—in a desperate attempt to flower, produce seeds, and survive for another generation.

Conserving water

Water is a valuable asset at any time of year but when rain is scarce it is particularly precious. It is important that you collect and conserve whatever water you can. When it does rain, think about what measures you can take to gather as much as possible. Water butts fed from drainpipes can be used to collect rainwater from the roofs of sheds, greenhouses, and outbuildings. Recycled household water

Plastic water butts are easy to set up so that they collect and store rainwater from the roofs of sheds. A cover on top keeps out leaves and other debris, and reduces evaporation. A faucet at the bottom allows you to fill watering cans.

(far left) **Newly planted seedlings** have immature root systems and need to be kept well watered. If they are allowed to dry out they may be so weakened that they are unable to recover.

(center) **Water generously** in order to give the ground a good soaking. Merely dampening the surface is a waste of time. Avoid the heat of the day when evaporation will be at its height and when any water splashed on leaves can cause scorching owing to strong sunlight.

(left) **Open-ended plastic bottles** sunk into the soil allow you to direct water right down to the roots and the underground tubers of potatoes and sweet potatoes.

("gray" water) can be used on the kitchen garden, provided you haven't been using bleach and have containers for transporting it. And surface mulches will minimize evaporation in hot weather and help retain moisture in the soil.

How to water effectively

The motto here is: soak don't sprinkle. It's far better to give a few plants a really thorough drink than to give everything a few meager sips. A good soaking will get water right down into the soil so that it reaches the roots, which is where the plants are able to take it up and make use of it. In gardens, leaky pipes or seep hoses are an economical way of making a little water go a long way, but they may not be practical on kitchen gardens if you are restricted to shared faucets or hand pumps.

When is the best time to water? The answer is at the beginning or end of the day, when both sun and air temperatures are fairly low. At midday or in the heat of long summer afternoons, you'll lose most of the water through evaporation.

WHICH PLANTS NEED WATER THE MOST?

In a drought, when water is scarce, you may have to take some tough decisions: if you are unable to water everything, which of your crops take priority? Below are the plants to target.

■ **Young seedlings** and newly established plants, which still have shallow roots (1).

■ **Fruit and fruiting vegetables** that are in the process of swelling—strawberries, raspberries, tomatoes, cucumbers (2).

■ **Podded vegetables** such as peas and beans as soon as the first flowers start to form (3).

■ **Leafy vegetables** such as spinach, lettuces, celery, and salads that are prone to bolting (4).

■ **Potatoes**, especially when they are in flower (5).

■ **Plants growing in containers**—herbs, strawberries, blueberries, and cranberries, for example (6).

■ **New fruit trees** planted within the last year or two.

August

It's a cliché, but August really is the month of plenty. Almost everything you've sown, planted, and nurtured through the spring and early summer will be coming to fruition now. Daily harvests should include everything from peas, beans, carrots, beets, corn, peppers, potatoes, onions, and salads to berries, currants, plums, peaches, figs, and perhaps even early apples and pears. And tomatoes! Determinate varieties, also known as bush tomatoes, bear all their fruit within the space of two weeks, so August is the month to put up your tomato store for the entire winter—whether you can or freeze them, or make spaghetti sauce instead.

Top tasks for August

■ **Harvest** your last broad beans and your first corn, plus summer fruiting vegetables such as tomatoes, peppers, chilies, and eggplants.

■ **Check** French beans, runner beans, and zucchinis every day, and harvest them regularly. They seem to double in size overnight.

■ **Pick** plums, greengages, and blackberries, and perhaps your first apples, pears, and figs.

■ **Sow** your last batch of carrots and turnips for this year, plus Japanese onion seeds and spring cabbages for next year.

■ **Feed** your pumpkins if you want to produce Halloween giants.

■ **Dry out** garlic, onions, and shallots so that they can be stored for the winter.

■ **Check** potatoes and tomatoes for signs of blight, and spray in warm, humid weather.

Sun-ripened tomatoes that you have grown yourself are hard to beat for sheer flavor. Vine tomatoes ripen gradually so you can pick them as you need them and eat fresh from the plant.

Vegetables

1 Carrots
August is likely to be a crossover month for harvesting the last of the fast-growing early varieties and the first of the slower-maturing maincrop carrots.

2 Kohlrabi
Harvest kohlrabi by slicing off the swollen globes at the root and trimming away all but the smallest, youngest leaves that grow from the center. Eat them raw or cooked.

3 Potatoes
August is still the time for second earlies—both the wonderful, floury baking potatoes, such as 'Estima' or 'Wilja', and classic, waxy, salad varieties, like 'Charlotte'.

4 Beets
Harvest beets regularly, lifting them carefully so that you don't disturb the roots of their neighbors. Those that remain in the ground will keep on swelling once they've been given more space.

5 Cabbages
Both summer and red cabbages should be hearting up by now. As soon as the heads are solid and dense, they are ready for harvesting.

6 Bok choy
Like many other Oriental brassicas (see p.226), bok choy is extremely fast-growing. You could be picking baby leaves in August from seed sown as recently as last month.

7 Garlic
Lift the last of your garlic this month. Dry it out and hang it up ready to use as and when you need it during the next few months.

8 Summer squashes
Zucchinis (such as the round one shown here) and other summer squashes come in many different-shaped varieties. August is the height of the season for them: they grow so rapidly that they will need to be harvested every couple of days.

2

3

6

7

10

11

14

15

9 Florence fennel
Fennel is prone to bolting in dry weather, so cut your bulbs before they become elongated and too tough to eat. If you leave the stumps in the ground you should find that they sprout; you can use the new feathery leaves in salads and stir-fries.

10 French beans
Harvest both dwarf and climbing varieties now. If you're going to eat the pods whole (like the 'Purple Queen' pods shown here) rather than shell them or keep them for drying, pick them while they are still young and slender.

11 Globe artichokes
Keep picking globes once they swell up but before they open, working your way down the plant from top to bottom. 'Purple Globe' (shown here) is a beautiful, lilac-colored variety.

12 Eggplants
In the heat of August, eggplants will be fattening up—as long as you're able to give them the water they need. Harvest them when they are at their blackest and glossiest.

13 Turnips
In addition to lifting the roots, try harvesting the young leaves. They're called "turnip tops" and can be cooked and eaten like spring greens or spinach.

14 Chilies and peppers
Most peppers become sweeter as they ripen, and most chilies become hotter. Yet the rule barely applies to these innocent-looking, peach-colored 'Habaneros'; they are blisteringly hot at whatever stage you pick them.

15 Shallots
Lift any remaining shallots by the end of the month. If you dry them thoroughly, clean them off, and discard any damaged bulbs, they should keep for several months in a cool, well-ventilated store.

16 Broad beans
Harvest the last of your broad beans this month. When they're finished, cut plants down to ground level and leave the nitrogen-rich roots in the soil.

17 Onions
Onions are ready to be harvested when their leaves turn yellow and start to bend over. Lift and dry them thoroughly before bringing them in.

18 Leaf beet
All the leaf beets—perpetual spinach (shown here) and the various varieties of Swiss chard—can be harvested throughout the summer, provided they don't bolt and go to seed.

19 Corn
Harvest corn when the tassels or silks go brown or black, and when the juice from the kernels is milky rather than clear.

20 Broccoli
Continue cutting heads of calabrese and spears of sprouting broccoli. Harvest them before the flower buds open.

21 Cauliflowers
The first summer and autumn cauliflowers should be developing heads by now. Modern, colored varieties make a change—although it's debatable whether they taste any different.

ALSO HARVEST

Peas
Pick snow, snap, and regular, maincrop shelling peas while they're still young and tender. Keep them netted to fend off birds.

Runner beans
Harvest beans every day or two. If any become too large and stringy, pick them anyway, and compost them; don't leave them on the plants.

Marrows
Vegetable marrows should be starting to swell to their full, competition-winning size during this month.

Spinach
In hot, dry summers, spinach bolts very readily. Pick the leaves often and be prepared to water daily.

Salads

1 Salad leaves
Corn salad, summer purslane, rocket, and land cress (variegated 'Fire and Ice' shown here) are all welcome alternatives to lettuce and should crop throughout the summer.

2 Tomatoes
Cherry or grape tomatoes, such as the plum-shaped 'Santa' (shown here), are bite-sized and bred to be especially sweet.

3 Scallions
Lift scallions before the bulbs grow too fat, especially if they're to be eaten in salads. The larger they are, the stronger the taste.

4 Cucumbers
Keep an eye on ripening cucumbers. Don't let them start to turn yellow. If they do, pick them and compost them immediately or you'll delay the plant producing new fruits.

5 Lettuces
August is a tricky time for lettuces. If it's hot and dry—which it often is—they'll almost certainly bolt. Keep them well watered, and harvest them regularly.

6 Chicory
For salads, pick sugarloaf chicory while it's still fairly young. Older, larger plants can become very bitter-tasting.

7 Radishes
Provided you sowed several successive batches of radish seeds in late spring, you'll still be harvesting new crops now.

ALSO HARVEST
Celery
Harvest self-blanching or green celery before the leaves go yellow, otherwise the stems will become too stringy.

Fruit

1 Plums
This month and next are when most varieties of plum and gage are ready for picking. Dessert plums don't keep for long, so pick them when they're just ripe.

2 Cherries
One or two late-season cherry varieties ripen in August ('Sweetheart' and 'Morello', for example) but most will have been ready to pick last month.

3 Raspberries
Summer-fruiting raspberries are likely to finish this month, but with luck you may find you can harvest the first autumn-fruiting varieties. If so, your supply of freshly picked fruit will go uninterrupted.

4 Peaches and nectarines
Both peaches and nectarines will be ripening this month. Pick the fruits when they're slightly soft and pull away easily. 'Duke of York' (shown here) is a good choice for temperate climates; it thrives in a sheltered, south-facing position.

5 Blackberries and hybrid berries
'Sylvan' (shown here) is an early-fruiting hybrid blackberry that ripens this month; numerous other varieties should also be ready for picking. So, too, will more unusual hybrid berries, such as boysenberries, loganberries, tayberries, and veitchberries.

6 Black currants
Watch for the moment when the berries swell to full size and turn a shiny blue-black, and pick them within a week.

7 Melons
As trailing melons begin to ripen, lift them off the ground and slip plastic sheeting under them (as shown here) to protect them from damp soil and slugs.

8 Apples
Early-cropping varieties are ready to eat this month. How do you know when they're ready? The appearance of windfalls is one sign; a deepening, or change in color is another. But the only true test is to pick one and taste it.

1

5

8

9

11

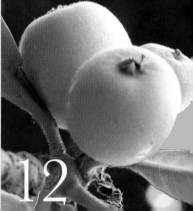

12

9 Pears
It is notoriously difficult to be sure of the right moment to pick pears. If you're uncertain, pick them when they are under-ripe rather than over-ripe. Both early-cropping apples and pears should be eaten soon after harvesting, as they don't keep.

10 Figs
The first figs should ripen this month, if you grow them in a warm, sunny, sheltered spot. Pick the fruits when their color darkens and they feel slightly soft. A bead of nectar appearing at the base is another sure sign.

11 Strawberries
Summer-fruiting strawberries probably finished sometime last month, but modern perpetual varieties will go on cropping from now until the autumn.

12 Apricots
Outdoor-grown apricots need warm, sunny weather to ripen properly. When the fruit is ready to pick, it will feel slightly soft and should pull away without resistance.

13 Tayberries
A cross between blackberries and raspberries, tayberries are perhaps the best of all the hybrid berries. They're at their peak in August. Eat them raw in fruit salads or use them for jams, pies, and tarts.

14 Red and white currants
Inspect the berries regularly, and try to pick them when they are at their most plump and juicy, but before they become too soft. Cut off the entire truss or "strig" and, when you get home, use a fork to "comb" off the ripe berries into a bowl or dish.

ALSO HARVEST

Blueberries
The berries all tend to ripen at different rates, so you'll need to inspect blueberry bushes regularly and harvest at least once a week to catch them at their best.

Kale seedlings raised in modules are now ready for transplanting. Take care not to damage the root system.

VEGETABLE
SEEDS TO SOW

- Cabbages (spring)
- Carrots
- Kohlrabi
- Onions
- Oriental leaves
- Radishes (winter)
- Spinach
- Swiss chard/Spinach beet
- Turnips

SALAD SEEDS
TO SOW

- Arugula
- Chicory (sugarloaf and red)
- Lettuces
- Radishes
- Salad leaves
- Spring onions
- Winter purslane

Sow or plant in August

There is not much you can still sow or plant now in time for harvesting this year. Perhaps a few lettuces and salad leaves, and some of the faster-growing roots and leaf vegetables. That's about it. However, space on your plot should become vacant once broad beans, onions, and shallots are all finished, so you can begin to plant out overwintering crops such as brussels sprouts, spring cabbages, and winter cauliflowers.

Cauliflowers
August is the month for transplanting winter and spring cauliflowers that were sown in the spring. If they overwinter successfully they should give you a harvest in the new year, from January onward.

Cabbages, broccoli, and kale
Sow a few more cabbages now for harvesting next spring—in a temporary seedbed if you are tight for space, or even in pots or modules. They can be kept out of the way somewhere as long as you remember to cover them with nets or fleece to keep off birds and caterpillars. In addition, plant out any remaining kale or sprouting broccoli still in pots.

Chicory
Continue sowing both sugarloaf and radicchio forms of chicory. They are hardy and should last well into the autumn.

Leaf vegetables
Now is your last chance to sow Swiss chard, as well as most of the Oriental leaves. But, if it's not too hot, there are certain varieties of spinach that can be sown this month or next for an autumn crop.

Lettuces and other salad crops
It's still possible to sow lettuces, though they may not germinate if the weather is very hot. For late autumn and winter salads,

VEGETABLES & FRUIT TO PLANT

- Cauliflowers (winter and spring)
- Kale
- Sprouting broccoli
- Strawberries

(right) **Oriental mustard seedlings** sown outside will need thinning. Young leaves can be harvested for salads after six to eight weeks.

continue to succession sow arugula, land cress, corn salad, and winter purslane to keep up supplies.

Onions

Japanese onions are specially bred, hardy varieties able to withstand most winters. Sow seeds now, in drills marked with a string to remind you where you put them, and simply leave them until the spring, when you can thin them out. They should be ready for harvesting in the summer.

Root vegetables

It really is now or never this year for sowing carrots, turnips, winter radishes, and—although it's not strictly speaking a root vegetable—kohlrabi.

Strawberries

Plant new strawberry plants as soon as they become available from garden centers and nurseries. Or as soon as your own runners have rooted (see p.128). Plant them in soil where you haven't grown strawberries for at least the last three years.

(below) **Transplant strawberry runners** with strong roots for cropping next year. Planting through a plastic sheet will help conserve warmth through the winter.

Jobs for August

August is mostly about harvesting—and reaping the benefits of the work you've put in earlier in the year. However, there are still a number of routine tasks that shouldn't be neglected. Weeding, watering, and mulching head the list, as always. Many of your crops will be growing flat-out now, and climbing beans, tomatoes, cucumbers, peppers, and even fruit trees may need to be supported as they become more heavily laden. Other crops will be over, and you can begin cutting them down or pruning them.

Weed and water

In a dry summer, weed growth should slow down. But the time you save hoeing will probably be taken up with watering. It's important to water regularly to promote normal, healthy growth and prevent plants from bolting prematurely.

Spread surface mulches

If you have any rotted-down compost left, use it up now. Next month you'll want to start a new heap with this year's waste material. Spread mulches immediately after rain to keep the moisture in the soil.

"Ripen" garlic, onions, and shallots

Dry out or "ripen" any bulbs you intend to store. A few days before you harvest them, carefully loosen the roots from the soil. Lift them and lay them on the ground in the sun, or spread them out on wire racks to dry.

Harvest regularly

At this time of year, zucchini, runner beans, and French beans are notorious for the speed at which they grow. Check them every day and harvest regularly, picking them before they grow too large and become stringy.

Pinch out tops of climbing beans

Continue pinching out the growing tips when climbing beans reach the top of your canes. This prevents them from becoming top-heavy and encourages new growth lower down.

Bean flowers

However many beans you pick, as long as flowers are still appearing, new pods should continue to grow. Water plants regularly or spray the flowers to prevent them falling.

Pinch out and feed tomatoes

Continue to remove any side shoots that keep appearing in the "V" between leaf stems and the main stems, and nip out the growing tip at the top of vine tomatoes once four or five trusses have formed. Feed with tomato fertilizer when you water.

Tie up tomatoes, peppers, and cucumbers

As the fruits develop, they can become very heavy. Tall vine tomatoes and outdoor cucumbers in particular may need extra support by tying their main stems to additional stakes or sturdy canes.

Earth up brassicas, potatoes, and celery

Keep earthing up potatoes to stop tubers being exposed, trench celery to keep stems out of the light, and brassicas to support unsteady stems.

(left to right) **Well-rotted compost** spread as a mulch will retain moisture during hot weather. **Dry shallots** on the ground, or on a chicken wire rack to allow air to circulate. **Pinch out** the tips of climbing beans to stop them flopping over at the top of their supports.

GREEN MANURES

A green manure is a crop grown specifically to be dug back into the soil. There are three main reasons for growing it:

- To improve the structure of the soil by opening it up and providing valuable organic matter.
- To release nutrients—particularly nitrogen—in a form that subsequent crops can utilize.
- To act as a protective covering, smothering weeds and sheltering soil from the leaching or compacting effects of heavy rain.

Green manures are ideal for areas of your plot freed up after harvesting crops such as broad beans, early potatoes, or onions and shallots.

Sow crimson clover, buckwheat, or mustard now for digging in this autumn, and alfalfa, field beans, grazing rye, or phacelia for overwintering and digging in next spring. It's best to allow about four weeks between digging in and sowing seeds for edible crops.

(left to right) **Clover** is good for adding nutrients to the soil. **Alfalfa** has long taproots, ideal for breaking up hard ground. **Grazing rye** opens up heavy soil and is best left undisturbed over winter.

Feed pumpkins and winter squashes

For Halloween-sized growth, feed once a week with high-potash tomato fertilizer. In damp weather, lift them off the soil onto bricks or planks of wood so that they don't rot.

Propagate strawberries

Strawberry runners that you have pegged down into pots to root should be ready for transplanting now. Plant in a sunny position, in ground that has had plenty of organic material dug in, and keep them well watered. Plastic sheeting stretched over the bed (see p.141) will also conserve warmth and moisture.

Summer-prune gooseberries and currants

Finish summer-pruning once all the fruit has been picked. Your bushes will need to be pruned again in winter.

Prune summer-fruiting raspberries

If you didn't do so last month, cut down to the ground all the canes that have borne fruit this year. Tie in the new, green canes that will produce fruit next summer.

Tie in blackberries and hybrid berries

Continue to tie in vigorous, new, nonfruiting canes. Old canes will be removed in autumn.

Prop up heavily laden fruit trees

In good years, apples, pears, and plums can bow so severely that branches are in danger of breaking. Support with rope ties or props.

Pick early apples and pears

Test early varieties for ripeness by gently twisting—not pulling—them. If they come away easily, without tearing the stalk, pick them and eat at once, since they won't store.

Summer-prune wire-trained fruit trees

Finish tying in or trimming new growth on all espalier, cordon, and fan-trained trees.

Grapevines

Continue pruning side shoots and removing some of the foliage to expose fruit to the sun.

(below, left to right) **Prune raspberries** by cutting out all this year's spent fruiting canes. **Tie in new** raspberry canes so they grow strongly upward and fruit well next summer. **Support fruit-laden** branches with a sturdy home-made prop.

August pests & diseases

Vegetables

Carrot flies are laying their eggs again this month. Protect crops with fleece or physical barriers.

Slugs and snails still need to be controlled, especially in wet summers and immediately after rain when the ground is damp.

Powdery mildews can be a problem in warm, dry summers, particularly on peas, zucchini, squashes, and cucumbers. Regular watering and a fungicide spray may help.

Spray potatoes and tomatoes against blight, especially if it's very humid. If your crop is infected, cut down the foliage and destroy it. Lift potatoes at once—they may still be edible.

Water tomatoes regularly to prevent splitting and blossom end rot. Take care not to splash the fruits to avoid ghost spot.

Magnesium deficiency is often the cause of tomato or potato leaves turning yellow between the veins. Spray with a solution of Epsom salts (magnesium sulfate).

Check corn for smut and remove any affected cobs. Protect others from birds and mice with clear plastic bottles.

Inspect peas for caterpillars of the pea moth feeding inside the pods. They will have laid their eggs in June and July.

Check for blackfly on globe artichokes, beets, and broad, French, and runner beans.

Look under cabbage and other brassica leaves for the caterpillars of cabbage white butterflies. Pick them off and squash them by hand, or spray. Keep nets in place.

Fruit

Look for brown rot on apples, pears, plums, and quinces. Remove and destroy infected fruits.

Apple bitter pit is caused by calcium deficiency. Watering regularly and spraying with calcium nitrate solution may help.

Pheromone traps in apple, pear, and plum trees may need their capsules to be replaced in order to continue being effective in attracting codling moths.

Spray plums, cherries, apricots, and peaches with Bordeaux mixture or other copper-based fungicide to treat outbreaks of bacterial canker. Spray after harvesting but before pruning, and spray again next month.

Check raspberries, blackberries, and hybrid berries for the small, yellow-brown larvae of raspberry beetles.

(top to bottom) **Mesh barriers** higher than 2-ft (60 cm) will keep carrot flies well away from your crop. **Potato leaves** deficient in magnesium appear yellow and blotched. **Brown rot** on plums will soon spread to healthy fruit. **Corn** cobs can be stripped by hungry birds.

September

September marks the onset of autumn, and people living in northern regions or at high elevations will see the first frosts at the end of the month, while those in the Deep South will barely feel the change in seasons. It may be the last month for French and runner beans, zucchini, tomatoes, peppers, chilies, eggplant, cucumbers, and corn. On the other hand, later crops are coming into harvest now, and you should be lifting maincrop potatoes, pulling leeks, cutting your first winter squashes, and picking apples, pears, late-season plums and damsons, and autumn raspberries. You may even have your first brussels sprouts, celeriac, rutabagas, and leeks. The year certainly isn't over yet.

Top tasks for September

- **Harvest** remaining summer vegetables (beans, tomatoes, peppers, corn, globe artichokes) and the first of your autumn crops (leeks, pumpkins, and maincrop and sweet potatoes).
- **Pick** late plums, midseason apples and pears, and autumn-fruiting raspberries.
- **Sow** the last of your Oriental and salad leaves and spinach for this year.
- **Plant** spring cabbages and Japanese onion sets to overwinter for next year.
- **Clear away** dead foliage and other plant remains as soon as crops have finished.
- **Add** everything you can to your compost heap—provided the plant material has no signs of disease.
- **Check** apples, pears, and plums for brown rot and discard any infected fruit.

Apple trees laden with ripening fruit are a sure sign that autumn is beginning. Cup the fruit in your palm, give it a gentle twist, and pull: if it comes away easily, it's ready for picking.

Vegetables

1 Eggplants
Pick eggplants while the skins are unblemished and still have a glossy shine. Once they lose that shine, they begin to go downhill, and may develop an unpleasantly bitter taste.

2 Swiss chard
Harvest the leaves before they grow too large, cutting them from the outside of the plants and discarding any that are damaged. New leaves will shoot up in the center.

3 Onions
Lift any remaining onions this month. Dry them out and hang them up somewhere cool and well ventilated. They should last for several months.

4 Corn
Modern "supersweet" varieties are so sweet that, when perfectly ripe, you can eat them raw, straight from the plant. Otherwise, hurry home to cook and eat them as soon as possible, before the sugars turn to starch.

5 French beans
Late sowings should be providing you with plenty of beans to harvest. 'Goldfield' (shown here) is an unusual, bright yellow, climbing variety with wide, flat, straplike pods that may be eaten whole.

6 Rutabagas
The first rutabagas of the year should be ready this month. They will, of course, grow bigger if left in the ground, but it's tempting to lift a few as soon as they are large enough to use.

7 Globe artichokes
Established plants may well produce a second crop of flower heads that can be harvested now—but pick them all by the end of the month.

8 **Cabbages**
Red cabbages such as 'Red Jewel' (shown here) are usually sown and planted at the same time as summer and autumn cabbages. They should be ready for harvesting between August and November.

9 **Carrots**
Lift carrots carefully to avoiding snapping off the roots. Use a handfork if the soil is hard and compacted.

10 **Calabrese**
The 'Romanesco' calabrese (or cauliflower, as it is sometimes called) shown here is remarkable. Not only is its head formed from seemingly infinite spirals of lime-green, fractal-like flower buds but it's also one of the sweetest and tastiest of all the broccolis.

11 **Chilies and peppers**
Many chilies and peppers turn from green to red as they mature and ripen. The red ones will be both hotter and sweeter than immature green ones.

12 **Beets**
Keep lifting the roots before they get too large. By all means pickle them if you wish, but first try them cut into chunks, doused generously in olive oil and balsamic vinegar, and then roasted.

13 **Leeks**
If you've timed things well, your first leeks should be ready about now—just as the last of the year's onions are finally finished.

14 **Winter squashes**
Begin harvesting pumpkins and winter squashes such as the small, nutty 'Uchiki Kuri' (shown here). They'll keep for longer if you dry or "cure" them in the sun to harden their skins.

15 Peas
Maincrop peas should still be producing. Keep picking regularly and remove any overlooked overgrown pods.

16 Winter radishes
The roots of winter radishes such as 'Mooli' (shown here) are much larger than those of the salad varieties.

17 Oriental leaves
You can still pick mustard greens, mibuna, and komatsuna as baby salad leaves but, as autumn approaches, leave some to grow on, to steam or stir-fry.

18 Potatoes
Maincrop potatoes will be ready to lift this month. Old-fashioned, knobbly 'Pink Fir Apple' (shown here) is regarded as one of the best salad potatoes.

19 Runner beans
Pick the new, young beans still forming. Discard any that have grown too large; they'll be tough and stringy.

20 Cauliflowers
Cut cauliflowers once the heads have developed but while the tiny flower heads (or "curds") are still tightly closed.

ALSO HARVEST

Florence fennel
Lift the whole plant and cut off the roots and foliage, leaving just the edible bulb.

Kohlrabi
Slice off the swollen stems at root level and trim off the larger, outer leaves.

Brussels sprouts
The first of the year—although they may still be very small.

Zucchini and summer squashes
Late sowings should still be going strong and will still need frequent harvesting.

Spinach
Keep harvesting regularly if you still have plants that haven't bolted.

Marrows
To store vegetable marrows, leave them in the sun to "cure" so their skins harden.

Sweet potatoes
Dig up your first crop this month.

Turnips
Continue lifting turnips before the roots grow too large.

Celeriac
If you can't wait, lift a few early celeriac, but they're unlikely to be fully grown yet.

Salads

1 Chicory
Early summer sowings of red and sugarloaf chicory should be ready to harvest now. Pick individual leaves or uproot the entire plant.

2 Celery
Dig up self-blanching or green celery after first watering it. Trim off the roots and any outer shoots, and keep the heads in the refrigerator. Stand stems in cold water to crisp them before eating.

3 Tomatoes
Large, beefsteak tomatoes take longer to develop than smaller, fast-maturing varieties. 'Country Taste' (shown here) is a modern hybrid that bears huge fruits over a long period.

4 Land cress
American or upland cress sown in early summer will be ready to harvest. Pick the leaves as a cut-and-come-again crop and eat them raw in salads or use for cooking, as you would watercress.

5 Lettuces
Harvest lettuces such as the red semi-cos shown here either by uprooting the whole plant or by slicing through the main stem just above soil level.

6 Cucumbers
Regularly harvest cucumbers, before any of them grow too large. And make sure you have picked them all before there's any danger of frost.

ALSO HARVEST

Radishes
Late-summer radishes can be harvested now from sowings made around July.

Salad leaves
Corn salad, summer purslane, rocket, and baby-leaf Oriental brassicas should still be cropping this month.

Endive
Start harvesting both the blanched frisée and the broad-leaved endives.

Scallions
This is probably the last month for salad onions—but any left in the ground may well grow on and fatten up to provide you with a few extra regular onions.

Fruit

1 Apples
There's no shortage of apples to pick this month—both the last of the early varieties and the first of the mid- or late varieties. Fruit that is ripe and ready to pick should come away with a gentle twist of the hand, and with its stem still attached.

2 Strawberries
Perpetual strawberries should continue cropping this month and—if there are no early frosts—next month, too. Keep them netted and watch out for slugs. The fruits remain as tempting as they were earlier in the year.

3 Grapes
September marks the start of the grape harvest. Early varieties may be picked now, although the longer you leave them on the vine, the higher their sugar content will be—especially in warm, sunny Indian summers.

4 Melons
Late-season melons grown under cover—in polytunnels or cold frames, for example—should ripen this month.

5 Pears
Like apples, this month sees the first of the late-season pears (such as 'Conference', shown here). It's trickier to tell when they're ready to pick than it is with apples, but the same technique applies: if, when gently twisted, the fruit pulls off the tree easily, complete with its stem, that's good. If it doesn't, leave it for a little longer.

6 Blackberries
Late-season blackberries should ripen this month. Pick the berries when they are fully colored and soft but not squishy. Unlike raspberries, the core or plug usually pulls away with the berry instead of staying on the bush.

7 Cranberries
The first cranberries should be ready for picking this month, although there's no hurry. You may prefer to leave them on the bush until they are all ripe, and harvest them together in one go.

1

4

7

8

10

11

8 Blueberries
If you have one of the late-season varieties, you may be lucky enough to have a few remaining blueberries ready to harvest this month.

9 Figs
Leave figs to ripen on the tree for as long as possible, but harvest any that still remain by the end of the month. If you're careful not to bruise the fruits, they should keep for a surprisingly long while—up to two or three weeks if you cover and store them somewhere cool.

10 Plums, damsons, and gages
Late-season plums ripen in September. So, too, do most damsons: 'Merryweather' (shown here) has the typical blue-black skin and the characteristic bloom. Because damsons are used for cooking, they may be picked while still slightly unripe.

11 Peaches and nectarines
Late-season peach and nectarine varieties may not be ready for picking until September. Not a problem if they're grown in a warm climate or under cover, but they're probably not the cultivars to choose to grow outdoors in temperate regions, where they are unlikely to ripen.

12 Raspberries
Autumn-fruiting raspberries should continue cropping from August until the first frosts next month—or, in mild areas, even later.

13 Apricots
Harvest your remaining apricots early this month. Wait any longer and, as the days shorten and temperatures drop, it becomes increasingly unlikely that any still left on the tree will ripen.

ALSO HARVEST

Cape gooseberries
Cape gooseberries, also known as physalis, should begin to ripen this month. Start picking them when the outer husks dry up and turn brown, revealing the bright orange fruits inside.

Sow or plant in September

There are very few seeds that can still be sown this month: winter lettuces, salad leaves, a few Oriental leaves, and spinach. It is, however, the month to begin planting sets of overwintering autumn onions. Like the Japanese varieties for which seeds could be sown last month, they stay in the ground all winter, grow on in the spring, and will be ready for lifting from June onward next year.

Plant onion sets in a shallow drill about 1 in (2.5 cm) deep and make sure the tips are only just visible. If you don't plant them deep enough, they may well be uprooted by birds and their delicate roots will be damaged.

Cabbages

Transplant your spring cabbages this month or next. Whether you've raised them in pots or in a temporary seedbed, it's now time to move them to their final growing positions. Make sure that they go into ground that has been well firmed down.

Leaf vegetables

This is your last chance to sow spinach, as well as hardy Oriental leaves such as mizuna, mibuna, and komatsuna. You may need to cover them with cloches if the temperatures are low at night.

Lettuces and other salad crops

Sow winter lettuces, and further batches of salads such as arugala, land cress, corn salad, and winter purslane—under cloches of necessary. A few last-minute radishes may give you a final crop before the end of the year. And scallions sown now may overwinter, ready for next spring.

Onions

Plant overwintering autumn onions sets this month or next. Prepare the ground first so the sets go in easily, and add an all-purpose fertilizer. Bury the sets about 3–4 in (7–10 cm) apart with their tips at or just below the surface of the soil. Although large sets may look stronger and more promising, small or medium-sized sets are less likely to bolt in the spring.

Cranberries

Plant new cranberry bushes at any time from September to November, or wait until next spring. However, bear in mind that they need acid soil. It may be best to grow them in tubs full of special ericaceous soil.

Peaches and nectarines

Container-grown peaches and nectarines can be planted at any time of the year, although between September and December is probably best. Plant bare-root trees later, preferably in November. Remember that peaches and nectarines will only thrive in the warmth of a sheltered, sunny, south-facing site.

Strawberries

If you didn't do so last month, plant new strawberry plants— either those you've bought or those you've propagated from runners. The sooner you plant them, the sooner they will get established and the bigger your crop next year.

"Sow arugala seeds and other salads now for a supply of fresh homegrown leaves."

VEGETABLE SEEDS TO SOW
- Oriental leaves
- Spinach

SALAD SEEDS TO SOW
- Arugala
- Lettuces
- Radishes
- Salad leaves
- Scallions
- Winter purslane

VEGETABLES & FRUIT TO PLANT
- Cabbages (spring)
- Cranberries
- Onion sets
- Peaches and nectarines
- Strawberries

(below, left to right) **Arugala seeds** will germinate reliably this month. Thin seedlings when true leaves show. At two weeks plants show healthy growth.

Make your own compost bin

Kitchen gardeners often make an art out of constructing homemade compost bins from recycled materials—wooden pallets, packing crates, old doors, sheets of corrugated iron, even straw bales. Such creations display a wonderful sense of ingenuity but, more importantly, they get the job done: they are solid enough to contain growing piles of decomposing material, they can be easily disassembled when the compost is ready, and they can be covered with a plastic sheet or a piece of old carpet to keep the heat in and the rain out.

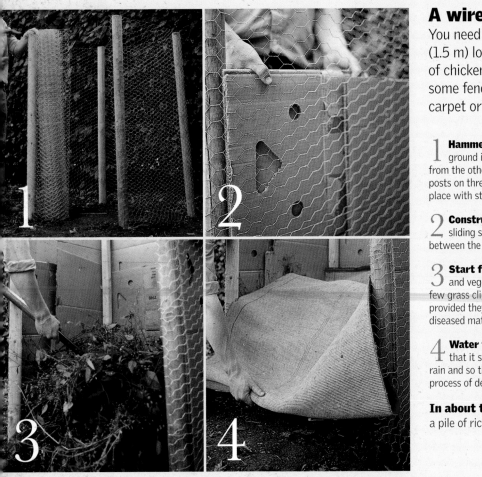

A wire and cardboard bin

You need four wooden posts about 5 ft (1.5 m) long; 8 ft (2.5 m) x 4 ft (1.2 m) of chicken wire; thick cardboard boxes; some fencing staples; a square of old carpet or plastic sheeting for a lid.

1 **Hammer the posts** 12 in (30 cm) into the ground in a square, each corner 30 in (75 cm) from the others. Wrap the chicken wire around the posts on three sides of the square, and secure it in place with staples.

2 **Construct walls** on three sides by sliding several layers of flattened cardboard between the chicken wire and the posts.

3 **Start filling the bin** with old plant material and vegetable kitchen waste. You can add a few grass clippings, and some woody prunings provided they're well shredded, but don't compost any diseased material.

4 **Water the heap** from time to time to ensure that it stays damp, but cover it to keep off heavy rain and so that heat builds up and hastens the process of decomposition.

In about twelve months, you should have a pile of rich, dark, sweet-smelling compost.

A wooden "beehive" box

A better-looking option than the wire and cardboard bin, this beehive box is fairly easy to construct and can even be stained or painted with a nontoxic product. For a box four tiers high, you need sixteen wooden boards about 3 ft (1 m) long x 8 in (20 cm) wide x 1 in (2.5 cm) thick; sixteen wooden battens 8 in (20 cm) x 2 in (5 cm) x 2 in (5 cm); plenty of nails; a square of old carpet or plastic sheeting for a lid.

1 **Construct a wooden square** from four of the boards by nailing them to the wooden battens. Each corner post should protrude by about 1 in (2.5 cm) so that the square above will "lock" in place on top of the one below.

2 **As the box begins to fill up**, add another wooden square in order to increase its height.

3 **Uncover the heap from time to time** and add a little water if it is in danger of drying out. It will decompose more quickly in a warm, humid atmosphere.

4 **Turning the pile mixes everything up** and reactivates it. Simply lift off the top square, set it down alongside, and fill it up from the top of your original heap. Do the same with the second square then carry on until you've moved the whole bin into its new position.

"Homemade garden compost is one of the very best things you can add to your soil."

Jobs for September

If August was all about harvesting, then September is more about neatening and composting. As soon as you finish harvesting, clear away old foliage and vegetation and put it right onto your compost heap. Don't leave it to rot on the soil, where it may spread disease. Even this late in the season weeds will still be growing, especially on areas of your plot that you've just cleared of crops. Sowing green manure is one way of keeping them down.

Vine tomatoes will finish ripening if untied and laid flat on a bed of straw. Cover with a tunnel cloche to speed up the process.

Water when necessary

September can be dry, particularly in a warm Indian summer. If rainfall is scarce and temperatures remain high, continue to water all crops regularly.

Sow green manures

If you haven't already done so, field beans, annual ryegrass, and phacelia can be sown in September. They will overwinter and can be dug into the ground next spring (see p.143).

Turn your compost heap

As you add this autumn's mass of dead and dying plant material to your heap, turn it regularly with a fork to aerate it and stimulate decomposition. Water it if it's dry, and cover to keep it warm.

Harvest any remaining onions

Lift any onions that are still in the ground, and dry them thoroughly before storing them.

Ripen and pick tomatoes

To prompt tomatoes to fatten up and ripen, cut off all the lower leaves (especially if they are turning yellow). Cover bush tomatoes with fleece or a cloche. Untie vine tomatoes from their canes, carefully bend them over, and lay them flat on a layer of clean straw. Pick all remaining green tomatoes by the end of the month and finish ripening them indoors.

Cut down asparagus

Tall, feathery asparagus foliage will be starting to turn yellow now and should be cut right down to just 1 in (2.5 cm) above the ground.

Earth up or stake brussels sprouts

As brussels sprouts and other autumn and winter brassicas grow steadily taller they may become top-heavy and need supporting. Earth up the stems or tie them in to stakes.

Ripen pumpkins and winter squashes

Remove a few leaves so that the sun can get to the fruits. Continue watering and feeding until you're ready to harvest, this month or next.

Feed and trim celeriac

Feed regularly with liquid manure and remove any old, damaged leaves from around the stem.

Harvest apples and pears

Continue testing for ripeness and pick when the moment is right. Early pears can be picked while still slightly firm, then ripened indoors. Eat early season fruit right away, and store mid- and late-season varieties.

(below, left to right) **Cut asparagus** stems and their ferny foliage right down and compost them. **Expose squashes** to sunlight by removing a few leaves to encourage ripening. **Old or damaged celeriac** leaves can be pulled from the base to expose the swelling crowns.

HARVESTING CORN

Cobs are usually ready for picking when the silks at the top turn brown or black. Pick cobs just before you need them because the sweet flavor deteriorates with storage.

1 Test for ripeness and make sure that corn is at its most succulent by peeling back the outer leaves and digging a fingernail into one of the kernels. Ripe corn exudes a milky, not clear, juice.

2 Harvest cobs from the plant by gripping them firmly and pulling them downward, while holding the main stem steady with your other hand. Ripe cobs should snap off fairly easily.

LIFTING MAINCROP POTATOES

Dig up most if not all of your potatoes by the end of this month. Although leaving them in the ground longer will result in larger tubers, there is a greater risk of attack by slugs. Dry them out, remove any damaged tubers, and store in lightproof potato sacks.

1 As potato haulms (stems and leaves) die down, cut them off with a sharp knife to leave about 2 in (5 cm) of stem on each plant.

2 Wait for a dry day to lift your crop so the potatoes will be easier to uproot and store.

3 When digging up potatoes, you never know how many or how few you're going to find underneath. The stems above ground give absolutely no indication.

Prune blackberry canes that have borne fruit this year and take out any old or dead wood. Leave new canes unpruned to carry next year's crop.

Prune blackberries and hybrid berries

As soon as you have finished picking, cut out all the old canes that carried this year's fruit. New, nonfruiting canes should be tied in to take their place, ready for next year.

Order new fruit trees and bushes

November is the best month for planting many new bare-root trees and bushes, so it's worth ordering the plants from specialist nurseries this month for the widest choice.

Collect and save seeds

It's worth saving certain seeds for sowing next year—especially plants you're fond of and that may be hard to find commercially. Bean, pea, squash, pumpkin, melon, and tomato seeds can all be saved, dried, stored, and sown again— although not F1 hybrid varieties. It's difficult to predict how these seeds will turn out.

September pests & diseases

Vegetables

■ **Check potatoes** for blight, particularly in wet or humid weather. It may be too late now for preventive sprays. If you spot diseased foliage, cut the haulms down immediately and destroy them; do not compost them. Lift potatoes at once in case they are still edible.

■ **Carrot flies** are still laying eggs this month. When they hatch the maggots can attack late crops. Protect plants with fleece or physical barriers.

■ **Powdery mildews** may affect peas, zucchini, squashes, and outdoor cucumbers. Water regularly and perhaps spray with an appropriate fungicide.

■ **Tomato blight** can kill off a whole crop in warm, wet weather. You may still have time to spray with mancozeb or Bordeaux mixture early in the month, but infected crops must be destroyed.

■ **Cabbage whiteflies** can continue to infest brassicas through the autumn and into winter. If there are only a few, pick them off and squash them. Otherwise, spray under the leaves.

■ **Leek moth caterpillars** feed on the leaves of leeks and burrow into the stems. Spray or pick them off.

■ **Slugs and snails** still need to be controlled, especially in wet weather when the ground is damp.

Fruit

■ **Look for brown rot** on apples, pears, plums, and quinces. Remove and destroy infected fruits. A few healthy windfalls can be left as bait to attract wasps.

■ **Apple bitter pit** is caused by calcium deficiency. Watering regularly and spraying with calcium nitrate solution may help.

■ **Remove apples and pears** affected by scab and pick up any infected leaves. Destroy them rather than composting them.

■ **Spray apples and pears** against canker only after you have picked all the fruit.

■ **Prune out mildewed foliage** on apples, pears, and gooseberries and destroy it.

■ **Spray plums**, cherries, apricots, and peaches for a second time with Bordeaux mixture or another copper-based fungicide to treat bacterial canker.

■ **Do not prune cherries or plums** now or at any time until next spring—pruning cuts may allow silver leaf fungus to enter.

(clockwise from top left) **Potato blight** is a fungal infection that begins on the leaves. **Tomato blight** destroys leaves and eventually causes fruit to rot. **Leek moth caterpillars** in cocoons will pupate. Pick them off. **Scab** on apples can be due to damp conditions and overcrowded branches. **Brown rot** is a fungus, often spread by birds and insects. **Cabbage whiteflies** do not pose a serious problem unless plants become heavily infested.

October

October is the month when it feels as if the year is starting to turn. The days are noticeably shorter, the sun is lower in the sky, and temperatures are dropping. Leaves are changing color and beginning to fall. The first frosts are likely, too, and if you still haven't yet harvested your last tomatoes, peppers, eggplants, and zucchini, the frosts will mean the end for them—unless they're under cloches. Carrots too should be dug before the first frosts, while parsnips are better after a frost. October is the right month to sow and plant one or two crops for next year, and garlic can be planted throughout the fall if the ground isn't frozen. In the South, cool-loving greens such as kale, mustard, and turnips can be sowed. However, at this time of year the work is primarily about clearing away the remains of the summer's harvest and taking care of overwintering plants.

Turk's turban squashes, like other winter pumpkins and squashes, are best left to ripen on the vine, and then cut down to harden further. Toughening the skin will extend their "shelf life."

Top tasks for October

■ **Harvest** remaining summer vegetables before the first frosts. Lift potatoes and beets.

■ **Cut** pumpkins and winter squashes. "Cure" the fruits by leaving them in the sun for their skins to harden and the flesh inside to ripen.

■ **Cover** autumn salads and Oriental leaves with cloches or fleece if there is a danger of night frosts.

■ **Sow** broad bean seeds for next year.

■ **Plant** garlic, onions, rhubarb, and bare-root fruit bushes such as currants and gooseberries.

■ **Take down** supports used for climbing beans, peas, and tomatoes.

■ **Clear away** dead plant material and compost it. Begin winter digging.

Vegetables

1 Cabbages
Harvest autumn cabbages this month and next. Keep nets in place.

2 Parsnips
Traditionally, parsnips are not lifted until after a couple of frosts have concentrated and improved their flavor.

3 Peas
Harvest any remaining peas before the arrival of the first frosts.

4 Broccoli
October is probably the last month for calabrese, but sprouting broccoli may continue cropping until later in the year.

5 Eggplants
You may get a late crop of eggplants from plants grown under cover. Outdoor plants should have been harvested last month.

6 Oriental leaves
Leaves such as the loose-headed Chinese cabbage shown here will continue cropping for a while, but may need covering with cloches or frames.

7 Turnips
You can leave turnips in the ground for a few more months yet, but lift and eat them before they become too large.

8 Sweet potatoes
Dig up any remaining sweet potatoes this month. They'll be attacked by slugs if they stay in the ground much longer. They will keep indoors for a while if they're dried in the sun—like pumpkins and squashes.

9 Celeriac
The swollen stems will be reaching full-size and can be harvested any time now. Pick off the outer leaves to keep the crowns clear and reduce the risk of slug damage.

10 Pumpkins and winter squashes
Harvest this month. Cure them in the sun to harden the skins, and bring the fruits indoors before the first frosts.

11 Leeks
Harvest leeks just before you require them, and earth up any that remain in the ground.

12 Beets
Finish lifting any remaining beets this month, before they become too large and woody to be appetizing.

13 French beans
Harvest beans left for drying this month. Strip them from their pods and store them in airtight containers.

14 Cauliflowers
Continue cutting autumn cauliflowers. The heads will keep longer if you leave some outer leaves in place.

ALSO HARVEST

Brussels sprouts
Start harvesting at the base of the stalks and work your way upward.

Carrots
Continue pulling maincrop carrots or, if they're not being attacked by slugs, leave in the ground for later in winter.

Chilies and peppers
You may have a few left to pick if the autumn has been warm, or if you've grown them under cover.

Florence fennel
Fennel can withstand light frosts, but use cloches to protect your last bulbs.

Kohlrabi
Crops grown from seed sown in the summer should be ready to harvest now.

Leaf beets
Continue harvesting both Swiss chard and spinach beet leaves.

Runner beans
Harvest any remaining runner beans.

Spinach
Fast-growing, autumn varieties sown in late summer should be cropping now.

Rutabagas
Rutabagas should be at their best during October and November.

Vegetable marrows
If you harden off their skins, you can store vegetable marrows for a couple of months—but they're better eaten fresh.

Winter radishes
Hardy autumn and winter radishes sown in the summer will be ready to lift now.

Zucchinis and summer squashes
Harvest any remaining crops early this month—they won't survive a frost.

Salads

1 **Lettuces**
Autumn lettuces grown from seed sown in midsummer can be harvested now, although they may need to be protected with fleece or cloches.

2 **Celery**
Harvest self-blanching or green celery before the arrival of the first winter frosts.

3 **Tomatoes**
Late-ripening tomatoes can be left outside if they're under cloches or fleece, but this is really the end of the season; they won't survive a frost. It's better to bring in any remaining fruit and attempt to ripen it indoors.

4 **Chicory**
Harvest any remaining red or sugarloaf chicory now—unless you have hardy winter varieties that you're growing on in a cold frame or under cover.

5 **Salad leaves**
Land cress (shown here), corn salad, rocket, and most of the Oriental brassicas are still a valuable source of leaves for salads. Cover them at night, if necessary.

6 **Endive**
Harvest broad-leaved (or Batavian) and frisée endives throughout autumn and winter, provided your plants are covered with fleece or cloches as the weather turns colder.

ALSO HARVEST

Radishes
There may still be a few salad radishes waiting to be harvested from late summer sowings.

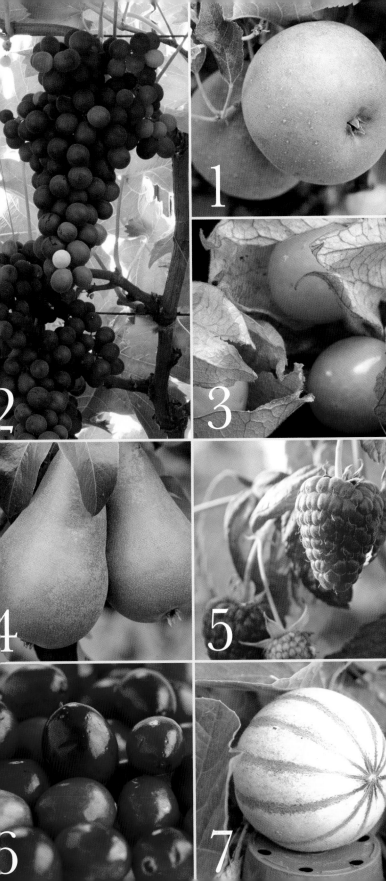

Fruit

1 Apples
Aim to harvest all remaining apples by about the middle of the month. Check them carefully for any signs of damage, discard the rejects, and bring the rest indoors for storage (see pp.174, 190).

2 Grapes
Traditionally, mid-season varieties are harvested in the middle of the month, and late-season varieties at the end, but let the weather dictate. If summer and autumn have been hot and sunny, grapes will be ready for picking earlier. If not, then leave them on the vine as long as possible.

3 Cape gooseberries
Leave the berries for as long as you can: they'll get sweeter the longer they remain on the plants. However, be sure to harvest them all before the first frost.

4 Pears
Most will have been harvested or blown off the tree by now, but pick any pears that are still holding on. Inspect them meticulously and be ruthless if any are damaged or evenly slightly bruised. They will rot if you try to store them.

5 Raspberries
Autumn-fruiting raspberries should go on cropping until the arrival of the first serious frosts.

6 Cranberries
You can pick cranberries this month if they are beginning to ripen, or they may be left until they are all ripe and then harvested together at one time.

7 Melons
Harvest any remaining late-season melons grown under cover now.

ALSO HARVEST

Plums, damsons, and gages
October is too late for ordinary plums but not for some of the late-ripening, less familiar damsons and bullaces.

Strawberries
Pick the last of the year's perpetual strawberries. They won't survive a frost.

Sow or plant in October

At this time of year, plants are beginning to enter their winter dormancy period. If you're buying bare-root (as opposed to container-grown) fruit bushes, any time in the next six months is a good time to plant them—provided your soil is not frozen or waterlogged. October is also the month for sowing and planting crops that don't mind the winter cold: broad beans, spring cabbages, garlic, onion sets, and rhubarb. Greens such as kale can be planted in the milder South.

Broad beans

Sow seeds of "early" varieties now or next month. Except in very cold regions, they should overwinter and give you a crop from around June onward next year.

Cabbages

October is your last chance for transplanting spring cabbages. Plant them in ground that has been well firmed down, and cover with nets to protect them from birds, especially pigeons.

Cauliflowers

If you have a cold frame, you might try sowing a few seeds of early summer cauliflowers in

VEGETABLE SEEDS TO SOW
- Broad beans
- Cauliflowers (early summer)
- Peas

pots or modules. Keep them under cover all winter, and plant them out in early spring.

Garlic

Plant garlic cloves this month or next. As long as they don't get waterlogged, they will survive a cold winter. The longer they are in the ground, the bigger your next year's bulbs should be. It's

PLANTING GARLIC

For reliable cropping, garlic requires an initial period of cold (but not freezing) weather, so autumn is the ideal time to sow.

1 Break up the head to separate the individual cloves.

2 Make holes with a dibber—roughly twice the depth of the cloves and 7 in (18 cm) apart.

3 Plant cloves individually, pointed end uppermost.

possible to grow garlic from a bulb bought in the supermarket, or from cloves you've saved from your own crop, but it's much safer to buy commercially grown bulbs that you know are guaranteed disease-free.

Onions

Plant overwintering autumn onion sets now if you didn't do so last month (see p.154).

Peas

For an early crop next year, sow a hardy, overwintering pea variety in a warm, sheltered spot. Except in very mild regions, protect plants with cloches over the winter.

Rhubarb

Rhubarb plants should be entering their dormant period now. They will last right through the winter to early spring and October is the best time to plant new sets or divide and replant old crowns (see p.192).

Currants and gooseberries

Plant new, bare-root bushes this month or next. Container-grown bushes can be planted at any time of year, but autumn is a good time for them to get their roots established, too.

Grapevines

New, bare-root vines can be planted this month or next, although according to traditional wisdom it's better to wait until spring, ideally March.

Strawberries

New strawberry plants can still be planted out this month, but they may not crop generously next year if planting is left this late.

Bare-root fruit bushes will establish well at this time of year when the soil is still warm. Make sure the top of the planting hole is level with the top of the root ball, using a cane or stick.

VEGETABLES TO PLANT
- Cabbages (spring)
- Garlic
- Onion sets
- Rhubarb sets

FRUIT TO PLANT
- Black currants
- Cranberries
- Gooseberries
- Grapevines
- Peaches and nectarines
- Red currants and white currants
- Strawberries

Construct raised beds

Raised beds are a good way of permanently separating the areas of your plot that you cultivate from those that you walk on. The shape of the beds is entirely up to you, but restrict their width to 3–4 ft (90–120 cm); any wider and you may have trouble reaching the center without treading on the soil. Every year, top up the bed with bulky organic matter and you should end up with rich, fertile soil that is well structured and free-draining.

If your plot is on heavy clay the structure of your soil may be poor and it will retain water, making it slow to warm up in time for spring sowing. Making a double-height raised bed containing soil enriched with well-rotted organic matter is a good solution.

"Make sure you can reach the center of your bed from the path."

1 **From edging boards measuring** at least 4 in (10 cm) wide by 1 in (2.5 cm) thick, cut two 4-ft (1.2-m) lengths, one for each end of the raised bed. The bed can be any length, but this width allows easy access. Nail a 12-in (30-cm) long wooden peg about 4 in (10 cm) in from the end of each of the boards.

2 **Hammer the strips** of wooden edging into the ground, with the pegs facing inward, in order to make a rectangle, or a diamond—whatever shape you prefer.

3 **Check** that each edging board is level, making any adjustments by carefully hammering down the higher of the two ends.

4 **Lay a length of wood** diagonally across the two edging boards, and check with a spirit level to ensure that one isn't higher than the other.

5 **Top up the raised bed** with a thoroughly mixed combination of good-quality topsoil and well-rotted garden compost or barnyard manure.

6 **Use a garden fork** or a rake to spread the soil evenly.

7 **Wrap a length of string** around two bricks and stretch it diagonally across the bed in various different places to ensure that the surface of the soil is level.

Jobs for October

October should see you harvesting the last of many of the year's crops—those that may not survive the first frosts of the winter: beans, pumpkins, squashes, apples, pears, and even autumn raspberries and strawberries. Much of the work to be done this month involves clearing away and composting old plant material that's now dead or dying off, taking down bean and pea supports and storing them away, and making a start on your winter digging.

Clear old vegetation

Remove all dead foliage and old, dying plants. Unless there are signs of disease, add it all to your compost heap. Shred or pulverize thick, woody stems such as corn, beans, and brassicas so that they decompose more quickly.

Remove plant supports

Clear away bean poles, canes, pea sticks, and tomato stakes, and store them somewhere under cover. If you leave them out all winter, they'll quickly rot.

Break up heavy soil

Dig over beds where the soil has become hard and compacted. Pull out any weeds as you go.

Dig in green manures

Chop and dig in green manures that will not overwinter (see p.143). They will swiftly rot down and become incorporated into the soil.

Cover beds with plastic sheeting

Spreading plastic sheets over the soil keeps off the worst of the rain and suppresses weeds, as well as allowing you to sow earlier next spring.

Cut down asparagus and Jerusalem artichokes

If you didn't do it last month, chop down to the ground yellowing asparagus foliage and the stems and foliage of Jerusalem artichokes. Compost it all.

Earth up brussels sprouts

Keep earthing up the stems of brussels sprouts, cabbages, and other brassicas to give them support as they become increasingly top-heavy. Cut off any yellow leaves.

"Cure" pumpkins and squashes

Cut and leave pumpkins and squashes to dry in the sun. This "curing" hardens their skins, and the tougher the skins, the longer they'll keep.

Lift carrots and other roots

Potatoes and beets should all be harvested now. Carrots, turnips, and rutabagas can stay in the ground for longer, but it may be wiser to lift them and store them.

Mulch celeriac and parsnips

Parnips and celeriac are reasonably safe to leave in the ground. Indeed, parsnips are said to taste better after cold weather. Protect the plants by mulching them with straw or bracken.

(below, left to right) **Green manures** such as phacelia are killed by frost so dig them in now. **Support brussels sprouts** by piling up earth around the stem. **Raise pumpkins** and squashes off damp ground, on a brick or flat stone, and let them "cure." **Protect celeriac crowns** from frost with a mulch of dry straw.

MAKING A VEGETABLE CLAMP

Now somewhat old-fashioned—but none the worse for that—a homemade vegetable clamp is a way of insulating and storing root vegetables such as potatoes, rutabagas, turnips, carrots, and beets for use during the winter.

1 In a dry, sheltered spot, spread out a 8 in- (20 cm-) thick layer of clean straw and stack vegetables on top in a pyramid, with necks facing outward and the largest roots at the bottom.

2 Carefully cover the pyramid with more clean straw—at least 8 in (20 cm) to keep vegetables frost-free.

3 If very cold weather is forecast, add a 6 in (15 cm) layer of soil to act as further insulation for the vegetables inside.

4 Firm down the sides of the clamp, making it as stable as possible, and keep a close watch on it for any signs of attack by rodents.

Earth up leeks and celery

Draw earth up around leeks and trench celery to keep the stems blanched.

Lift chicory for forcing

After the first frosts, you can start digging up chicory and replanting the roots to force them (see p.183).

Cover late crops with cloches

If temperatures drop, especially at night, protect autumn salads and Oriental leaves with cloches or fleece.

Dry out beans for storage

If the weather is dry, leave bean pods on the plants to dry. If it's wet, cut them down and hang them up indoors or somewhere dry and sheltered. When they are completely dried, pod

Storing apples successfully depends on rejecting blemished fruits, which will infect the whole batch. Wrap singly in paper or store unwrapped, but make sure the fruits are not touching.

them and store the beans in airtight containers, ready to use in soups and casseroles.

Harvest apples and pears

Pick the last of your apples and pears this month. Cook or eat right away any that are damaged. Store only perfect fruit; blemished ones will simply rot and infect the others.

Finish pruning blackberries and summer raspberries

By now you should have cut out all the old canes that carried this year's fruit. New, nonfruiting canes should be tied in ready for next year.

Order new fruit trees and bushes

Next month is a good time for planting many new, bare-root trees and bushes, so order plants from nurseries now if you didn't do so last month.

PREPARING GLOBE ARTICHOKES FOR OVERWINTERING

Plants are not always frost hardy so take steps to help your crop survive cold winter weather.

1 Cut down dead stems and also remove any yellowing foliage.

2 Spread a mulch of well-rotted compost around the base, and top this with straw in very cold spells.

October pests & diseases

Vegetables

■ **Dig over** your potato patch thoroughly to ensure that no potatoes are still left in the ground. It's easy to miss a few, especially the small ones. If you don't remove them, they will survive the winter to sprout again next year and may carry over viruses or other diseases.

■ **Remove yellow leaves** from brussels sprouts, cabbages, and other brassicas. Leaving them to rot on the ground risks spreading gray mold.

■ **Rake up fallen leaves** and spent foliage. If any material shows signs of powdery mildew or disease, destroy or dispose of it. Don't add it to your compost.

■ **Cabbage aphid** attacks are likely to be at their worst this month and next, and cabbage whitefly can continue to infest brussels sprouts, cabbages, and other brassicas through the autumn and into winter. Spray with an organic or inorganic insecticide if necessary.

■ **Leek moth caterpillars** may finish feeding and spin themselves a lacelike cocoon in which to pupate. Now is the time to examine your leeks and pick off the insects.

■ **Net winter cabbages** and other brassicas to protect them from pigeons.

Fruit

■ **Look for brown rot** on any remaining apples and pears. Remove and destroy infected fruits rather than composting them.

■ **Spray apples and pears** against canker when about half their leaves have fallen.

■ **Prune out** any diseased or damaged branches from apple and pear trees.

■ **Rake up leaves** and destroy them if there are any signs of scab or rust.

■ **Fit grease bands** to the trunks of fruit trees to prevent insects such as winter moths from climbing up and laying their eggs.

■ **Spray peaches and nectarines** with copper fungicide to protect them against peach leaf curl.

■ **Do not prune cherries or plums** until next spring— pruning cuts may allow silver leaf fungus to enter.

(top to bottom) **Yellowing leaves** on brussels sprouts can spread fungal disease. **Remove aphids** from cabbages before they become heavily infested. **Grease bands** around fruit trees act as a barrier to egg-laying pests.

November

Along with the shortening days, November is a thoroughly wet month—unless you live in colder regions, in which case you may have snow rather than rain. This is the month to ensure that you have a sharp pair of pruning shears. Fruit trees and bushes have shed their leaves and are now dormant. So, with the exception of cherries and plums, now is a good time to prune them, before the weather turns very cold. For the same reasons, it's the best time of the year to plant new, bare-root fruit trees and bushes. The soil will still be warm, and if you prepare the planting holes by adding a generous helping of compost or manure, the roots will be able to establish themselves before winter really sets in. And for those in the South, lettuce and cabbage seeds can be sown in a cold-frame.

Kale survives the harshest of winter weather and will flourish as long as your soil isn't waterlogged. There are several varieties, and this "black" kale, 'Cavolo Nero', is one of the best.

Top tasks for November

- **Harvest** root vegetables, autumn brassicas, Oriental leaves, and late-season salad crops.
- **Pick** autumn raspberries and cranberries. Sow broad bean seeds outdoors, and plant garlic and rhubarb sets.
- **Plant** new, bare-root fruit trees, bushes, and canes before the ground becomes too cold and wet.
- **Prune** apple and pear trees and soft-fruit bushes while they are dormant.
- **Dig** over your plot, removing any perennial weeds and adding plenty of well-rotted organic material.
- **Cover** beds with polythene, carpet, or cardboard to protect the soil from heavy rain.
- **Remove** nets from fruit cages but keep them over brussels sprouts, cabbages, and other brassicas.

Vegetables, salads, and fruit

1 Brussels sprouts
The young leaves at the stalk tops are known as "sprout tops"; harvest, cook, and eat them like spring greens.

2 Cauliflowers
Harvest cauliflowers as you need them. Unless it is very cold, there's no hurry—they'll have stopped growing.

3 Winter radishes
Orientals, such as 'Mantanghong' (shown here), sown in July may be lifted or left alone for a couple of months.

4 Jerusalem artichokes
At last, patience is rewarded: after nine months in the ground, the first artichokes should finally be ready to lift.

5 French beans
Beans intended for drying may be left on the plants until the pods have completely dried out.

6 Endive
Both curly-leaved or frisée varieties (shown here) and flat-leaved, Batavian types will continue cropping through the winter if protected by fleece or cloches.

7 Spinach
Winter spinach varieties are fast-growing and bred to tolerate shorter days; they should crop this month. Provide protection in severe weather.

8 Oriental brassicas
Komatsuna, mibuna, mizuna, chop suey greens, Chinese broccoli, mustard greens, and choy sum (shown here) will all last until now, if given protection.

9 Kale
Harvest full-grown leaves now, and over the winter. Kale is extremely hardy.

10 Kohlrabi
Modern varieties are reasonably hardy and will withstand moderate

frosts, but if temperatures are very low, protect plants with fleece or cloches.

11 Sprouting broccoli
Pick any remaining spears, before hardier types take over in the new year.

12 Turnips
Lift turnips if there is any danger of the ground freezing. You can store them for use later in winter (see p.190).

13 Swiss chard
All leaf beets are fairly foolproof. They're hardy, withstand neglect, and resist attacks from pests and diseases.

14 Raspberries
Autumn raspberries will produce fruit until the first frost. In mild regions or sheltered spots, that might be now.

ALSO HARVEST

Carrots
Continue lifting maincrop carrots to eat or to store—although they can be left in the ground for later in the winter.

Cabbages
Both autumn and winter cabbage varieties are ready for cutting now.

Celeriac
Dig up entire roots and trim before use.

Celery
Harvest trench-grown celery now.

Cranberries
Pick the berries when their color darkens to a rich, deep red.

Leeks
Use a fork to dig up leeks or you'll risk snapping off the stem.

Lettuces
Pick the last autumn lettuces now.

Parsnips
Harvest, or leave them in the ground.

Radishes
Pull any remaining summer radishes now or they'll turn woody and unpalatable.

Rutabagas
Lift rutabagas now or leave them if they are not becoming too large.

Salad leaves
Land cress, corn salad, rocket, winter purslane, and some of the Oriental brassicas will still provide leaves for salads if protected against frost.

Spinach
Autumn and winter varieties sown in late summer should be cropping now.

Sow or plant in November

November is a key month for planting new fruit trees, especially if you have bought bare-root plants, which can only be planted when dormant. The same applies to new fruit bushes and canes, and to outdoor grapevines. As far as vegetables go, there's little you can sow or plant. Unless you have a heated greenhouse, broad beans, garlic, and rhubarb are all you'll need to think about.

Broad beans

Sow seeds of "early," overwintering varieties now—either in the ground or in pots in a cold frame—if you didn't do so last month. Otherwise, wait until the new year, when you can sow "late" broad beans for harvesting in July and August.

Garlic

Plant garlic cloves (see p.168). If you leave it until next month, the ground may become too hard or too wet, in which case you should wait until February or even March—although that won't leave as long for the bulbs to fatten up.

VEGETABLE SEEDS TO SOW
- Broad beans

VEGETABLES TO PLANT
- Garlic
- Rhubarb sets

FRUIT TO PLANT
- Apples, cherries, pears, and plums
- Apricots, peaches, and nectarines
- Blackberries and hybrid berries
- Black currants
- Blueberries
- Cranberries
- Figs
- Gooseberries
- Grapevines
- Raspberries
- Red currants and white currants

Rhubarb

Rhubarb is dormant now, so it is a good time to buy and plant new sets or propagate from established plants. Spread well-rotted compost around the stems but don't cover the crowns.

Fruit trees

Bare-root cherries and plums can be planted at any time between November and January, and apples and pears between November and March. That said, November is considered to be the optimum time, especially in areas where the ground is likely to freeze hard.

Raspberries and blackberries

Plant new, bare-root canes of raspberries, blackberries, and hybrid berries—preferably in holes or trenches that you have previously dug and filled with well-rotted compost or manure.

Currants and gooseberries

Plant new, bare-root bushes this month or next. Container-grown bushes can be planted at any time of year, but autumn is an ideal month to get them in the ground.

Grapevines

Plant new, bare-root vines this month or wait until next spring, ideally March.

PLANTING A BARE-ROOT FRUIT TREE

This month, while the soil is still warm, is ideal for planting fruit trees so their roots get well established.

1 Check that the tree will be planted at the right depth—the same level as the soil mark on the stem.

2 Drive in a stout stake to a depth of about 2 ft (60 cm) to support the growing tree.

3 Replace the tree in the hole and fill, moving it around to make sure the soil settles in around the roots.

4 Firm down as you backfill the planting hole, but try not to compact the ground.

5 Tie the tree to the stake using a belt tie, so the trunk is close to the stake, but not touching.

6 Water well, then spread a mulch of well-rotted compost around the stem.

(top to bottom) **Spreading lime** on your soil will increase its pH value, or alkalinity. Brassicas, in particular, prefer alkaline soils. **Cover** beds with plastic sheets anchored firmly and the ground will be ready for sowing or planting early next year.

Jobs for November

November is a good month for giving your soil some time and attention. Next month it may be too cold or too waterlogged to do much with it at all—in which case you'll have to wait until next spring before you can begin to work it again. So, remove all the old plant debris still remaining on your plot, including any weeds, and turn over the soil with a spade or fork, working in as much compost or manure as you can lay your hands on. All this material will be drawn down by worms and become incorporated over the winter, replacing nutrients and improving the structure of the soil.

Clear away old plants

Continue to remove all remains of plants that have finished cropping. Provided there are no signs of disease, add everything to your compost heap.

Take down bean supports

Dismantle any cane or wigwam supports you've left standing while climbing beans finish drying out.

Weed and dig

Remove any surviving weeds (especially perennials such as bindweed or couch grass) and turn over the soil if it has become hard and compacted.

Dig in manure and compost

Wherever you can, dig in plenty of well-rotted compost or farmyard manure. In the case of raised or "no-dig" beds, simply spread it over the surface.

Lime your soil if necessary

Before the ground becomes too wet, test the pH value of your soil (see p.47). If it's too acid, spread some powdered lime over the surface and rake it in. But don't add it at the same time as manure because they react chemically with one another.

Cover vegetable beds

As you clear your plot, continue to spread plastic sheeting or membranes over the soil in order to keep off the worst of the rain and to suppress weeds. If you can't get hold of plastic sheeting, old carpets or even cardboard will offer some protection.

Make leafmold

Leaves take a long time to rot down if simply added to a regular compost heap. It's better to pile them into specially constructed wire cages so they won't blow away. You can also combine them with a little moist soil and pack into plastic bin liners punctured with small holes.

Mulch celeriac and globe artichokes

Spread a thick mulch of straw or bracken around celeriac stems (see p.173) and also over globe artichoke crowns to protect them from frost damage in cold weather.

(above) **Fallen leaves for leafmold** are best collected after rain. If your leaves are dry, water them. After a year, use the leafmold as a moisture-retaining mulch on your beds.

Protect cauliflowers

Bend over a few leaves and tie them in place to protect the heads or curds from frost—just as you protected them from the sun in summer.

Cover late crops with cloches

Protect late-season salads and Oriental leaves by covering them with cloches.

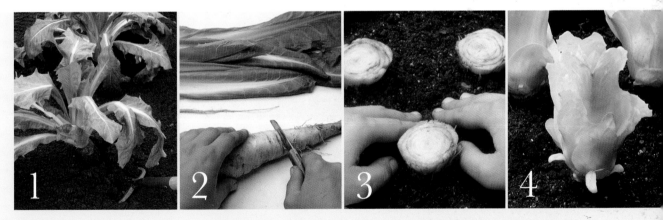

FORCING CHICORY

The leaves of Belgian, or Witloof, chicory are excessively bitter, but the roots can be "forced"—by excluding light—to produce the familiar blanched shoots, called chicons, that are an important winter salad crop.

1 Dig up mature plants that you grew over the summer, ideally after the first frost of the season.

2 Trim the leaves leaving about 1 in (2.5 cm) above the crown, then slice off the tapering end of the roots to leave 8–9 in (20–22 cm) lengths.

3 Plant three roots in a 10 in (25 cm) pot of moist compost. Line a second pot of the same size and invert it over the first to block out any light.

4 After three or four weeks in a warm, dark place, the blanched chicons will be ready for harvesting.

Weed around fruit trees and bushes

Carefully weed around all established fruit trees, bushes, and canes. Spread mulches around the base of the plants.

Remove nets from fruit cages

Now is the time of year when you actually do want birds in your fruit cage. Take off the nets to allow them in to pick off and eat any lurking insects and their eggs. Removing nets also saves them from damage by heavy snowfalls.

Prune gooseberries and currants

Start winter-pruning gooseberry and currant bushes when the leaves have fallen and you can more easily see what you are doing. They can be pruned between now and next spring. Always cut out any dead, diseased, or damaged branches (the three D's) and remove any shoots that cross over in the center of the bush.

Pruning black currant bushes

Remove between a quarter and a third of the oldest stems, cutting them right down to just 1 in (2.5 cm) above the soil. Also remove any weak, crowded, or diseased branches. This way you'll stimulate new growth and open up the bush so that light and air can circulate when the weather improves next spring.

Start winter-pruning apples and pears

Once most of the leaves have fallen and the trees have entered their period of winter dormancy, begin pruning (see pp.34–35).

Remove unripened figs

Take off and discard any figs as large or larger than a cherry. They won't ripen now and will fall off in due course. Leave the small embryo figs in place. They should fruit next year.

Prune vines

Once you've picked your last grapes, begin to winter-prune vines. Spread the task over the next two months and aim to finish by January.

(left to right) **Hard prune** established black currant bushes, taking out old unproductive stems. **Small figs** must be removed so the embryo figs have the best chance of ripening next year.

November pests & diseases

Vegetables

■ **Check stored vegetables** such as potatoes, beets, celeriac, and squashes for signs of rot. Discard any affected crops.

■ **Continue to collect** up fallen leaves and spent foliage. If it shows any signs of mildew or disease, burn or dispose of it. Don't add it to your compost.

■ **Remove yellow leaves** from brussels sprouts, cabbages, and other brassicas. Leaving them to rot risks spreading gray mold.

■ **Check brussels sprouts** and other brassicas for cabbage whitefly. They can still be a problem, even this late in the year. They're impossible to miss since they fly up in a cloud when the leaves are disturbed. Pick off or spray.

■ **Net winter cabbages** and other brassicas to protect them from pigeons. At this time of year, when there is increasingly little else to eat, the birds can completely strip the leaves.

■ **Inspect herbs** such as rosemary, sage, and thyme for mould and root or stem rot, especially if the autumn has been wet. They dislike damp, waterlogged conditions.

■ **Mice** can be a problem as winter approaches. They are particularly keen on digging up newly planted broad bean seeds, garlic, shallots, and onions.

(Clockwise from top) **Burn** fallen leaves that show signs of disease. **Brown rot** will quickly spread to any remaining apples. **Cabbage whitefly** are still active, even this late in the year.

Fruit

■ **Remove rotten fruit** that may still hang on your trees. Apples, pears, and plums affected by brown rot should be destroyed not composted. If you leave them in place in a withered state, they will spread disease.

■ **Prune out** any diseased or damaged branches from apple and pear trees.

■ **Rake up leaves** and destroy them if there are any signs of scab or rust.

■ **Fit grease bands** to the trunks of fruit trees to prevent insects such as winter moths from climbing up and laying their eggs.

■ **Check stored fruit** and discard any that show signs of rot.

■ **Spray peaches and nectarines** with copper fungicide to protect them against peach leaf curl.

■ **Do not prune cherries or plums** until next spring because pruning cuts may allow silver leaf fungus to enter.

December

Surprisingly, December is not necessarily as lean a month, particularly in the warmer regions, as you might expect. With luck, your winter brassicas should be at their peak now: brussels sprouts, cabbages, cauliflowers, and the almost indestructible kale. Fresh root vegetables—parsnips, celeriac, rutabagas, and turnips—should still be in good supply, and you'll have a hoard of potatoes, beets, and carrots in storage. You may still be picking salads such as endive, winter purslane, and corn salad, and perhaps even lettuces, arugula, and a few Oriental leaves if you've been growing them in a cold frame or under cloches. Winter, which officially begins on the solstice, December 21, delivers cool temperatures and rain to the South, snow and ice to the North. The silver lining: in addition to inducing dormancy, the cold temperatures kill off most infestations.

Frost-hardy brussels sprouts come into their own this month and may even taste better after a cold snap. Pick them while still fairly small, starting from the bottom of the plant.

Top tasks for December

■ **Harvest** leeks, root vegetables, autumn and winter brassicas, and perhaps a few hardy salad crops.

■ **Plant** garlic, rhubarb, and new, bare-root fruit trees and bushes—provided the ground is not frozen or waterlogged.

■ **Prune** apple and pear trees, soft-fruit bushes, and outdoor grapevines if it's not too cold.

■ **Dig** over your plot, add plenty of well-rotted organic material, and cover beds to protect the soil.

■ **Check** nets over brussels sprouts, cabbages, and other brassicas.

Vegetables and salads

1 Celeriac
Harvest the roots now or, if you don't need them yet, leave them in the ground. Pull off any dead or dying leaves, and if temperatures are very low protect them with some straw or bracken.

2 Jerusalem artichokes
Dig up the last of your Jerusalem artichokes this month. Unless you want another crop next year, make sure you find and remove all the tubers.

3 Endive
One of the hardiest of all the salad plants, endive withstands most winters if you cover it with frames or cloches to protect from the worst of the weather.

4 Kale
Although you may have been growing kale earlier in the year for baby salad leaves, it really comes into its own during the winter months. 'Cavolo Nero', sometimes known as 'Black Tuscan' (shown here), is tough enough to survive almost anything.

5 Winter radishes
Oriental and other winter radishes are much larger than the small summer radishes grown for salads. They are also hardier, and can be left in the ground during all but the most severe winters.

6 Cauliflowers
If frosts are severe, protect curds of winter cauliflowers by wrapping a few of the outer leaves around them.

7 Carrots
Theoretically, carrots can be left until the end of the year, but if the ground is in danger of freezing hard, or if they are starting to look a little worse for wear, lift them now and store any that are in good condition (see p.190).

8 Rutabagas
Although rutabagas may be left in the ground until the end of this month, beyond that they tend to become woody.

It's better to lift them all now and, if necessary, store them (see p.190).

9 Brussels sprouts
Sprouts should be plentiful this month. Either harvest them one by one, working up the stem from the bottom to the top, or uproot the entire plant. They'll keep for a few days if you stand the stalk in a bucket of water.

10 Leeks
Harvest leeks just before you need them because they don't store well once lifted. Cut off the roots and wash the stems carefully to remove any soil trapped between the leaves.

11 Savoy cabbages
Winter-season Savoy cabbages (shown here) have distinctive, crinkly leaves and are hardy enough to survive the coldest weather.

12 Parsnips
Lift parsnips when you need them. Either leave the remainder in the ground or harvest them all and store them for later in the winter, laying them out in shallow boxes and covering them with moist sand (see p.190).

13 Turnips
Lift any remaining turnips by the end of the month; otherwise, they will grow too large and turn woody. Store them indoors in sand-filled boxes or outdoors in "clamps" (see p.190).

ALSO HARVEST

Celery
A late crop of trench-grown celery can be harvested now—provided the plants have been protected against frost.

Kohlrabi
Harvest the last of your kohlrabi by the end of the year. While it's true that plants can survive moderate frosts, especially if protected with fleece or cloches, their flavor does not improve with age.

Salad leaves
Just a few hardy salad plants can still be persuaded to provide fresh leaves, if they are protected beneath fleece or under cloches: they include corn salad, rocket, land cress, and winter purslane.

Store crops for the winter

By December, you'll need to make some decisions about whether to leave your remaining crops in the ground or lift and store them. Brussels sprouts, winter cabbages, broccoli, and kale can certainly stay where they are. Leeks, too. And, in theory, parsnips, celeriac, rutabagas, and winter radishes can remain in the ground over the winter—although they may appreciate a protective covering of straw or bracken. But if there's any chance of the ground freezing solid, it's probably best to have lifted your root crops, such as carrots, turnips, and beets, before the end of the year.

Where to store crops

To ensure that crops last as long into the winter as possible, they need to be stored somewhere cool, dry, and if possible, dark. An outhouse or shed should be fine—as long as it's frost-free and secure against attack from mice and rats. A cellar or garage might be suitable, too, but only if it's not too warm. Good ventilation is important. Stale, humid air is the perfect breeding ground for disease.

Regular health checks

Before you store any vegetables or fruit, inspect each one carefully for any signs of damage or disease. Be ruthless. Discard any produce that isn't perfect. If you don't, not only will it rot, it will also contaminate the rest of your harvest—and you could lose everything. Each time you take something out of storage for use in the kitchen, check on the crops remaining and remove any that look as if they are in danger of deteriorating.

1 **Storing carrots and parsnips**
Spread a layer of sand in the bottom of a shallow wooden box, lay the roots on top so that they do not touch, and then cover them completely with another layer of sand. The sand should be moist enough to keep the roots from shriveling but not so wet that they rot.

2 **Storing cabbages**
Solid-headed, winter cabbages can be hung up in net bags or spread on wooden slats covered with straw. Keep them apart from other crops in case any of them are harboring slugs.

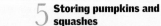

3 Storing potatoes

Maincrop potatoes should be kept in thick paper sacks. Avoid plastic, which will make the roots sweat and perhaps even sprout. The bags should be sealed or folded over at the top to exclude light, and kept in a frost-free place.

4 Storing apples and pears

One of the keys to keeping apples and pears successfully is to choose the right varieties. Only late-season fruit can be stored. Pack them in single layers in trays or boxes, wrapped in tissue or shredded paper, somewhere cool, dry, and well ventilated. Keep apples and pears apart from one another.

5 Storing pumpkins and squashes

If properly cured so their skins dry out and harden, winter squashes should store well. They need good ventilation and should sit on straw or on paper that has been shredded.

6 Storing beans

Lay haricot and other beans out to dry completely before storing them. Keep them in screw-top containers, but check on them from time to time because they may sometimes contain tiny weevils or other insects.

7 Storing onions, shallots, and garlic

Provided that they have been thoroughly dried out, onions, shallots, and garlic can be made into traditional strings or braids and hung up to store. Alternatively, stack them in single layers in wooden boxes or on slatted shelves.

8 Storing rutabagas and other root crops

A "clamp" is a traditional method of storing root vegetables outdoors by covering them with straw and a layer of soil (see p.173 for details of how to construct a clamp for potatoes).

Sow or plant in December

This is without question the quietest month of the year for sowing and planting. Seeds of overwintering crops should have been sown at least a month or two ago, and it will almost certainly be too cold and damp to sow or plant anything successfully. The only exceptions are garlic cloves, rhubarb sets, and bare-root fruit trees, bushes, and canes, but only if the ground is not wet or frozen.

Garlic
Plant only in mild areas and only if the soil is not frozen or waterlogged. Otherwise, wait until February or March.

Rhubarb
Rhubarb is dormant now, so plant new sets or divide and replant old crowns. Rhubarb will tolerate the cold—in fact it needs a certain number of cold days—but doesn't like being waterlogged.

Fruit trees and bushes
Plant new, bare-root trees and bushes now. Prepare the ground in advance by clearing all weeds and digging in plenty of well-rotted manure or compost. December is your last chance for planting young, bare-root peaches and nectarines.

Raspberries and blackberries
Plant new, bare-root canes of raspberries, blackberries, and hybrid berries if you didn't do so last month.

VEGETABLES TO PLANT
- Garlic
- Rhubarb sets

FRUIT TO PLANT
- Apples, cherries, pears, and plums
- Apricots, peaches, and nectarines
- Blackberries and hybrid berries
- Black currants
- Blueberries
- Figs
- Gooseberries
- Raspberries
- Red currants and white currants

DIVIDING RHUBARB
Rhubarb can last for years but may lose vigor, so divide the rootstock to make new "crowns."

1 Lift the crown and use a sharp spade to divide it into sections, each with a bud.

2 Replant each section with the bud just showing, in well-manured ground.

Jobs for December

December is a month for housekeeping. Out on your plot, there's not much to do except digging and mulching, and winter-pruning of fruit trees, bushes, and vines. If the weather has already turned very cold it's probably best not to do even that. Instead, clean up all your tools and neaten your kitchen garden shed. Order the packets of seed you want for next spring. And—provided your brussels sprouts, cabbages, and other brassicas are securely netted—perhaps take a moment to go out and scatter some food for the birds.

Continue winter digging

As long as your soil is not frozen or waterlogged, you can still dig. But if the earth sticks to your boots when you walk on it, it's too wet and you risk compacting the soil. Either keep off your beds altogether, or work from planks to distribute your weight.

Dig in rotted manure or compost

If you've already worked out next year's planting plan, it's worth digging plenty of organic matter into the beds where you intend to grow beans and peas. Even more than most vegetables, they need rich, fertile soil.

Top up compost and leafmold bins

Continue adding any of last season's old plant material to your compost heap, and collect any fallen autumn leaves for your leafmold pile or sacks. But burn or otherwise destroy any plant debris that looks as if it may be diseased.

Cover beds with plastic sheeting

As long as the earth isn't waterlogged, it's not too late to spread sheets or even old carpets over the soil in order to keep off heavy rain, suppress weeds, and help warm the ground ready for early sowing and planting next year.

Lift root vegetables for storage

Harvest the last of your carrots, turnips, kohlrabi, and any remaining beets. They can be stored if necessary (see pp.190–91). Celeriac and parsnips can stay in the ground if there's no risk of their being "frozen in," although a mulch of straw or bracken will help protect them.

(top to bottom) **Stand on** a plank to spread your weight evenly over beds. **Add plant material** to your compost bin and then cover it to keep in any warmth.

Force chicory

Continue lifting chicory roots for forcing indoors, to keep you supplied with fresh winter salad ingredients (see p.183).

Check spring cabbages and brussels sprouts

Remove any brown or yellow leaves, earth up brussels sprouts stems that are unsteady, and ensure that nets are in place to keep off birds.

Prepare ground for new fruit trees and bushes

If it has not become too cold, prepare planting holes for new fruit trees and bushes (see p.181). If the ground is frozen, you can wait—but no longer than the end of March.

Weed around fruit trees and bushes

If you didn't do so last month, carefully weed and mulch around all established fruit trees, bushes, and canes.

Winter-prune apple and pear trees

Unless it is very cold, continue pruning dormant apple and pear trees (see pp.34–35), taking out dead, diseased, and damaged branches.

(left to right) **Prune gooseberries** by removing the oldest branches. This will prevent overcrowding and open up the center of the bush. **Vines** trained along wires should have any vertical growth pruned back so that three or four strong buds remain.

Winter-prune fruit bushes

If you didn't do so last month, winter-prune gooseberries and thin established blueberry and currant bushes, removing about a third of older wood on black currants (see p.184).

Prune grapevines

Now that the leaves have fallen, winter-prune outdoor grapevines. Some say the job should be completed by Christmas. Certainly, next month is your last chance before the sap starts rising and it will be too late.

Check wires and ties

Inspect all stakes, wires, and ties on your fruit trees and bushes. Replace any that are worn or broken, loosen any that are too tight, and ensure that others are secure.

Clean tools, pots and seed trays

Give all this year's pots, seed trays, and other equipment a thorough cleaning. It will help prevent any diseases or viruses from infecting next year's new seedlings.

December pests & diseases

Vegetables

■ **Check nets** on winter cabbages, cauliflowers, brussels sprouts, kale, and broccoli. You'll need to keep them in place all winter to keep off birds. Repair any holes and refasten any nets that have become loose.

■ **Remove dying leaves** from brussels sprouts, cabbages, and other brassicas as soon as they start to turn yellow. Leaving them to rot on the ground risks spreading gray mold.

■ **Digging over your soil** during the winter will help expose hibernating grubs to the watchful eyes of hungry birds.

■ **Slugs** can still be a problem even this late in the year. Check for them in the outer leaves of cabbages and cauliflowers.

■ **Mice and rats** can be a problem as winter approaches. They are partial to digging up newly planted broad bean seeds, garlic, and shallot and onion sets.

■ **Check stored crops** such as potatoes, rutabagas, squashes, onions, shallots, and garlic for signs of rot.

Fruit

■ **Check stored fruit** such as apples and pears, and discard any that show signs of rot.

■ **Spray fruit trees** and bushes with a plant-oil-based winter wash to help control aphids, mites, scale insects, and winter moths.

(left to right) **Remove** yellowing foliage on brussels sprouts to halt the spread of disease. **Canker** is a bacterial infection that can spread rapidly. Take out entire branches and burn.

If you spray thoroughly, the overwintering eggs should be destroyed. The best time to spray is this month and next, when the trees and bushes are completely dormant.

■ **Check apple and pear trees** for signs of canker. Cut out any diseased wood—as well as any other branches that have been damaged.

■ **Renew grease bands** on the trunks of fruit trees if necessary.

■ **Spray peaches and nectarines** with copper fungicide to protect them against peach leaf curl. Erecting a rainproof cover over espalier or fan-trained trees can shelter them and prevent rain from spreading the spores that carry the disease.

■ **Blackbirds and starlings** are notorious for eating newly forming buds—particularly on gooseberries, apples, pears, and plums. Nets are the only guaranteed solution.

■ **Do not prune cherries or plums** until next spring because pruning cuts may allow silver leaf fungus to enter.

Net winter kale and other brassicas or birds will strip the leaves. Food sources are scarce at this time of year so the birds can be particularly troublesome.

Crop planner

Most kitchen gardeners share a dream—one of an unbroken, year-long harvest in which not a month goes by without some form of fresh, home-grown produce coming to fruition, ready to pick and take indoors to the kitchen. Sadly, it's not as easy as it sounds. But it's not impossible either. The secret lies in planning. And planning in turn depends on knowing what to do and when. In this section, not only will you find detailed information about how to grow the vegetables and fruit most commonly found in kitchen gardens, you'll also find month-by-month cultivation charts outlining exactly when you should be sowing seeds, when you should be planting, and—most important of all—when you can harvest your crops.

Raised beds are a way of ensuring fertile, well-structured soil, and also help you stay organized, making it easier to rotate crops according to a well-planned planting schedule.

Vegetables

Vegetables are usually grouped according to what part of the plant we eat, whether it is the roots, tubers, leaves, stems, fruit, or seeds. Sometimes it's obvious: lettuces and spinach are clearly leaves, and beets and carrots are just as clearly roots. But sometimes it's not: Florence fennel, celeriac, and kohlrabi may look like roots but are in fact swollen stems. The issue is further complicated by the fact that certain botanical families contain vegetables you would never guess are related. Cabbages, rutabagas, and broccoli, for example, are all brassicas, although they look completely different from each other.

Vegetable families

- **Root and stem vegetables** include carrots, tubers such as potatoes, and stems such as celery and Florence fennel.
- **Cabbages, leaves, and other brassicas** encompass cauliflowers, broccoli, brussels sprouts, kale, and spinach.
- **Onion family members** are all alliums. In addition to onions themselves, shallots, leeks, and garlic are included.
- **Peas, beans, and other legumes** are all grown for their edible seeds and seedpods.
- **Salads** are all leaf vegetables, more often than not eaten raw.
- **Summer fruiting vegetables**, such as tomatoes, peppers, and eggplant, all need high temperatures and long hours of sunshine in order to ripen.
- **Cucumbers, pumpkins, and squashes**—sometimes known as cucurbits or gourds—are technically fruits.
- **Perennial vegetables** include artichokes, asparagus, and rhubarb. They all die down in the autumn but reappear in spring.
- **Herbs** may be annuals, biennials, perennials, or evergreen shrubs. They are grown for their aromatic leaves.

Closely planted rows of oak-leaf lettuce, onions, beets, carrots, and leeks make use of every available inch of space. With such intensively grown crops, weeds can't get a foothold.

Root and stem vegetables

This group of vegetables includes all those that are obviously roots: potatoes, carrots, beets, parsnips, turnips, and so on. But it also includes a couple of impostors that look like roots but are not. The knobbly, hairy celeriac and the bulbous Florence fennel with its fernlike foliage are in fact swollen stems. As a group, these vegetables are rightly prized not just for their taste but for the fact that many of them can be stored after harvesting and thus provide a valuable source of homegrown food during the lean winter months.

Root crops are fairly easy to grow and all will flourish in soil that has been improved with well-rotted compost or manure. Stem vegetables, particularly celery, need more attention, especially when it comes to watering.

(above left to right) **First early potatoes, turnips, Chantenay carrots**

(far left) **Celeriac 'Monarch'**
(left) **Radish 'French Breakfast'**

Potatoes

Hardly anyone grows potatoes from seed. Instead, they're grown from commercially cultivated tubers called "seed potatoes," which can be bought from garden centers or specialist nurseries, usually in January or February. Potatoes are classified according to the length of time they spend in the ground. "Earlies" will be ready for lifting first, then "second earlies," and in late summer and early autumn, "maincrop" varieties.

	spring			summer			autumn			winter		
	E	M	L	E	M	L	E	M	L	E	M	L
plant	■	■	■									
harvest				■	■	■	■					

New potatoes or "earlies" are the first of the season. Uprooting your first forkful from the ground is always an exciting moment.

Where to grow

Potatoes grow best on a sunny, well-drained site in ground that has had some well-rotted compost or barnyard manure dug in during the winter. They prefer a slightly acid soil, with a pH of 5–6.

Crop rotation is important. Don't plant potatoes in the same place as last year, or in a spot where you've just grown onions or other root vegetables. If you can, grow them where you grew beans or peas last summer.

Sowing and planting

■ WHEN TO PLANT Start planting seed potatoes in March or April, once the soil has warmed up to at least 45°F (7°C).

■ PLANTING DEPTH In trenches or holes, at least 6 in (15 cm) deep.

■ PLANTING DISTANCE Earlies 12–14in (30–35 cm) apart; second earlies and maincrops 15 in (38 cm) apart.

■ ROW SPACING Earlies 18 in (45 cm) apart; second earlies and maincrops 30 in (75 cm) apart.

Tips on growing

Potatoes will be ready to harvest sooner if you encourage them to develop shoots or sprouts before you plant them. This is known as sprouting and is best done by spreading them out in empty egg boxes indoors, somewhere cool and light (see p.36).

WHICH POTATOES TO GROW

Early
- ■ 'Accent'
- ■ 'Concorde'
- ■ 'Epicure'
- ■ 'Foremost'
- ■ 'International Kidney'
- ■ 'Pentland Javelin'
- ■ 'Red Duke of York'
- ■ 'Swift'
- ■ 'Kestrel'
- ■ 'Picasso'
- ■ 'Ratte'
- ■ 'Roseval'
- ■ 'Wilja'

Second early
- ■ 'Belle de Fontenay'
- ■ 'Charlotte'
- ■ 'Estima'

Maincrop
- ■ 'Desiree'
- ■ 'King Edward'
- ■ 'Maris Piper'
- ■ 'Navan'
- ■ 'Nicola'
- ■ 'Pink Fir Apple'
- ■ 'Yukon Gold'

(above) **Salad potatoes** such as knobbly 'Pink Fir Apple' (left) and yellow 'Nicola' (center) have firm, waxy flesh and hold their shape when cooked. **Floury potatoes**, such as 'Red Duke of York' (right), 'Maris Piper', and 'Wilja', have a fluffy texture ideal for baking, roasting, and mashing.

HERITAGE POTATOES

Recent years have seen a rebirth of interest in traditional or "heirloom" potato varieties, some of which are only now being made available again. Often sold as "microplants" instead of seed potatoes, they range from those with red, purple, or black skins to 'Salad Blue' with its shockingly bright blue flesh.

(below, left to right) **'Salad Blue'** is an early maincrop potato that retains its color when steamed. **'Burgundy Red'** another striking maincrop, has a mild taste.

Once planted, keep potatoes well watered (especially earlies) and earth up or cover young plants with fleece at night to protect them from late frosts. Continue earthing up regularly to keep the tubers covered with soil. If they are exposed to light, they turn green and become inedible.

Harvesting

As a rule of thumb, earlies should be ready to lift 100–110 days after planting, second earlies within 110–120 days, and maincrops after 125–140 days—although the only way to be sure is to dig up a few and take a look. It's usually best to wait until the first flowers appear.

Choose a dry day and, if you're lifting maincrop potatoes for storage, leave them out in the sun for a few hours before bringing them in. The drier they are, the better they'll keep.

Troubleshooting

■ PESTS Colorado beetle, cutworm, potato cyst eelworm, slugs, wireworm.
■ DISEASES common scab, potato blackleg, potato blight, powdery scab.

Sweet potatoes

Sweet potatoes aren't actually potatoes at all. In fact, they're related to bindweed, the mortal enemy of every kitchen gardener. In spite of this, the potato-like tubers, with their sweet-tasting orange or white flesh, are utterly delicious baked, roasted, or mashed. Sweet potatoes can be raised from seed, but it's easier to grow them from rooted cuttings called "slips."

	spring			summer			autumn			winter		
	E	M	L	E	M	L	E	M	L	E	M	L
sow indoors	■	■										
transplant			■	■								
plant slips out			■	■								
harvest							■	■				

Lift sweet potatoes if the leaves are beginning to turn yellow, and be gentle when using a fork—they are easily split.

Where to grow
A spacious, warm, well-drained site with rich, fertile soil that has a pH of 5.5–6.5.

Sowing and planting
■ WHEN TO SOW Indoors in March and April. Transplant in May and June.
■ WHEN TO PLANT Plant slips in earthed-up ridges in May or June, when the soil has warmed.
■ PLANTING DEPTH 2–3 in (5–8 cm) deep.
■ PLANTING DISTANCE 10–12 in (25–30 cm) apart.
■ ROW SPACING 30 in (75 cm) apart.

Tips on growing
Sweet potatoes need deep, fertile soil and are best grown in earthed-up ridges. And they need lots of water, so sink cut-off plastic bottles into the soil to get water right down to their roots. Feed every two or three weeks with a general fertilizer.

Harvesting
Tubers should be ready in September, although they need a warm summer to produce a good crop. If you plan to store them, dry them out in the sun to "cure" them first. Finish lifting before the first frosts.

Troubleshooting
■ PESTS aphids, whitefly.
■ DISEASES general fungal diseases and viruses.

Beets

It's hard to think of a vegetable that's easier to grow—and one that is so underrated (except the turnip, perhaps). We're all familiar with the standard, large, purple globes, but baby beets picked when they're no larger than golf balls and roasted with oil and balsamic vinegar are something else. Then there are the orange, golden-yellow, white, and even pink-and-white striped varieties...

	spring			summer			autumn			winter		
	E	M	L	E	M	L	E	M	L	E	M	L
sow under cover	■	■	■									
sow outdoors			■	■	■							
harvest					■	■	■	■	■			

Where to grow

Any sunny position with reasonably good soil that has a neutral pH of 6.5–7.

Sowing and planting

■ WHEN TO SOW Outdoors from March onward if sown in prewarmed soil under cloches. Further sowings from May throughout the summer. Sow direct—beets do not like being transplanted.
■ SOWING DEPTH 1 in (2.5 cm) deep.
■ SOWING DISTANCE 4 in (10 cm) apart.
■ ROW SPACING 12 in (30 cm) apart.

Tips on growing

Germination is sometimes hit-or-miss, so it's worth soaking seeds in warm water for an hour or so to soften them and rinse off any germination inhibitor residue. Don't be tempted to sow too early if the ground is still cold.

Harvesting

Pull beets from here and there along the length of your rows in order to give those that remain room to grow—but don't let them get too large.

Troubleshooting

■ PESTS aphids, cutworm.
■ DISEASES damping off, fungal leaf spot.

(far left) **'Alto'**, like the better known 'Chioggia', features striking rings and has a mild, sweet flavor.
(left) **Golden beets** have attractively colored flesh.
(opposite) **'Red Ace'** is a sturdy variety with deep red flesh.

WHICH BEETS TO GROW

■ 'Boltardy'
■ 'Burpees Golden'
■ 'Chioggia'
■ 'Pronto'
■ 'Red Ace'

Rutabagas

Rutabagas are often unjustly maligned. They can be trickier to grow than you'd think from their tough, sturdy, workmanlike appearance. They are slow-growing and prone to all the diseases and pests that afflict the brassica family, to which they belong. Yet, when roasted along with other root vegetables, or mashed with butter and pepper as the Scottish "neeps" traditionally served with haggis on Burns night, they are wonderful.

	spring			summer			autumn			winter		
	E	M	L	E	M	L	E	M	L	E	M	L
sow outdoors			■	■								
harvest							■	■	■	■	■	

Where to grow
Rutabagas are even less fussy than turnips, but like to grow in soil that has had compost or manure dug well in before sowing. Add lime to raise the pH to around 7 if the soil is acid.

Sowing and planting
■ WHEN TO SOW In May in warm regions, in June elsewhere.
■ SOWING DEPTH ¾ in (2 cm) deep.
■ SOWING DISTANCE Thin to 9 in (23 cm) apart.
■ ROW SPACING 15 in (38 cm) apart.

Tips on growing
Rutabagas take as long as six months to mature so it's tempting to sow seeds early, but if the soil is still cold and wet mildew can be a problem. It's wiser to wait until the soil has warmed up.

Harvesting
The first rutabagas should be ready to lift sometime in September, although they can be left in the ground right through to early next year. In cold winters they may need a covering of straw to protect them. However, the roots tend to turn woody the older they get, so it may be better to lift and store them (see pp.190–91).

Troubleshooting
■ PESTS cabbage root fly, flea beetle, mealy cabbage aphid.
■ DISEASES clubroot, downy mildew, and powdery mildew.

New rutabaga varieties now available to growers are much sweeter than the old garden stalwarts.

WHICH RUTABAGAS TO GROW
■ 'Best of All'
■ 'Invitation'
■ 'Marian'
■ 'Ruby'

Radishes

The radish family is one of the great undiscovered secrets of the vegetable world. There are hundreds of different varieties. The small, bright-red salad radishes familiar to all of us represent only a fraction of them. Not only are there white, yellow, purple, and black versions of those, there are also huge white Oriental mooli (or daikon) and innumerable, turnip-sized winter radishes.

(above, left to right) **Fast-growing** summer radishes can be ready to pick in just over a month after sowing. **'Mantanghong'**, an Oriental winter radish, is delicious raw in salads or added to stir-fries.

Tips on growing
For a spring crop of summer radishes, sow seeds indoors and grow on under cover or transplant in April. Sow directly outdoors when warm enough, from April onward, and harvest through to November.

Sow winter radishes in summer for harvesting in autumn and winter.

Harvesting
Pick summer radishes before they grow too large and become woody and fiercely hot. Larger winter radishes can stay in the ground until midwinter although they may need protecting in hard frosts.

Troubleshooting
■ PESTS cabbage root fly, flea beetle, slugs and snails.
■ DISEASES clubroot.

	spring E	spring M	spring L	summer E	summer M	summer L	autumn E	autumn M	autumn L	winter E	winter M	winter L
Summer radishes												
sow indoors										■	■	
sow under cover	■											
sow outdoors		■	■	■	■	■	■					
plant out		■										
harvest				■	■	■	■	■	■	■		
Winter radishes												
sow outdoors					■	■						
harvest								■	■	■	■	■

Where to grow
Radishes are obliging and will grow nearly anywhere, although they dislike recently manured soil.

Sowing and planting
■ WHEN TO SOW Sow summer radishes indoors at the start of the year for a very early crop. Keep sowing outdoors until September. Sow winter radishes in July and August.
■ SOWING DEPTH ½ in (1 cm) deep.
■ SOWING DISTANCE Thin summer radishes to 1 in (2.5 cm) apart, winter radishes to 6 in (15 cm) apart.
■ ROW SPACING Summer radishes 6 in (15 cm) apart, winter radishes to 12 in (30 cm) apart.

WHICH RADISHES TO GROW

Summer
■ 'Cherry Belle'
■ 'French Breakfast'
■ 'Munchen Bier' (for edible pods)
■ 'Scarlet Globe'
■ 'Sparkler'

Winter
■ 'Black Spanish Round'
■ 'China Rose'
■ 'Mantanghong'

Mooli
■ 'April Cross'
■ 'Minowase Summer Cross'

Parsnips

Parsnip seeds are notoriously hit-or-miss to germinate, but once they have they are extremely easy to grow. Unless you're growing baby parsnips, they stay in the ground for up to nine months—although they need little beyond watering and weeding during that time. Pull them in the autumn after the first frosts and roast them with other roots.

WHICH PARSNIPS TO GROW
- 'Avonresister'
- 'Gladiator'
- 'Javelin'
- 'Tender and True'
- 'White Gem'

	spring			summer			autumn			winter		
	E	M	L	E	M	L	E	M	L	E	M	L
sow outdoors	■	■										
harvest	■							■	■	■	■	■

Parsnip leaves will die down when the roots are left to over-winter, so always mark the position of your crop with canes.

Where to grow
Parsnips like an open site and light soil with a slightly acid pH of 6.5. Make sure the ground is not compacted as the roots can grow deep.

Sowing and planting
- WHEN TO SOW In March or April as soon as the soil is workable.
- SOWING DEPTH ¾ in (2 cm) deep.
- SOWING DISTANCE 2–3 seeds together then thin to 4–6 in (10–14 cm) apart for medium roots, 12 in (20 cm) for large ones.
- ROW SPACING 12 in (30 cm) apart.

Tips on growing
Sow seeds directly into the ground. Parsnips dislike being transplanted, so it's not worth trying to start them in pots or modules. Weed carefully and water regularly when seedlings are still young.

Harvesting
Parsnips can be harvested in summer when they are still young and small, but they're traditionally left in the ground until autumn. Leaving them in the ground until after the first frosts is said to improve their flavor. Once lifted, they can be stored over the winter (see pp.190–91).

Troubleshooting
- PESTS carrot fly, celery leaf miner.
- DISEASES downy mildew, parsnip canker, powdery mildew, violet root rot.

Celeriac

Gnarled, knobbly, misshapen, and trailing a tangled mass of hairy roots: when it comes out of the ground, celeriac is unsettlingly ugly. But once you clean it up and peel it, the globe (which is actually a swollen stem, not a root) has a wonderful nutty, mild, celery-like taste whether it is roasted, mashed, or eaten raw in salads.

	spring			summer			autumn			winter		
	E	M	L	E	M	L	E	M	L	E	M	L
sow indoors	■	■										
plant out			■	■								
harvest	■						■	■	■	■	■	■

WHICH CELERIAC TO GROW
- ■ 'Brilliant'
- ■ 'Giant Prague'
- ■ 'Monarch'
- ■ 'Prinz'
- ■ 'Snow White'

Swelling crowns of celeriac topped with celery-like green leaves can be lifted throughout the winter, but mulch around the stems with straw if there is any danger of severe frosts.

Where to grow
Celeriac is pretty tolerant but grows best in soil that has had a generous amount of well-rotted manure or compost dug into it the previous autumn.

Sowing and planting
- ■ WHEN TO SOW Indoors in March or April at a temperature of at least 50°F (10°C).
- ■ WHEN TO PLANT Transplant in May or June.
- ■ PLANTING DISTANCE 12 in (30 cm) apart.
- ■ ROW SPACING 18 in (45 cm) apart.

Tips on growing
Celeriac is slow-growing, so start early by sowing seeds indoors, in a propagator if necessary. After planting out, seedlings need a lot of moisture if they are to swell up to a reasonable size, so it's important to water regularly—as often as twice a week in dry weather.

Harvesting
Celeriac can be harvested from September onward. Use a fork to lift the whole plant, and then cut off the leaves and roots. Celeriac can be stored over the winter (see pp.190–91).

Troubleshooting
- ■ PESTS celery leaf miner, slugs.

Celery

Celery is not an easy crop to grow. It needs a lot of water and it needs it regularly, without interruption. Moreover, the stems are tender only when blanched —that is, kept out of the light. Old-fashioned trench celery is planted in trenches and then earthed up or wrapped in collars to keep it white. Modern self-blanching or green celery is grown in closely sown blocks rather than rows, and may still need collars.

WHICH CELERY TO GROW

Self-blanching
- 'Green Utah'
- 'Lathom Self Blanching'
- 'Pink Champagne'
- 'Tango'
- 'Victoria'

Trench
- 'Giant Red'
- 'Pascal'

	spring			summer			autumn			winter		
	E	M	L	E	M	L	E	M	L	E	M	L
Self-blanching/Green celery												
sow indoors	■	■										
plant out				■	■							
harvest						■	■	■	■			
Trench celery												
sow indoors	■	■										
transplant				■	■							
harvest										■	■	

(left to right) **For tender white** celery, wrap collars round the stems to deprive them of light. **Trench** varieties need to have earth mounded up around the stems as they grow.

Where to grow

Celery needs rich, fertile, moisture-retentive soil with a slightly acid pH of around 6.7.

Sowing and planting

■ WHEN TO SOW Indoors in March or April at a temperature of at least 59°F (15°C).
■ WHEN TO PLANT Transplant in May or June.
■ PLANTING DISTANCE Self-blanching 10 in (25 cm) apart in blocks, trench 12–18 in (30–45 cm) apart.
■ ROW SPACING Trench 12 in (30 cm) apart.

Tips on growing

After planting out, seedlings need regular watering to prevent them from becoming stringy. Mulching helps conserve moisture. As it grows, earth up trench celery to keep the stems out of the light, and construct lightproof collars for self-blanching celery, especially those plants around the outside edges of the blocks (see p.89).

Harvesting

Pick self-blanching celery from midsummer onward, giving it a good watering first to keep it crisp and fresh. Trench celery is harvested much later—provided you've protected it from frosts.

Troubleshooting

■ PESTS carrot fly, celery leaf miner, slugs.
■ DISEASES fungal leaf spots, foot and root rots, violet root rot.

Florence fennel

Strictly speaking, the large white bulbs of Florence (or sweet) fennel are not really bulbs at all. They are swollen, overlapping leaf stems. So, as a vegetable, fennel is closer to celery than it is to the onion family. It has a unique aniseed taste and can be eaten either raw in salads or cooked.

WHICH FLORENCE FENNEL TO GROW
- 'Finale'
- 'Romanesco'
- 'Rudy'
- 'Zefa Fino'

	spring			summer			autumn			winter		
	E	M	L	E	M	L	E	M	L	E	M	L
sow indoors	■	■										
sow outdoors			■	■	■							
plant out			■	■								
harvest				■	■	■	■	■				

Where to grow
Fennel likes a well-drained site with rich, fertile, slightly sandy soil with a neutral pH.

Sowing and planting
- WHEN TO SOW Indoors in March or April at a minimum of 59°F (15°C) or outdoors, but only when temperatures are as high. Transplant in May or June.
- SOWING DEPTH 1 in (2.5 cm) deep.
- SOWING/PLANTING DISTANCE 12in (30 cm) apart.
- ROW SPACING 12 in (30 cm) apart.

Tips on growing
Seeds need warmth to germinate and so may be hit-or-miss. Sow three or four together and thin out if necessary. Water regularly, mulch to retain moisture, and earth up around the stems to blanch and stabilize them as they grow.

Harvesting
Cut the bulbs just above soil level when they are nicely rounded, before they elongate and bolt.

Troubleshooting
Fennel is particularly prone to bolting if it is allowed to dry out or get too cold.
- DISEASES rhizoctonia is a fungus that stunts the plants and produces yellow, red, or dark green–black lesions on the bulbs and leaf stems. There is no treatment, so crops must be destroyed.

Cut fennel bulbs when they are well rounded and about the size of an apple.

Carrots

As a general rule, early carrots are those sown in spring, and maincrop varieties are sown from about May onward. If you sow some of each, in batches, you should be able to harvest carrots from June until the end of the year. There are plenty to chose from: Amsterdam types are small, narrow, and cylindrical; Nantes are slightly broader and longer; Chantenay are short and conical; and Autumn King are the longest of all. There are yellow and purple varieties too.

	spring			summer			autumn			winter		
	E	M	L	E	M	L	E	M	L	E	M	L
sow under cover	■											
sow outdoors		■	■	■	■	■						
harvest				■	■	■	■	■	■	■	■	

Where to grow

Carrots like an open, dry site and light, fertile soil with a pH of 6.5–7.5. Dig in some manure or compost and make sure the ground is free of stones and not compacted—otherwise the roots tend to fork. For this reason, raised beds are ideal.

Sowing and planting

- WHEN TO SOW Start indoors or under cover in March and succession sow right through into summer.
- SOWING DEPTH ½–¾ in (1–2 cm) deep.
- SOWING DISTANCE 1 in (2.5 cm) steadily thinning to 4 in (10 cm) apart.
- ROW SPACING 12 in (30 cm) apart.

WHICH CARROTS TO GROW

Early
- 'Adelaide'
- 'Amsterdam Forcing'
- 'Flyaway'
- 'Nairobi'
- 'Nantes'
- 'Parmex'
- 'Sytan'

Maincrop
- 'Autumn King'
- 'Bangor'
- 'Chantenay Red Core'
- 'Sugarsnax'

Tips on growing

In the early stages, seedlings are easily overrun by weeds. Weeding needs to be done by hand, at close quarters. The same goes for thinning—nipping off the leaves of unwanted, weaker seedlings and carefully removing them without releasing the scent that attracts carrot flies (see p.85).

Harvesting

Early varieties may be ready within just seven weeks of sowing. Maincrops may take 10–11 weeks. If the soil is dry or compacted, use a fork to loosen the roots before pulling them out.

Troubleshooting

- PESTS aphids, carrot fly.
- DISEASES downy mildew, powdery mildew, violet root rot.

(far left) **Heritage varieties** come in a range of colors from yellow to scarlet and deep purple.
(left) **Chantenay hybrids** are crunchy and sweet.
(opposite) **Quick-growing Nantes varieties** are smooth-skinned and store well.

Turnips

Like rutabagas, turnips are in fact brassicas, relatives of the cabbage family. Yet they're grown in exactly the same way as other root vegetables. Admittedly, they don't have a wonderful reputation as a gourmet food, but if harvested when they are still young and small, then steamed, roasted, or eaten raw in salads, they have a deliciously sweet and nutty flavor.

WHICH TURNIPS TO GROW
- 'Atlantic'
- 'Blanc de Croissy'
- 'Golden Ball'
- 'Ivory'
- 'Market Express'
- 'Oasis'
- 'Tokyo Cross'
- 'White Globe'

	spring			summer			autumn			winter		
	E	M	L	E	M	L	E	M	L	E	M	L
sow under cover	■	■										■
sow outdoors			■	■	■	■	■					
harvest			■	■	■	■	■	■	■	■		

Where to grow
Turnips are not fussy but grow well in soil high in nitrogen and with a neutral pH of 6.5–7.

Sowing and planting
- WHEN TO SOW Early varieties can be sown in multiblock modules outdoors in a cold frame from late February. Direct sow once the soil is warm enough to work, in batches from April through to August.
- SOWING DEPTH ¾ in (2 cm) deep.
- SOWING DISTANCE Thin to 2–4 in (5–10 cm) apart.
- ROW SPACING 9–12 in (23–30 cm) apart.

Tips on growing
Try multisowing in module trays, four seeds to each cell. Transplant each cell as a cluster and leave the turnips to grow closely without thinning them out.

Harvesting
Turnips grow quickly. Pick early varieties as soon as 5–6 weeks after sowing, when they are no more than 1½–2 in (4–5 cm) in diameter. Pick the leaves or "turnip tops," too; cook and eat them like spring greens. Later in the year, maincrop varieties can be left to grow larger and can be stored in winter.

Troubleshooting
- PESTS cabbage root fly, cutworm, flea beetle, mealy cabbage aphid, wireworm.
- DISEASES clubroot, downy and powdery mildew.

(below) **Pick early purple-skinned turnips** when golf-ball sized. **White turnips** (right) usually crop very early.

Unusual root vegetables

There are plenty of unusual root vegetables to try growing if you are feeling mildly adventurous. Scorzonera and salsify are both long, tapering roots with an attractive, subtle flavor. Hamburg parsley, as its name suggests, is a member of the parsley family but one grown for its roots rather than its leaves. And horseradish is the hot, pungent ingredient that gives horseradish sauce its special, sinus-clearing quality.

1 Salsify

Sow seeds outdoors in April or May in light, well-drained soil—the roots must be able to grow through it easily. Salsify won't grow well in compacted or waterlogged ground. Harvest in the autumn if the roots are thick enough. If not, leave them in the ground over winter and lift them the following spring. When cooked, they have a mild, oysterlike flavor.

2 Scorzonera

Sometimes called black salsify, scorzonera can be grown from seed sown in spring, in the same way as salsify. It grows slowly, however, and can be left in the ground until the autumn after next— a full eighteen months. Like salsify, it's a vegetable that's perhaps harder to prepare for cooking than it is to grow. Its long, skinny roots are hard to peel, so it's best to skin them after they've been boiled.

3 Hamburg parsley

These roots look like parsnips, taste like parsnips, and are grown like parsnips. Sow seeds direct outdoors in March or April as soon as the soil is workable. Weed and water in summer, then harvest at any time from September through to the following spring.

4 Horseradish

It's hard to grow horseradish from seed. Instead, propagate it by dividing an existing plant, or by taking or buying a root cutting called a "thong." Plant it in spring and in the first year dig up the roots for harvesting in the autumn. Once established, harvest as and when you need it.

Cabbages, leaves, and other brassicas

Most of the vegetables in this group belong to the family known as brassicas.
They include cabbages, cauliflowers, broccoli, brussels sprouts, and kale.
There's also an odd-man-out: kohlrabi, although it is also a brassica, is grown
not for its leaves but for its round, fat stem. All brassicas have certain features
in common: they are slow growing, they are large and therefore take up a lot
of space, and unfortunately most are prone to the same pests and diseases—
clubroot, cabbage root fly, caterpillars, and birds.

Brassicas like cool growing conditions
and all are prone to bolting if the
weather is hot and dry. Water your
crops regularly to keep the soil moist.

(above left to right) **Young kohlrabi,
Calabrese 'Romanesco', Cabbage
'Red Jewel'**

(far left) **Curly winter kale**
(left) **Summer cauliflower**

Cabbages

Generally, cabbages are categorized according to when they are harvested. Spring and summer cabbages tend to be small, are round or pointed, and are eaten right after picking, sometimes even before the leaves have formed heads. Autumn and winter cabbages are larger, have dense, solid heads, and can be stored. Savoy cabbages are the ones with deeply veined, sometimes bubble-textured leaves.

	spring			summer			autumn			winter		
	E	M	L	E	M	L	E	M	L	E	M	L
Spring cabbages												
sow					■	■						
plant out							■	■				
harvest	■	■	■									
Summer, autumn, and red cabbages												
sow	■	■	■									
plant out			■	■								
harvest						■	■	■	■			
Winter cabbages												
sow		■	■									
plant out				■	■							
harvest	■									■	■	■

Red cabbages grown from seed can be transplanted into their final positions in early summer once they have been hardened off.

Where to grow
Cabbages will grow happily in most fertile soils. Dig in compost or manure the previous autumn, add lime in the winter if the pH of the soil is below 6.8, and firm it down well. Don't plant cabbages where you've grown brassicas within the last three years.

Sowing and planting
■ WHEN TO SOW Sow in pots or modules, or in a special seedbed, for later transplanting. Start under cover in March for summer, autumn, and red cabbages. Sow in April and May for winter cabbages, and in July and August for spring cabbages the following year.
■ SOWING DEPTH ¾ in (2 cm) deep.
■ PLANTING DISTANCE 12–18 in (30–45 cm).
■ ROW SPACING 16–24 in (40–60 cm) apart.

Tips on growing
When you plant out cabbage seedlings, fit them with brassica collars to combat cabbage root fly, and net them to keep off birds and cabbage white butterflies. Sadly, both birds and butterflies are so persistent that it's quite likely your crops may need to spend their whole lives under nets. As the cabbages grow and become increasingly heavy, earth up their stems to give them some additional support.

HARVESTING CABBAGES

Spring or early-summer cabbages can be harvested while immature or left until heads have developed.

1 Pick spring greens while the leaves are still young and the plants have no central heart.

2 From late summer onward, harvest cabbages with well-formed heads by cutting right through the tough stem with a sharp knife.

(below, left to right) **Summer red cabbages**, such as this early, dense-headed variety, add vibrant color to your plot and have delicious peppery-tasting leaves. **Savoy cabbages** are very tough plants and can be left in the ground, however cold the weather.

Harvesting

Pick spring cabbages when the leaves are still loose and have not yet formed heads—they are then known as "spring greens." Wait for others to heart up into firm, dense heads. Either cut through the stems with a sharp knife or dig up the whole root.

Troubleshooting

■ PESTS birds, cabbage moth, cabbage root fly, cabbage white butterfly, cutworm, flea beetle, leatherjackets, mealy cabbage aphid, slugs and snails, whitefly.
■ DISEASES clubroot, downy mildew, powdery mildew, white blister.

WHICH CABBAGES TO GROW

Spring
■ 'Duncan'
■ 'Myatt's Offenham'
■ 'Pixie'
■ 'Spring Hero'
■ 'Wheeler's Imperial'

Summer/Autumn
■ 'Derby Day'
■ 'Hispi'
■ 'Minicole'

■ 'Stonehead'

Winter
■ 'Celtic'
■ 'January King'
■ 'Protovoy'

Red
■ 'Red Drumhead'
■ 'Red Jewel'
■ 'Savoy King'
■ 'Tundra'

Brussels sprouts

Brussels sprouts excite strong opinions. They are generally either loved or loathed. There's no middle ground. To their detractors, they are bitter and foul-tasting. To their evangelists, they have a wonderful, unique, nutty flavor. Even if you remain unconvinced, please try them just once more—but this time homegrown, picked when young and small, and cooked lightly while still fresh and tender.

WHICH BRUSSELS SPROUTS TO GROW

- 'Cascade'
- 'Darkmar'
- 'Maximus'
- 'Red Delicious'
- 'Revenge'
- 'Rubine'
- 'Trafalgar'

	spring			summer			autumn			winter		
	E	M	L	E	M	L	E	M	L	E	M	L
sow indoors	■											■
sow outdoors		■	■									
plant out				■	■	■						
harvest	■						■	■	■	■	■	■

Where to grow

Grow in soil with a pH of at least 6.8, enriched with compost or manure the previous autumn, and firmed down well. Don't plant sprouts where you've grown them within the last three years.

Sowing and planting

- WHEN TO SOW For early autumn crops, sow indoors in February or March and plant out in May. For winter crops, sow in April and May and transplant before the end of July.
- SOWING DEPTH ¾ in (2 cm) deep.
- PLANTING DISTANCE 24 in (60 cm) apart.
- ROW SPACING 24 in (60 cm) apart.

Tips on growing

Give seedlings plenty of space and plant them deeply—they'll have a lot of weight to support when fully grown. Fit brassica collars to deter cabbage root fly, and net them to keep off birds and butterflies. Feed in summer with a nitrogenous fertilizer or organic liquid feed.

Harvesting

Begin picking sprouts from the bottom, where they

(left to right) **Deep red sprouts** retain their wonderful color, especially if you steam them. **Regular green varieties** are sweet-tasting and reliable and store well.

mature first, and gradually work your way up to the top. Alternatively, dig up the whole plant and stand it in water for a few days or hang it up somewhere cool for a couple of weeks.

Troubleshooting

- PESTS birds, cabbage moth, cabbage root fly, cabbage white butterfly, cutworm, flea beetle, leatherjackets, mealy cabbage aphid, slugs and snails, whitefly.
- DISEASES clubroot, downy mildew, powdery mildew, white blister.

Cauliflower

Choose the right variety, sow and plant it at the right time, and there's no reason why you shouldn't have your own homegrown cauliflowers almost all year round. They're not the easiest vegetables to grow, requiring very regular watering, but modern cultivars are less demanding—and the new lime-green, purple, and orange-colored heads are fun.

(above) **Tight heads**, known as "curds," are made up of florets—unopened flower buds.
(right) **Purple-headed varieties** need less protection from the sun than regular white ones.

	spring			summer			autumn			winter		
	E	M	L	E	M	L	E	M	L	E	M	L
Early summer cauliflowers												
sow indoors											■	
sow under cover								■				
plant out	■											
harvest				■								
Summer/autumn cauliflowers												
sow indoors	■	■										
sow under cover	■	■	■									
plant out				■	■	■						
harvest							■	■	■	■		
Winter/spring cauliflowers												
sow		■										
plant out					■							
harvest	■	■	■							■	■	■

Where to grow
Grow in firm ground, in fertile soil with a pH of at least 6.8. Don't plant cauliflowers where you've grown them within the last three years.

Sowing and planting
■ WHEN TO SOW Sow early summer varieties in October and keep in a cold frame all winter, or sow indoors in January, then plant out in March. Sow summer/autumn varieties indoors or outdoors in April or May. Sow winter/spring varieties in May, transplant in August, and overwinter.
■ SOWING DEPTH ¾ in (2 cm) deep.
■ PLANTING DISTANCE 24 in (60 cm) apart.
■ ROW SPACING 24–28 in (60–70 cm) apart.

Tips on growing
Give plants plenty of space, fit brassica collars around seedlings, and cover with nets to keep off birds and butterflies. Water regularly to avoid any check to their growth and to prevent bolting.

Harvesting
Pick your moment: cut the heads when the curds are fully grown but still firm and tight, before the florets start to go to seed.

Troubleshooting
■ PESTS birds, cabbage moth, cabbage root fly, cabbage white butterfly, cutworm, flea beetle, leatherjackets, mealy cabbage aphid, slugs and snails, whitefly.
■ DISEASES clubroot, downy mildew, powdery mildew, whiptail (molybdenum deficiency).

WHICH CAULIFLOWERS TO GROW

Early summer
■ 'Candid Charm'
■ 'Mayflower'
■ 'Graffiti'
■ 'Gypsy'
■ 'Snowball'

Summer/autumn
■ 'All The Year Round'
■ 'Autumn Giant'
■ 'Clapton'

Winter/spring
■ 'Galleon'
■ 'Maystar'
■ 'Medallion'

Broccoli

The term broccoli encompasses two slightly different vegetables: calabrese, which forms large, green, cauliflower-like heads, and sprouting broccoli, which grows as a mass of smaller, separate florets on long stems. Originally, calabrese was a summer crop, while sprouting broccoli was reserved for the autumn and winter months, but modern cultivars can supply an almost year-round harvest.

	spring			summer			autumn			winter		
	E	M	L	E	M	L	E	M	L	E	M	L
Calabrese												
sow outdoors	■	■	■	■	■							
harvest				■	■	■	■	■				
Sprouting broccoli												
sow indoors	■	■	■									■
sow outdoors	■	■	■	■	■							
transplant under cover	■	■										
plant out			■	■	■	■						
harvest	■	■		■	■	■	■	■	■		■	■

WHICH BROCCOLI TO GROW

Calabrese
- ■ 'Belstar'
- ■ 'Chevalier'
- ■ 'Romanesco'
- ■ 'Trixie'

Sprouting broccoli
- ■ 'Bordeaux'
- ■ 'Claret'

- ■ 'Rudolph'
- ■ 'Early Purple Sprouting '
- ■ 'Late Purple Sprouting '
- ■ 'Early White Sprouting'
- ■ 'White Star'

Early white-sprouting broccoli is among the first of the spring varieties to mature and tastes just as good as the purple form.

Where to grow
Broccoli should grow well on a sheltered site in most fertile soils. Dig in compost or manure the previous autumn, add lime in the winter if the pH of the soil is below 6.8, and firm it down well. Don't plant broccoli where you've grown any other brassicas within the last three years.

Sowing and planting
■ WHEN TO SOW Sow calabrese directly outdoors from March to July. Start off sprouting broccoli in February, in trays or modules indoors to begin with, then outdoors from March onward, under cover if necessary.
■ SOWING DEPTH ¾ in (2 cm) deep.
■ SOWING/PLANTING DISTANCE Calabrese 12 in (30 cm), sprouting broccoli 24 in (60 cm) apart.
■ ROW SPACING Calabrese 18 in (45 cm), sprouting broccoli 24 in (60 cm) apart.

Tips on growing

Calabrese doesn't like being transplanted so sow it where it's going to grow. Sprouting broccoli is more amenable and can be raised in pots and modules or in special seedbeds before it is transplanted to its final growing position. Early summer varieties can be raised from seed indoors and planted out in spring, under cover until the frosts are over. Succession-sow in batches from March through to July for a crop that lasts most of the year—the hardy, late varieties will survive most winters.

Harvesting

Cut the main central head of calabrese before it grows too large and the flower buds have a chance to open. Side shoots should give you a second harvest a little later.

Harvest sprouting broccoli regularly, cutting off the flowering shoots before they open. The more you pick, the more will grow.

Troubleshooting

■ PESTS birds, cabbage moth, cabbage root fly, cabbage white butterfly, cutworm, flea beetle, leatherjackets, mealy cabbage aphid, slugs and snails, whitefly.
■ DISEASES clubroot, downy mildew, powdery mildew.

Harvest calabrese while still dense and firm and no larger than about 4 in (10 cm) across. Cool summers produce the best heads.

(right, top to bottom) **Acid green 'Romanesco' calabrese** is particularly nutritious. **Purple-sprouting broccoli** spears are good in stir-fries. **Calabrese head** in top condition.

Swiss chard and spinach beet

Although they're grown for their leaves not their roots, both these vegetables are related to the beet family—which explains why collectively they're often called "leaf beets." Individual names can add even more confusion. Swiss chard is also known as seakale beet or silver beet. And spinach beet is sometimes called perpetual spinach.

	spring			summer			autumn			winter		
	E	M	L	E	M	L	E	M	L	E	M	L
sow outdoors		■	■	■	■	■						
harvest	■	■	■	■	■	■	■	■	■			

(top to bottom) **Young spinach**, multicolored **Swiss chard**, vibrant **Ruby chard**.

Where to grow
Leaf beets like rich, moisture-retentive soil. Dig in compost or manure the previous autumn or add a general fertilizer. Lime the soil if the pH is lower than 6.5.

Sowing and planting
■ WHEN TO SOW April to June for harvesting until November; then July and August for crops the following spring.
■ SOWING DEPTH 1 in (2.5 cm) deep.
■ SOWING DISTANCE 4 in (10 cm) apart for salads, or 12 in (30 cm) apart for full-grown crops.
■ ROW SPACING 18 in (45 cm) apart.

Tips on growing
Sow seeds directly into the ground, and weed and water regularly. Plants that are overwintering for harvesting next spring may need cloches in harsh winters.

Harvesting
Pick young leaves as a cut-and-come-again crop for salads. Cut fully grown leaves as and when you need them and cook and eat them like spinach. Thick chard stems can be cooked separately.

Troubleshooting
Problems are very rare.

WHICH LEAF BEETS TO GROW
■ 'Bright Lights'
■ 'Lucullus'
■ 'Rainbow Chard'
■ 'Rhubarb Chard'

(left) **Eye-catching yellow-stemmed chard** is sure to liven up any kitchen garden.

Must-try Oriental brassicas

Seeds for Oriental leaves are increasingly available in regular garden centers. If not, they can be obtained from specialist nurseries by mail order. They are not difficult to grow—provided that you don't plant them too soon, when the soil is still cold, and that you water them regularly to keep them from bolting. Used for salads, for steaming, and for stir-fries, they are well worth a try.

(left) **Bok choy**, or pak choi, grows quickly and you will be able to harvest young leaves within a month of sowing. Leave plants to heart up for thick-ribbed leaves.

1 Chinese cabbage
Also known as Chinese leaves, these are tall, cylindrical heads of densely packed leaves. Sow from May onward, and harvest from July until the first frosts. Later sowings are less likely to bolt.

2 Bok choy
Sow in summer to reduce the risk of bolting. Water well, and start picking young leaves within as little as a month. Steam or stir-fry larger leaves.

3 Choy sum
A generic name for Chinese flowering greens or flowering cabbage, these plants are in fact flowering forms of bok choy. Sow only when temperatures reach a reliable 68°F (20°C).

Pick flowering stems before the buds open and cook and eat like broccoli.

4 Chinese broccoli
Like choy sum, Chinese broccoli or Chinese kale is grown for its flowering stems, which taste similar to purple sprouting broccoli. Sow in summer, harvest in autumn, and steam or stir-fry.

5 Tatsoi
A close relative of bok choy, tatsoi has spoon-shaped leaves that splay out in the shape of a rosette. Grow and eat in the same way as bok choy.

6 Oriental saladini
Special selections of brassica seeds are often sold in mixed packets as "Oriental saladini." These selections usually include mustard greens as well as other leaves such as bok choy, mizuna, komatsuna, and nonheading Chinese cabbage.

7 'Red Giant' mustard
'Red Giant' is one of the larger—and most attractive—of the Oriental mustard greens. Its young leaves add a peppery tang to salads; older leaves are better cooked.

8 Komatsuna
Confusingly, komatsuna is sometimes referred to as either mustard spinach or spinach mustard. Its upright dark-green or red leaves taste midway between spinach and cabbage. Grow for cut-and-come-again salads or as leaves for steaming and stir-frying well into the winter.

9 Mizuna
Mizuna leaves look somewhat like a deeply serrated form of rocket and have an equally peppery, mustardy taste. Grow it in summer for salads and in winter (under cover if necessary) for stir-fries. It may need protecting from flea beetles.

10 Mibuna
Although closely related to mizuna and with a similar taste, mibuna's leaves are smooth-edged, not serrated. It too can be grown under cover to provide fresh greens throughout the winter.

Kohlrabi

There's no getting away from the fact that the kohlrabi is one of the weirdest-looking vegetables of them all. Yet its bulbous, swollen stems from which sprout large cabbagelike leaves are oddly beautiful—and, at least to its fans, the green, white, or purple globes are surprisingly tasty.

	spring			summer			autumn			winter		
	E	M	L	E	M	L	E	M	L	E	M	L
sow indoors	■											■
sow outdoors		■	■	■	■	■						
plant out		■	■									
harvest					■	■	■	■	■	■	■	

Where to grow

Grow in nonacid soil with a pH of about 7, enriched with compost or manure the previous autumn, and firmed down well. Don't plant kohlrabi where you've grown brassicas within the last three years.

Sowing and planting

- WHEN TO SOW For early crops, sow indoors in February or March and plant out in April or May. As the soil warms up, sow direct outdoors.
- SOWING DEPTH ¾ in (2 cm) deep.
- SOWING/PLANTING DISTANCE 9 in (23 cm).
- ROW SPACING 12 in (30 cm) apart.

Tips on growing

Kohlrabi is fast growing, so sow in batches throughout the spring and summer to give a continuous crop. Plants are prone to bolting if they are sown too early—when the soil is still cold—and need regular watering to prevent them from becoming woody.

Harvesting

Slice the bulbs off at the root when they are still small—ideally, somewhere between a golf ball and a tennis ball. Modern varieties can be left in the ground until the end of the year but may need cloches if it's a cold winter.

Troubleshooting

- PESTS birds, cabbage root fly, flea beetle, slugs and snails.
- DISEASES clubroot.

(far left) **Sitting above soil level**, this perfect kohlrabi is just ready for picking.

(left) **Leave the central shoots** on the plant when you harvest to prolong freshness.

WHICH KOHLRABI TO GROW

- 'Azur Star'
- 'Kolibri'
- 'Logo'
- 'Purple Delicacy'
- 'Superschmelz'
- 'White Danube'

Spinach

In theory, spinach is the ideal crop for cold, wet, northern latitudes. It likes cool weather, it loves rain, and it will even tolerate partial shade. If that sounds like your kind of climate, you should try it. Just be prepared to water at least once a day in summer if the weather suddenly turns hot and dry because spinach will bolt given the slightest chance.

	spring			summer			autumn			winter		
	E	M	L	E	M	L	E	M	L	E	M	L
sow indoors										■	■	
sow outdoors	■	■	■		■	■						
plant out	■											
harvest			■	■	■	■	■	■	■			

Where to grow
Spinach will grow almost anywhere, even in partial shade in summer. But it does need a fertile soil into which lots of compost or manure has been dug or a nitrogenous fertilizer added.

Sowing and planting
■ WHEN TO SOW Summer spinach: sow indoors in January and February, for planting out in March; outdoors from March to May. Autumn and winter spinach: sow in late August and September.
■ SOWING DEPTH ¾ in (2 cm) deep.
■ SOWING DISTANCE Thin to about 3–6 in (7–15 cm) apart.
■ ROW SPACING 12 in (30 cm) apart.

Tips on growing
Especially in the early days, weed carefully and thoroughly. Water generously and regularly.

WHICH SPINACH TO GROW
■ 'Bloomsdale'
■ 'Giant Winter'
■ 'Medania'
■ 'Reddy'

■ New Zealand spinach is a different species but is grown in the same way.

(above, left to right) **True spinach** is at its best when the leaves are young and succulent. **New Zealand spinach** is a versatile crop that, unlike regular spinach, will tolerate heat as well as dry conditions.

Spinach has a notorious thirst, and will bolt the moment you let it dry out.

Harvesting
Begin picking outer leaves about eight weeks after sowing—earlier if you want young leaves for salads. Treat the plants as a cut-and-come-again crop or harvest the whole plant at one time, cutting it just above ground level.

Troubleshooting
■ PESTS aphids, birds, slugs and snails.
■ DISEASES downy mildew.

Kale

Kale has a reputation for indestructibility. It is able to survive both the sub-zero temperatures of very cold winters and, in the case of some varieties, hot summers too. It's not even particularly demanding when it comes to watering. As a member of the brassica family, however, it is prone to clubroot and may need netting to keep off birds and butterflies.

	spring			summer			autumn			winter		
	E	M	L	E	M	L	E	M	L	E	M	L
sow indoors		■	■	■								
sow outdoors					■	■	■					
plant out						■	■	■				
harvest	■	■							■	■	■	■

Where to grow

Kale is not fussy, although it likes a firm, well-drained soil and plenty of room to spread.

Sowing and planting

■ WHEN TO SOW Indoors from April, outdoors from May, then plant out from June onward.
■ SOWING DEPTH ¾ in (2 cm) deep.
■ PLANTING DISTANCE Thin to 18–24 in (45–60 cm) apart.
■ ROW SPACING 18 in (45 cm) apart.

Tips on growing

Seeds can be raised in pots or modules, or sown in a special, out-of-the-way seedbed, then transplanted when space on your plot becomes available—perhaps after you've harvested your first early potatoes or broad beans.

Harvesting

Pick young leaves in summer for salads when they are only about 4 in (10 cm) long, and leave full-grown leaves for harvesting throughout the winter.

Troubleshooting

■ PESTS birds, cabbage moth, cabbage root fly, cabbage white butterfly, mealy cabbage aphid, slugs and snails, whitefly.
■ DISEASES clubroot, downy mildew.

WHICH KALE TO GROW

■ 'Cavolo Nero' ('Black Tuscan')
■ 'Dwarf Green Curled'
■ 'Pentland Brig'
■ 'Redbor'
■ 'Red Russian'

(top to bottom)
Curly kale leaves, both purple and green, are packed with Vitamin C.
'Cavolo Nero' has crinkled strap-shaped leaves.

The onion family

Onions, shallots, garlic, and leeks are all alliums. Although they may be grown for their flowers in the garden, they are valued for their edible bulbs or stems. Leeks and green onions are raised from seed. Bulb onions and shallots can be grown either from seed or from small, young bulbs called "sets." Although sets are more expensive to buy, they are easier to grow because they're less fussy about soil conditions, and less prone to certain diseases. They may, however, bolt and start to produce flowers more readily. Garlic is very rarely grown from seed; instead, it is raised by planting individual cloves.

The alliums are kitchen garden staples, and easy to please in fertile, well-drained soil. To ensure healthy, disease-free crops each year, add members of the onion family to your rotation plan and keep them moving around the plot, perhaps following crops of brassicas, such as cabbages, cauliflowers, or broccoli.

(above, left to right) **Onion, Green onion, Garlic** (far left) **Leek** (left) **Shallot**

Onions

Onions can be raised from seed—it's certainly not hard—but they're more often grown from "sets," commercially produced baby onions guaranteed free from viruses. Onions are slow-growing and need several months in the ground before they're ready to harvest, so either sow or plant them early in the year or choose special Japanese or overwintering varieties that you can sow the previous year.

	spring			summer			autumn			winter		
	E	M	L	E	M	L	E	M	L	E	M	L
sow indoors										■	■	
sow outdoors	■	■			■							
transplant	■	■										
plant sets outdoors	■	■					■	■				
harvest					■	■	■	■				

(above) **Multisown onions** are grown in clumps to make maximum use of space. (opposite) **Red onions** often have a mild, sweet flavor and can therefore be used raw in salads.

Where to grow
An open site with well-drained, fertile soil. Add lime if the pH is lower than about 6.5. Don't plant onions where you've grown other members of the onion family in the previous two years.

Sowing and planting
■ WHEN TO SOW For maincrop onions, sow seed outdoors, transplant seedlings raised indoors, or plant sets in March and April. For earlier crops, sow special varieties in August or plant sets in September and October the previous year.
■ SOWING DEPTH ¾ in (2 cm) deep.
■ SOWING/PLANTING DISTANCE 2–4 in (5–10 cm) apart.
■ ROW SPACING 12 in (30 cm) apart.

Tips on growing
Weed regularly but don't overwater. Onions are prone to rot if too wet. Cut off flower buds as soon as they appear.

Harvesting
When the leaves turn yellow and collapse, loosen the roots, lift the bulbs gently, lay them on their sides, and leave them to dry in the sun. If it's wet bring them under cover and spread them out, preferably on racks.

Troubleshooting
■ PESTS onion fly, onion thrips.
■ DISEASES downy mildew, onion neck rot, onion white rot.

WHICH ONIONS TO GROW
Maincrop onions
■ 'Golden Bear'
■ 'Red Baron'
■ 'Setton'
■ 'Sturon'

Overwintering onions
■ 'Keepwell'
■ 'Radar'
■ 'Senshyu'

Shallots

Shallots look like small onions but have a slightly milder, more subtle taste. Unlike onions, they grow in handful-sized clumps instead of as stand-alone bulbs. They can be raised from seed, but it's easier to grow them from sets, which are more reliable and may be planted outdoors earlier in the year than seeds can be sown.

(left) **Lay shallots** out to dry in the sun after lifting them, if the weather is dry.
(right) **'Longor'** bulbs are long and pointed, with a superb flavor.

	spring			summer			autumn			winter		
	E	M	L	E	M	L	E	M	L	E	M	L
plant outdoors	■											■
harvest					■	■						

WHICH SHALLOTS TO GROW

- 'Delvad'
- 'Golden Gourmet'
- 'Jermor'
- 'Longor'
- 'Mikor'
- 'Picasso'
- 'Pikant'
- 'Red Sun'

Where to grow
An open site with well-drained, fertile soil. Add lime if the pH is lower than about 6.5. Don't plant shallots where you've grown them in the previous two years.

Sowing and planting
- WHEN TO PLANT Plant sets in February or March.
- PLANTING DEPTH 1 in (2.5 cm) deep.
- PLANTING DISTANCE 6–8 in (15–20 cm) apart.
- ROW SPACING 12 in (30 cm) apart.

Tips on growing
Birds may pull up some of your newly planted sets. If they do, simply replant them. Weed regularly but water only if the soil becomes very dry.

Harvesting
When the leaves turn yellow and start to fall, loosen the roots, lift the clumps of shallots gently, and leave them to dry in the sun. If it's wet bring them under cover. Discard any that show signs of rot or damage.

Troubleshooting
- PESTS birds, onion fly, onion thrips.
- DISEASES downy mildew, onion neck rot, onion white rot.

Garlic

Garlic couldn't be easier to grow. Split a bulb or head into separate cloves, plant them out in the ground just below the surface, and within a few months each one will have produced a complete new bulb. Don't be tempted, though, to use supermarket garlic. Invest in special, commercially grown varieties that are guaranteed to be free from viruses or other diseases.

	spring			summer			autumn			winter		
	E	M	L	E	M	L	E	M	L	E	M	L
plant cloves outdoors	■								■	■	■	■
harvest				■	■	■	■					

Where to grow

An open, sunny site with light, well-drained soil. Add lime if the pH is lower than about 6.5. Avoid planting garlic where you've grown any other members of the onion family in the previous two years.

Sowing and planting

■ WHEN TO PLANT It's best to plant cloves in October or November for harvesting the following summer, but you can plant at any time through the winter as long as the ground is not completely frozen.
■ PLANTING DEPTH 1 in (2.5 cm) deep (or more in light soils).
■ PLANTING DISTANCE 7 in (18 cm) apart.
■ ROW SPACING 12 in (30 cm) apart.

Tips on growing

Garlic will happily survive the harshest of winters, so plant in autumn if possible—you should get larger bulbs than if you plant in the new year.

Harvesting

Autumn-planted garlic will be ready before crops planted in spring. When the leaves turn yellow, lift the bulbs and leave them to dry in the sun. In wet weather bring them under cover.

Troubleshooting

■ PESTS onion fly, onion thrips.
■ DISEASES downy mildew, onion neck rot, onion white rot, rust.

Garlic stores well, but dry the bulbs out first to prevent rotting.

WHICH GARLIC TO GROW

■ 'Lautrec Wight'
■ 'Purple Wight'
■ 'Solent Wight'
■ 'Sultop'

Leeks

Although leeks are members of the onion family, they grow long, thick stems or "shanks" instead of fat, rounded bulbs. The shanks are earthed up to exclude light and keep them white. Leeks are a valuable crop in that they are an uncanny fit with onions: the first leeks are ready to harvest in autumn just as the onions are finishing, and they last through to the following year until the new season's onions are ready for lifting.

WHICH LEEKS TO GROW

- 'Apollo'
- 'Giant Winter'
- 'Hannibal'
- 'Jolant'
- 'Musselburgh'
- 'Toledo'

	spring			summer			autumn			winter		
	E	M	L	E	M	L	E	M	L	E	M	L
sow indoors											■	■
sow outdoors	■	■										
plant out			■	■	■							
harvest	■	■					■	■	■	■	■	■

Leeks keep better in the ground, so harvest as and when you're ready to use them. Use a fork to lift them gently and try to avoid trapping soil between the leaves.

Where to grow

Leeks need a deep, well-drained soil enriched with well-rotted compost or manure. Don't plant them where you've grown onions, shallots, or garlic in the previous two years.

Sowing and planting

- WHEN TO SOW Sow indoors in modules during January and February, and outdoors in a seedbed in March and April. Transplant from May to July.
- SOWING DEPTH 1 in (2.5 cm) deep.
- PLANTING DEPTH 6 in (15 cm) deep.
- PLANTING DISTANCE 6–8 in (15–20 cm) apart.
- ROW SPACING 12–15 in (30–38 cm) apart.

Tips on growing

Leeks raised from seed are not generally planted out until the middle of the year, perhaps when space becomes available for them. The process is sometimes called "dibbing in" (see p.108). As they grow, they need earthing up to keep out the light.

Harvesting

Leave leeks in the ground until you need them, then lift them carefully with a fork. Trim, wash, and use right away because they don't store well.

Troubleshooting

- PESTS cutworms, leek moth, onion fly, onion thrips.
- DISEASES downy mildew, leek rust, onion neck rot, onion white rot.

Green onions

Green onions are easy to grow and very versatile. Nine times out of ten, of course, they're picked when slim and young, and eaten as salad onions (or "spring onions" as they are called in Britain), but if you leave them in the ground they'll keep on growing and eventually turn into delicious bulb onions that can be used either raw or for cooking.

	spring			summer			autumn			winter		
	E	M	L	E	M	L	E	M	L	E	M	L
sow outdoors	■	■	■	■	■	■	■	■				
harvest	■	■	■	■	■	■	■					

Where to grow
An open, sunny site with light, well-drained soil. Add lime if the pH is lower than about 6.5.

Sowing and planting
■ WHEN TO SOW Start sowing direct into the ground from March onward. Sow further batches through to early autumn. Seeds sown in August and September will overwinter for a crop the following spring.
■ SOWING DEPTH ½–¾ in (1–2 cm) deep.

■ SOWING DISTANCE ½ in (1 cm) apart.
■ ROW SPACING 12 in (30 cm) apart.

Tips on growing
Weed and water regularly. If necessary, cover overwintering green onions with cloches.

Harvesting
Begin picking onions when they are about 6 in (15 cm) high. Harvest them as if you were thinning them out, leaving the rest to grow on a little longer.

Troubleshooting
■ PESTS cutworms, onion fly, onion thrips.
■ DISEASES downy mildew, onion neck rot, onion white rot.

WHICH GREEN ONIONS TO GROW
■ 'Crimson Forest'
■ 'Eiffel'
■ 'North Holland Blood Red'
■ 'White Lisbon'
■ 'White Lisbon Winter Hardy'

Add color as well as flavor to salads by growing red and white varieties of green onion.

Unusual onions

If the onion-growing bug has bitten you, here are a few less well-known varieties that you might find both interesting and fun to try. You may have to search them out, but most can be found online or in mail-order catalogs for nurseries.

1 Welsh onions

These grow up to 18 in (45 cm) tall and look rather like giant green onions, although they grow in clumps rather than singly. They don't form bulbs at their base and are grown for their green, hollow stems, which may be cooked or eaten raw.

Sow seeds in spring for harvesting in the autumn. The plant is a perennial, so if it survives the winter it should continue cropping for at least two or three more years.

2 Japanese bunching onions

Like Welsh onions, from which they are derived, these also grow in clumps instead of individually. Some varieties are small, like green onions; others grow much larger, like leeks.

Japanese bunching onions are also perennials, but not reliably so. It's safer to sow new seeds each year. Sow outdoors from March to September—or earlier and later, if you protect seedlings and overwintering plants with covers or cloches.

3 Egyptian or tree onions

Somewhat surreally, the bulbs of these onions grow not at ground level but up in midair, at the top of tall stems where they form clusters in place of flowers. Perhaps because they can grow to knee or even waist height, they have been described as "lazy man's onions." As they become increasingly top-heavy, the stems bend over and the bulbs may take root, to produce new plants for the next year.

Plant new bulbs singly in spring or autumn, and harvest in summer. The onion bulbs can be dried and stored.

Peas, beans, and other legumes

"Legume" is the name of the plant family that includes peas, French beans, runner beans, broad beans, and a wide variety of others. In fact, lentils, peanuts, and lupins are part of the same family, too. Peas and beans are grown for their seeds and seedpods. They have always been popular crops for kitchen gardens not just because they're easy to grow but also because—if freshly picked and eaten before their natural sugars turn to starch—they taste so much better than their store-bought or frozen equivalents.

The legume family members are not only delicious, but their attractive flowers and pods will really brighten up your garden. Flowers come in a range of colors from white to bright crimson, and some French bean pods are multicolored with a distinctive, marbled appearance.

(above left to right)) **Climbing French bean, runner bean, snow pea**

(far left) **Broad beans in flower**
(left) **Sugar snap peas**

Peas

Just-picked, freshly shelled peas taste wonderful, either raw or cooked. But the moment you pick them the clock starts ticking because their natural sugars begin turning to starch and they lose their sweetness. So, harvest them at the last minute and try to get them to your plate as fast as you can. Snow peas and sugar (or snap) peas can be eaten just as they are, pods and all, raw or cooked.

	spring			summer			autumn			winter		
	E	M	L	E	M	L	E	M	L	E	M	L
sow indoors									■		■	■
sow under cover								■				■
sow outdoors	■	■	■	■	■							
plant out	■	■	■									
harvest				■	■	■	■	■				

Support young pea plants as soon as tendrils appear. Either use a row of canes and netting or peasticks.

Where to grow
Peas dislike extremes: they like sunshine but not intense heat; they need water but won't do well if they get waterlogged; and they do best in a rich soil that is neutral to slightly alkaline, with a pH of 6.5–7.

Sowing and planting
■ WHEN TO SOW For early crops, sow indoors in winter and plant out in spring. Start sowing direct outside only when the temperature reaches about 50°F (10°C), and then sow successively through to midsummer.
■ SOWING DEPTH 1½–2 in (4–5 cm) deep.
■ PLANTING DISTANCE 2 in (5 cm) apart in single or double rows.
■ ROW SPACING Same distance apart as the eventual height of the plants.

WHICH PEAS TO GROW

Peas
- ■ 'Cavalier'
- ■ 'Feltham First'
- ■ 'Hurst Green Shaft'
- ■ 'Kelvedon Wonder'
- ■ 'Purple Podded'
- ■ 'Waverex'

Snowpeas/ Mangetout
- ■ 'Oregon Sugar Pod'

Sugar/Snap peas
- ■ 'Sugar Ann'
- ■ 'Sugar Snap'

Tips on growing
Two things are essential. The first is some kind of support system up which the peas can climb in order to get off the ground and away from slugs—traditional hazel or birch peasticks are ideal. The second is netting to keep off birds. Otherwise, weed regularly and water as soon as the plants flower.

Harvesting
The first peas should be ready in June. Start picking at the base of the plant and work your way up. Pick regularly, pick when young, and remove any pods that have grown too old. To stimulate the development of more pods, pinch out the growing shoot at top of each plant as soon as the first pods are ready—and add the shoots to salads.

Troubleshooting
■ PESTS aphids, birds, mice, pea moths, pea thrips.
■ DISEASES downy mildew, pea leaf and pod spot, powdery mildew.

Runner beans

Growing runner beans could not be easier. The trickiest thing is probably constructing the wigwam or row of canes up which they'll climb. As soon as the soil is warm enough and there's no longer a danger of frost, plant a seed or two at the foot of each cane—they'll take it from there on their own. Watch out for insect pests, weed and water regularly, and stand by for harvest.

	spring			summer			autumn			winter		
	E	M	L	E	M	L	E	M	L	E	M	L
sow indoors		■	■									
sow under cover			■									
sow outdoors			■	■								
plant out				■								
harvest					■	■	■	■				

Where to grow

Runner beans are pretty tolerant, although they do best in a sunny, sheltered position where they are not buffeted by the wind. Because they grow so large and crop so heavily, they are hungry plants and appreciate a deep, fertile soil that has had lots of well-rotted compost or manure dug into it.

Sowing and planting

■ WHEN TO SOW Direct outside once the last frosts are over and the soil has warmed up to about 54°F (12°C). In cold areas or for an early crop, sow indoors or under cover in April and May, and plant out in June.
■ SOWING DEPTH 2 in (5 cm) deep.
■ PLANTING DISTANCE 9–12 in (23–30 cm) apart.
■ ROW SPACING 2ft (60 cm) apart.

Tips on growing

Runner beans are natural climbers and need strong supports to hold their weight. Traditionally, wigwams or double rows of strong bamboo canes are used. Sow or plant on the insides of the slanting canes, and if necessary tie in the growing seedlings with string until they coil around by themselves. Pinch out the growing tips when they reach the top. Water regularly as soon as flowers appear, and mulch around the base of the plants to help prevent roots from drying out.

Harvesting

At the height of the season, from about July onward, runner beans are unstoppable. Pick them every two or three days to catch them while they're still young and before they become too large, stringy, and tough. As long as there are still flowers, the more you pick, the more you'll get.

Troubleshooting

■ PESTS black bean aphids, slugs and snails.
■ DISEASES foot and root rots, halo blight.

(above) **Climbing frames** for runner beans must be sturdy enough to support fully laden plants.
(opposite) **Keep picking** and don't plant too many beans in the first place to avoid a glut.

WHICH RUNNER BEANS TO GROW

■ 'Enorma'   ■ 'Polestar'
■ 'Lady Di'   ■ 'Red Rum'
■ 'Painted Lady' ■ 'White Lady'

French beans

Also known as snap, string, Kenya, kidney, haricot, borlotti, and flageolet beans, French beans form a varied and extended family. Their pods may be green, yellow, gold, purple, red, or a multicolored mix, and the beans themselves come in just as many colors, too. Some pods are eaten whole; "flageolets" or "cannellini" are picked when half-ripe then shelled and eaten like peas; and "haricot" and "kidney" beans are generally left to dry so they can be stored. Generally, French beans are either climbers or dwarf bush plants.

	spring			summer			autumn			winter		
	E	M	L	E	M	L	E	M	L	E	M	L
sow indoors		■	■									
sow under cover			■									
sow outdoors			■	■	■							
plant out				■								
harvest					■	■	■	■	■			

Where to grow

French beans like warmth and sun and dislike wind and cold. A sudden frost, either at the beginning or the end of the year, will kill them. They grow best in a fertile soil with plenty of well-rotted compost or manure dug into it, and one that is neutral to mildly acid, with a pH of 5.5–7.

Sowing and planting

■ WHEN TO SOW To get started early, sow indoors or under cover in April and May and plant out in June. Sow direct outside only when the last frosts are over and the temperature reaches about 54°F (12°C).

■ SOWING DEPTH 2 in (5 cm) deep.

■ PLANTING DISTANCE Dwarf beans 4 in (10 cm) apart in single rows and 6–9 in (15–22 cm) apart in staggered double rows; climbers 12 in (30 cm) apart.

■ ROW SPACING 18 in (45 cm) apart.

Purple-podded climbing French beans
crop just as abundantly as the regular green varieties. Sadly, they tend to lose their purple color when they are cooked.

WHICH FRENCH BEANS TO GROW

Climbers
- 'Blue Lake'
- 'Borlotto Lingua di Fuoco'
- 'Cobra'
- 'Purple Podded Climbing'

Dwarf
- 'Goldfield'
- 'Masterpiece'
- 'Purple Queen'
- 'Rocquencourt'
- 'Sonesta'
- 'Speedy'
- 'The Prince'

Tips on growing

Climbing beans will need a row of canes or a wigwam to support them. Pinch out the growing tips when they reach the top. Dwarf beans can also become heavy and may need earthing up or supporting with twigs, peasticks, or short canes. Make sure you water regularly as soon as flowers appear and mulch around plants to retain moisture.

Harvesting

Your first beans should be ready to pick two or three months after sowing, which usually means July. Harvest them every few days when the beans are young, slender, and at their tastiest, and before they become overgrown and stringy. You'll continue to get more beans, however many you pick, as long as the plants still have flowers.

Troubleshooting

- PESTS black bean aphids, slugs and snails.
- DISEASES foot and root rots, halo blight.

French beans are at their tastiest when young so don't let the pods grow too large or the skin will become tough and stringy.

Broad beans

Fresh-picked, homegrown broad beans have a flavor that beats store-bought or frozen beans hands down. And if you grow them yourself you'll not only get a much bigger crop than you could afford to buy at the supermarket but you'll be able to pick them when they're young, tender, and at their absolute tastiest.

	spring			summer			autumn			winter		
	E	M	L	E	M	L	E	M	L	E	M	L
sow indoors											■	■
sow under cover								■	■		■	■
sow outdoors	■	■						■	■			■
plant out	■	■										
harvest					■	■	■					

Where to grow
Broad beans like fertile, well-drained soil, especially if some well-rotted compost or manure has been dug in before planting, but they're not fussy.

Sowing and planting
■ WHEN TO SOW Sow outside in the autumn, overwintering the plants for a crop early the following summer, or sow in the new year, between February and April, for harvesting slightly later in the summer. If your ground is frozen in January and February, sow indoors in pots and plant out in March and April.
■ SOWING DEPTH 2 in (5 cm) deep.
■ PLANTING DISTANCE 9 in (23 cm) apart.
■ ROW SPACING 18 in (45 cm) apart for single rows; 24 in (60 cm) for staggered double rows.

Tips on growing
Broad beans need regular watering when they are in flower. As soon as the first tiny pods appear, pinch out the top growing shoot, which should give you a heavier crop. As the pods develop, the plants can become top heavy and may need further support.

Harvesting
Pick when young while the beans are still small and tender; they are at their peak when the membranes that attach them to the insides of their pods are still green or white.

Troubleshooting
■ PESTS birds, black bean aphids, mice, pea and bean weevils.
■ DISEASES chocolate spot, foot and root rots.

Freshly harvested beans are tender and packed full of vitamins. They also freeze well.

WHICH BROAD BEANS TO GROW
■ 'Aquadulce Claudia'
■ 'Imperial Green Longpod'
■ 'Stereo'
■ 'Superaquadulce'
■ 'The Sutton'
■ 'Witkiem Manita'

Unusual beans

Here's a challenge. These beans originate mostly from tropical and subtropical regions such as the southern United States, Africa, or southeast Asia. They won't be easy to grow in temperate kitchen gardens, but don't dismiss them. If you start them off indoors, in a greenhouse, or in a polytunnel, and if you're lucky enough to get a long, hot summer, you may be successful.

Soybeans

Soybeans usually require a hot climate with summer temperatures consistently between 68°F and 86°F (20–30°C), but modern varieties such as 'Ustie' have been bred to withstand cooler, temperate conditions. Grow soybeans in the same way as you would French beans. Fresh pods can be boiled or steamed and the beans eaten as a snack (known as "edamame" in Japan) or they can be dried.

Lima beans

These large green or white beans are also known as butter beans. Grow the bush varieties in the same way as dwarf French beans and the climbers like runner beans. Seeds need a temperature of at least 64°F (18°C) to germinate, and the plants need a warm, sheltered position in full sun.

Yardlong beans

Also known as asparagus beans or Chinese long beans, these long, slender, green beans can be eaten boiled, steamed, or stir-fried. However, even in their native southeast Asia, they're unlikely to reach a full yard—or a meter—in length. In temperate climates, where they're best grown in a large polytunnel, half that length would be a triumph.

Soybeans are a staple food in many parts of the world, owing to their high protein content. Grow your own and you can choose to eat them fresh or dried.

Salads

These days a mixed leaf salad can contain pretty much anything—often the more unusual or exotic the leaves the better. But this doesn't mean that there's no longer a place for the humble lettuce—in all its many different forms—or for traditional leaves such as bitter endive and chicory, or hardy winter corn salad and land cress. It's more that if you're willing to experiment, and if you're happy to harvest otherwise familiar vegetables when their leaves are still young and small, you can make a salad using everything from kale and kohlrabi to broccoli, mustard greens, and even edible flowers.

Leafy salad crops are happy in most soils, but in hot, dry weather they do have a tendency to bolt and must be watered regularly. Many of the salads can be harvested from an early age as cut-and-come-again crops, providing tasty leaves throughout the growing season.

(above, left to right) **Kale** and **mizuna, lettuce, Greek cress** (far left) **Red chicory** (left) **Summer purslane**

Arugula

Also known as rocket, rucola, and sometimes even roquette, this leaf vegetable comes in two forms: salad arugula and wild arugula. Both are pleasantly peppery-tasting salad leaves. Salad arugula has larger leaves and a milder flavor. Wild arugula has narrow leaves and is hardier. It is also less prone to bolting in summer and lasts longer into the autumn and winter.

	spring			summer			autumn			winter		
	E	M	L	E	M	L	E	M	L	E	M	L
sow under cover	■	■					■					
sow outdoors			■	■	■	■						
harvest		■	■	■	■	■	■	■	■			

Where to grow
Arugula will grow in most fertile, moisture-retentive soils, but it doesn't like hot sun, and will appreciate any partial shade in summer.

Sowing and planting
■ WHEN TO SOW Sow direct outdoors as soon as the soil is warm enough, under cover if necessary. Sow further small batches throughout spring and summer.
■ SOWING DEPTH ½ in (1 cm) deep.
■ SOWING DISTANCE Thin to 6 in (15 cm) apart.
■ ROW SPACING 6 in (15 cm) apart.

Tips on growing
Water regularly to discourage arugula from bolting.

Harvesting
Harvest as a cut-and-come-again crop, or slice off the whole plant and wait for new shoots to sprout from the stump.

Troubleshooting
■ PESTS flea beetle, slugs and snails.

Both varieties of arugula are worthy of a place in the kitchen garden—and your salad bowl. Their distinctive flavor gives a peppery kick to mixed salads. (above right) **Salad arugula** (right) **Wild arugula**

Lettuce

There is a multitude of different types of lettuces with very different qualities: butterheads are soft and round; cos and semi-cos (sometimes called romaine) are upright and usually crisper; crispheads or icebergs have round, dense, crunchy heads; and loose-leaf lettuces are the open kind that don't form hearts at all.

	spring			summer			autumn			winter		
	E	M	L	E	M	L	E	M	L	E	M	L
sow indoors	■											■
sow under cover	■	■			■							
sow outdoors		■	■	■	■	■	■					
plant out		■	■									
harvest	■	■	■	■	■	■	■	■	■			

Where to grow

Lettuces will grow happily in most fertile, moisture-retentive soils, but avoid planting them where you have grown lettuces within the last three years.

Sowing and planting

■ WHEN TO SOW For early crops, sow in pots or modules indoors from February, outdoors under cover from March, or (if you are able to overwinter plants under cloches or in a cold frame) the previous September. Otherwise, sow directly in the ground from April or May onward, a few seeds at a time.
■ SOWING DEPTH ½ in (1 cm) deep.
■ SOWING/PLANTING DISTANCE small–medium 6–10 in (15–25 cm) apart; large 14 in (35 cm) apart.
■ ROW SPACING small–medium 9–12 in (23–30 cm) apart; large 15 in (38 cm) apart.

Tips on growing

Lettuce seeds can be difficult to germinate. If it's too cold or too warm, they simply won't, so don't sow seeds outdoors too early in the year and, if you're sowing in summer, wait till late afternoon or evening when the temperature has dropped. Water lettuces regularly to discourage them from bolting.

Harvesting

Harvest loose-leaf lettuces whole or as a cut-and-come-again crop. Pick butterheads, cos, and crisphead lettuces when they have hearted up but before they get a chance to bolt (in hot, dry weather) or to rot (if it is wet).

Troubleshooting

■ PESTS aphids (blackfly and greenfly), cutworm, leatherjackets, lettuce root aphids, slugs and snails, wireworms.

1 'Lollo Rossa' a loose-leaf with frilled leaves. 2 'Mottistone' a green-and-red mottled butterhead. 3 'Nymans' a beautiful purple-red cos. 4 Cos lettuce mix grown as cut-and-come again leaves. 5 'Sioux' a crisp, red-tinged iceberg. 6 'Winter Density' a semihardy cos that will overwinter.

WHICH LETTUCES TO GROW

Butterhead
■ 'All The Year Round'
■ 'Clarion'
■ 'Marvel of Four Seasons'
■ 'Mottistone'
■ 'Sangria'
■ 'Tom Thumb' (mini)

Cos
■ 'Freckles'
■ 'Little Gem' (mini)
■ 'Lobjoits Green Cos'
■ 'Nymans'
■ 'Pinokkio'

Crisphead
■ 'Black Seeded Simpson'
■ 'Iceberg'
■ 'Saladin'
■ 'Set'
■ 'Sioux'
■ 'Webb's Wonderful'

Loose-leaf
■ 'Cocarde'
■ 'Fristina'
■ 'Lollo Rossa'
■ 'Red Salad Bowl'
Overwintering
■ 'Arctic King'
■ 'Winter Density'

Corn salad

Also known as lamb's lettuce or mache, corn salad is a truly year-round crop and, if protected with cloches or grown in a cold frame, will provide you with fresh salad leaves right through the winter. There are two varieties: a large-leaved, floppy, light-green one, and an upright, dark-green one. Both have a mild, lettucelike flavor.

	spring			summer			autumn			winter		
	E	M	L	E	M	L	E	M	L	E	M	L
sow under cover		■	■				■					
sow outdoors				■	■	■						
harvest	■	■	■	■	■	■	■	■	■	■	■	■

Where to grow
Corn salad will grow in almost any soil, both in full sun and in partial shade.

Sowing and planting
■ WHEN TO SOW Sow from about April onward, under cover if necessary. Sow further small batches throughout spring and summer.
■ SOWING DEPTH ½ in (1 cm) deep.
■ SOWING DISTANCE Thin to 4 in (10 cm) apart.
■ ROW SPACING 6 in (15 cm) apart.

Tips on growing
Weed when seedlings are still small, and thin out if needed. Water regularly.

Harvesting
Pick leaves regularly as a cut-and-come-again crop, or slice off the whole plant and wait for new growth to sprout.

Troubleshooting
■ PESTS aphids, slugs and snails.
■ DISEASES powdery mildew.

Corn salad and other leafy crops grow quickly, so thin out the rows to reduce the number of plants competing for light and water. You can add the baby leaves from the thinnings to salads.

Endive

Endive is a form of leaf chicory and in Britain the frilly, curly-leaved kind that we call "chicory" is actually known as "frisée." There is also a type of endive with broader, flatter leaves called "escarole" or "Batavian." Both types are bitter by nature and are commonly blanched to mellow their flavor.

	spring			summer			autumn			winter		
	E	M	L	E	M	L	E	M	L	E	M	L
sow indoors		■	■									
sow outdoors				■	■							
plant out				■	■							
harvest	■						■	■	■	■	■	■

Where to grow
Endive will grow in most fertile, moisture-retentive soils. It is happy in full sun but will also tolerate partial shade in summer.

Sowing and planting
■ WHEN TO SOW Don't sow too early—wait until about April indoors, and June outside.
■ SOWING DEPTH ½ in (1 cm) deep.
■ SOWING/PLANTING DISTANCE 10–15 in (25–38 cm) apart.
■ ROW SPACING 10–15 in (25–38 cm).

Tips on growing
Weed and water regularly. Blanch curly-leaved plants by covering them with upturned plates to exclude the light and whiten the leaves. Blanch broad-leaved endives by bunching up the leaves and tying them with string.

Harvesting
Cut a few leaves at a time, or slice off the whole plant and wait for new leaves to sprout. Cover with frames or cloches in the autumn and winter.

Broad-leaved endives tend to be hardier than their showy curly relatives, so they are a good bet for an early winter harvest. (above, top) **'Jeti'** (above) **'Pancalieri'**

Troubleshooting
■ PESTS aphids, caterpillars, lettuce root aphids, slugs and snails.
■ DISEASES rot (if wet when blanched).

WHICH ENDIVE TO GROW
Curly endive
■ 'Frisée Glory'
■ 'Moss Curled'
■ 'Pancalieri'

Broad-leaved endive
■ 'Batavian Full Heart'
■ 'Jeti'

Chicory

Of the three types of chicory, Belgian or Witloof has the characteristic fat, cigar-shaped shoots or "chicons" that most people associate with the vegetable. Radicchio or red chicory has dense, tightly curled heads like small red iceburg lettuces, while sugarloaf chicory has larger leaves with looser heads. All three are bitter, but Belgian chicory is the only one that is normally blanched.

	spring			summer			autumn			winter		
	E	M	L	E	M	L	E	M	L	E	M	L
Witloof/Belgian chicory												
sow outdoors		■	■									
lift roots							■	■	■			
harvest forced	■										■	■
Sugarloaf chicory and radicchio												
sow indoors		■	■									
sow outdoors				■	■	■						
plant out				■								
harvest						■	■	■	■			

(opposite) **Radicchio 'Treviso Precoce Mesola'**
(below left) **Radicchio 'Palla Rossa Bella'**
(below right) **Witloof chicory**

Where to grow
Chicory will grow in almost any soil, and is happy in full sun or partial shade.

Sowing and planting
■ WHEN TO SOW Sow directly in May or June.
■ SOWING DEPTH ½ in (1 cm) deep.
■ SOWING DISTANCE Thin to 9–12 in (23–30 cm) apart.
■ ROW SPACING 12 in (30 cm) apart.

Tips on growing
Weed and water regularly to prevent bolting. To force Belgian chicory, lift the roots, trim them, replant them in a pot, and cover with a light-proof lid to blanch the new shoots (see p.183).

Harvesting
Red and sugarloaf chicories can be cut from July onward. They are fairly hardy and may even survive the first autumn frosts into late October.

Troubleshooting
■ PESTS aphids, lettuce root aphids, slugs and snails.

WHICH CHICORY TO GROW

Belgian chicory
■ 'Brussels Witloof'
■ 'Zoom'

Red chicory/radicchio
■ 'Rossa di Treviso'
■ 'Palla Rossa'

Sugarloaf chicory
■ 'Pan di Zucchero'
■ 'Sugar Loaf'

Must-try unusual salad leaves

Baby-leaf salads have been in vogue for some while. Now, in a move toward even further miniaturization, "microgreens" are the fashion. In truth, almost any vegetable can be grown and eaten as a salad if the leaves are picked while young, before they develop too strong a flavor. Beet, radishes, kohlrabi, broccoli, chard, and Oriental leaves may all be harvested as baby leaves. Here are a few others to try.

1 Land cress
Also known as American or upland cress, this is a larger, coarser, hardier version of watercress that doesn't need to be grown in water. It will last right into midwinter.

2 Summer purslane
Sow outdoors between March and July, and harvest its thick, fleshy stalks and crunchy, lobelike leaves from about May to September.

3 Winter purslane
Also known as miner's lettuce or claytonia, winter purslane is sown in August for harvesting in autumn and early winter. Start cutting the leaves once they are about the size of your fingernails. The more you harvest, the more it grows.

4 Oriental mustards
For salads, pick leaves young when they are tender and mild-tasting. If left to grow, they become coarse and the flavor is too strong to eat without cooking (see p.227).

5 Chop suey greens
A variety of chrysanthemum grown for its aromatic young foliage. Sow in spring in trays or directly outdoors, and harvest as a cut-and-come-again salad before it flowers.

6 Kale
Baby kale looks wonderfully decorative in salads and has a mild, cabbagelike flavor (see p.230). Try any of the readily available varieties: broad-leaved or curly, and green, red, or even the striking 'Cavolo Nero'.

7 Texsel greens
A fast-growing brassica specially developed from Ethiopian mustard. Sow from spring through to autumn, and harvest after about 6–7 weeks before plants bolt, especially in midsummer.

8 Mustard 'Red Frills'
Dark-red, deeply cut leaves with a mild mustardy taste that should be ready for picking within just a month after sowing.

9 Perilla
Also known by its Japanese name shiso, perilla is an herb that has both green- and purple-leaved forms. Baby leaves can be used in salads before the flavor becomes too strong.

10 Mizuna and mibuna
Just two of the many Oriental brassicas that can be picked for baby leaf salads (see p.227). Both are extremely fast-growing. Mizuna (shown here) has feathery, indented leaves, rather like wild arugula, and a mild mustardy taste. Mibuna has larger, more rounded leaves without any serrations and a slightly stronger taste.

11

11 Red-veined sorrel
This variety has thicker, darker green leaves than the standard sorrel and pronounced red veining. It has a similar lemony flavor.

12 Sorrel
All sorrels have a sharp lemony taste. They grow happily in shade but will bolt when allowed to dry out. If they do, cut them right down and they should reshoot.

13 Chicory
Sometimes called Italian dandelion, the leaves of upright 'Italiko Rosso' (shown here) are narrow and slightly jagged with a pronounced, bright red, central rib. They taste tangy and slightly bitter—a little like dandelion leaves.

14 Greek cress
Small, flat, parsleylike leaves with the distinctive peppery taste of cress. Grow in trays or raised beds, keeping it under cover if necessary at the start or the end of the year.

15 Red orache
Also known as mountain spinach, orache can be sown direct from spring through to autumn and picked regularly while leaves are small. Once they grow too large for salads, cook and eat them like spinach.

16 Par-cel
An herb that makes an interesting and unusual salad ingredient. Its small, finely cut leaves look like parsley but taste like celery.

"Microgreens are the latest fashion: leaves so young they are practically embryonic."

Summer fruiting vegetables

Tomatoes, eggplant, peppers, chilies, and corn are grown for their fruits rather than their leaves, stems, or roots. They're all native to hot climates and need heat for their seeds to germinate, a regular supply of water for healthy growth, and warmth and sunshine for the fruit to ripen. In temperate regions, it's no surprise that they are often grown under cover in a greenhouse or polytunnel. However, don't rule them out for a kitchen garden. Your garden center will be able to tell you which varieties grow best in your climate. No matter where you live, you'll be able to find varieties that will give you a bountiful harvest.

Most fruiting vegetables grown from seed require heat to germinate successfully. If space indoors for sowing is limited, opt for ready-grown plants, available in late spring from nurseries and garden centers.

(above left to right) **Plum tomatoes, eggplant, habanero chilies**

(far left) **Green chilies**
(left) **Corn cobs**

Tomatoes

Not all tomatoes can be grown in a kitchen garden—at least, not unless you have a polytunnel or a greenhouse. Many of them won't germinate, let alone ripen, unless they're raised and grown in a warm place. That said, there are plenty of outdoor varieties: large, small, plum, cherry, beefsteak, red, orange, yellow, black, and even striped. There are those that grow upright in vine or cordon forms, others that grow as spreading or trailing bushes, and some types are somewhere in between the two.

	spring			summer			autumn			winter		
	E	M	L	E	M	L	E	M	L	E	M	L
sow indoors	■	■										■
plant out			■	■								
harvest					■	■	■	■				

Where to grow
Tomatoes need full sun and rich, fertile soil that has either had compost or manure dug into it or had a general high-phosphorous fertilizer or pellets of poultry manure added to it. Add lime only if it is very acid—that is, with a pH of 5.5 or lower.

Sowing and planting
■ WHEN TO SOW Tomatoes need heat to germinate, so sow indoors in modules and pots between February and April and plant out only when it is warm enough in May and June.
■ SOWING DEPTH ¾ in (2 cm) deep.
■ PLANTING DISTANCE Vine 15–18 in (38–45 cm) apart, bush 12–36 in (30–90 cm) apart.
■ ROW SPACING 36 in (90 cm) apart.

Tips on growing
Outdoor tomato seedlings should be ready for hardening off and planting out when the first flowers form. Where there's a risk of late frosts, don't put them out too early unless you are able to cover them at night.

More than almost any other crop, tomatoes need regular feeding and watering. Begin feeding with a special liquid tomato fertilizer as soon as you see the first fruits, and never let plants dry out.

Bush tomatoes are available in dwarf varieties if space on your plot is tight. Sweet and tasty, they crop abundantly by midsummer.

Vine tomatoes need to be supported with canes, and their side shoots pinched out (see p.127). Once four or five trusses have formed, remove the growing tip from the top of the main stem.

Harvesting
If you can, leave tomatoes in place until they are ripe (see p.158). Toward the end of the season, when frosts become a danger, bring any remaining green tomatoes indoors and ripen them inside.

Troubleshooting
■ PESTS outdoors: leafhoppers, potato cyst eelworm; under cover: aphids, red spider mite, whitefly.
■ DISEASES blossom end rot, foot and root rots, leafmolds, tomato blight, tomato ghost spot.

Must-try tomato varieties

There is such a wide variety of tomatoes available that it's tempting to go wild and grow as many as you can. But before you do, check carefully what sort you are buying: vine, bush, or indeterminate; greenhouse or outdoor; cherry, plum, round, or beefsteak. And, although some of the more unusual cultivars are tempting, not all of them will ripen outdoors in cool climates.

1 Vine tomatoes
Cordon or vine tomatoes grow on trusses from a single upright stem. Sometimes called "indeterminate," they need to be supported as the fruits swell and ripen. Traditionally a greenhouse plant, there are now numerous varieties that will grow well outdoors
■ TRY 'Ailsa Craig', 'Alicante', 'Fantasio' (shown here), 'Outdoor Girl'.

2 Plum tomatoes
With their distinctive oval or elongated shape, plum tomatoes were once the classic, midsized Italian cooking tomato. These days they are much more varied. They are available in either vine or bush forms and can be grown indoors or out.
■ TRY 'Olivade', 'Roma', 'Summer Sweet' (shown here).

3 Cherry vine tomatoes
Most cherry tomatoes are bred to be very sweet and conveniently bite-sized. Cordon or vine varieties are often borne on long trusses laden with fruit.
■ TRY 'Gardener's Delight', 'Sun Cherry' (shown here), 'Sweet Million'.

4 Beefsteak tomatoes

These giants can grow to enormous sizes so, whether bush or vine, they usually need some form of support. Modern hybrids such as 'Country Taste' can easily weigh in at over 10 oz (300 g) each.

■ TRY 'Marmande' (shown here), 'Brandywine', 'Country Taste', 'Amaral'.

5 Striped tomatoes

There are plenty of tomatoes with distinctive patterning, many of them unusual heritage or heirloom varieties that are worth tracking down. 'Tigerella' looks and tastes good; it starts off green and orange, and then displays red and yellow stripes.

■ TRY 'Green Zebra', 'Tigerella' (shown here), 'Tiger Tom'.

6 Orange and yellow tomatoes

Bred and grown largely for their unusual coloring, these tomatoes can nevertheless be extremely tasty. 'Sungold' is claimed to be one of the sweetest tomatoes of all, and 'Yellow Brandywine' is a golden version of the famous nineteenth-century beefsteak.

■ TRY 'Yellow Brandywine', 'Golden Cherry', 'Golden Sunrise', 'Sungold' (shown here).

7 Bush tomatoes

Bush or "determinate" tomatoes tend to spread or trail and grow from multiple stems rather than a single one. They don't need pinching out. Smaller or dwarf cherry varieties can be grown in hanging baskets.

■ TRY 'Tornado', 'Tumbler' (shown here).

8 Black tomatoes

In the world of fashionable tomato growing, black is the new red. Black tomatoes, which originated in the Ukraine over 150 years ago, have a unique depth of flavor. Search out seeds from specialist nurseries and try something new.

■ TRY 'Black Cherry' (shown here), 'Black Krim', 'Chocolate Cherry'.

Peppers and chilies

All peppers and chilies are members of the capsicum family and it could be argued that the differences among the many varieties are merely a matter of taste. But what a taste! Sweet or bell peppers are large, sweet, and mild. Chilies, in contrast, are small and hot—sometimes so eye-wateringly hot that eating them is downright foolhardy. Growing them isn't difficult, however, provided you can give them the sunshine, warmth, and water they need.

	spring			summer			autumn			winter		
	E	M	L	E	M	L	E	M	L	E	M	L
sow indoors	■	■										
plant out			■	■								
harvest				■	■	■	■					

WHICH SWEET PEPPERS TO GROW

- 'Ariane'
- 'Atris'
- 'Bell Boy'
- 'California Wonder'
- 'Gourmet'
- 'Gypsy'
- 'Mavras'
- 'New Ace'
- 'Sweet Chocolate'

Where to grow

Peppers and chilies like a light, fertile soil that retains moisture. More importantly, because they are tropical or subtropical plants, they require heat and humidity. Unless you are growing them under cover, choose a planting position in a sheltered, sunny spot.

Sowing and planting

■ WHEN TO SOW Peppers and chilies need heat to germinate, so sow indoors in modules and pots in March and April, and plant out only when it is warm enough, in May and June. Sowing directly outdoors is hit-or-miss.

- SOWING DEPTH Just below the surface.
- PLANTING DISTANCE 15–18 in (38–45 cm) apart.
- ROW SPACING 24–36 in (60–75 cm) apart.

Tips on growing

Peppers and chilies need a long growing season in order to ripen fully, especially in temperate climates. Get ahead by raising seed indoors—at temperatures of 64–70°F (18–21°C) in order to guarantee germination. Harden off seedlings and plant them out only when all danger of frost has passed.

Weed and water regularly and feed every two weeks with general fertilizer or a special liquid tomato food once the first small fruits appear. Stake up plants if they become top-heavy.

Harvesting

Most sweet peppers change color as they mature. They start off green, then turn yellow, orange, red, or even dark purple when fully ripe. Picking them young will stimulate the plant to produce more fruits, but the young peppers won't taste as sweet.

Troubleshooting

- PESTS aphids, red spider mite, whitefly.
- DISEASES botrytis.

(above) **Chilies** on the same plant ripen at different rates. The color combinations can be very decorative.

(below, left to right) **Support ripening sweet peppers** with canes and twine. Leave a short length of stalk on the fruit when harvesting and consume fairly promptly—they don't store well.

Must-try chili varieties

Chilies vary in power from the very mild, which produce no more than a slight tingle on the tongue, to fruits so hot that you need to wear gloves to handle them. What gives them their heat? It's a chemical called "capsaicin," concentrated in the seeds and white pith. It stimulates the nerve endings in your mouth, throat, and skin.

1 **'Alma Paprika'** 〉
Mild, sweet, fleshy, and multicolored. Also try the similar 'Anaheim'.

2 **'Hungarian Hot Wax'** 〉〉
A medium-hot, thick-walled chili that starts off yellow, then turns red when ripe. Also try the smaller 'Apache'.

3 **'Aji Amarillo'** 〉〉
Long, thin, medium-hot chilies originally from South America. Also try the Mexican 'Jalapeno'.

4 **'Cherry Bomb'** 〉〉
Small, round, thick-walled fruits that ripen from green to red and have a medium-hot flavor.

5 **'Prairie Fire'** 〉〉〉
Fast-growing, small, fiery-tasting chilies. Try also 'Thai Dragon' and 'Ring of Fire'.

6 **'Habanero'** 〉〉〉
Unusual peach-colored variety of the notoriously hot Central American habanero family of chilies.

7 **'Dorset Naga Pepper'** 〉〉〉〉
Reputedly one of the hottest chilies in the world. Approach with extreme caution.

Eggplant

Like tomatoes, peppers, and chilies, eggplant originate in the warm, humid tropics and subtropics so they can be difficult to grow in cool temperate climates, unless we have a long, hot summer or you raise them in a polytunnel or greenhouse. If you can give them the conditions they need, try growing some of the more unusual creamy white, pale lilac, streaky violet, or even the yellow and red varieties.

	spring			summer			autumn			winter		
	E	M	L	E	M	L	E	M	L	E	M	L
sow indoors	■	■										
plant out			■	■								
harvest					■	■	■	■				

Where to grow
A warm, sunny, sheltered site and rich, fertile, moisture-retentive soil.

Sowing and planting
■ WHEN TO SOW Eggplant need a temperature of 70–86°F (21–30°C) to germinate, so sow indoors in March and April, and plant out only when it is warm enough, in May and June.
■ SOWING DEPTH Just below the surface.
■ PLANTING DISTANCE 24–30 in (60–75 cm) apart.
■ ROW SPACING 30–36 in (75–90 cm) apart.

Tips on growing
As soon as potted seedlings start to develop flowers, begin hardening them off. Plant out when there's no longer a risk of frost. Weed and water regularly and feed every two weeks with general fertilizer or a special liquid tomato food once the first small fruits appear. Stake up plants if they become top-heavy.

WHICH EGGPLANT TO GROW
■ 'Black Beauty'   ■ 'Moneymaker'
■ 'Bonica'   ■ 'Slim Jim'
■ 'Long Purple'   ■ 'Snowy'

Harvesting
Pick eggplant when they're still shiny. After that, they start to become bitter.

Troubleshooting
■ PESTS aphids, caterpillars, mealybugs, red spider mite, whitefly.
■ DISEASES botrytis.

(left to right) **Glossy and perfectly ripe**, this early variety of eggplant is compact and bushy. **Small "baby" eggplants** with attractive marbled skins are widely available.

Corn

Corn can grow up to 6 ft (2 m) in height and needs plenty of space. You must grow it in blocks of sufficient numbers for pollination to take place, but if you have the room, it's well worth it. Fresh corn eaten as soon as possible after picking is sweeter and juicier than any you'll ever buy. Indeed, you can eat perfectly ripe cobs raw, straight off the plant.

WHICH CORN TO GROW
- 'Incredible'
- 'Minipop'
- 'Sundance'
- 'Sweet Nugget'
- 'Swift'

	spring			summer			autumn			winter		
	E	M	L	E	M	L	E	M	L	E	M	L
sow indoors	■											
plant out			■									
plant out			■	■								
harvest						■	■					

Where to grow
Corn needs full sun and a site sheltered from strong winds. The plants grow very large so they need rich, fertile soil.

Sowing and planting
- WHEN TO SOW Indoors in April, outdoors only when the soil temperature reaches 50°F (10°C).
- SOWING DEPTH 1–1½ in (2.5–4 cm) deep.
- SOWING/PLANTING DISTANCE 14–18 in (35–45 cm) apart.
- ROW SPACING 18–24 in (45–60 cm) apart.

Tips on growing
Seedlings raised inside or under cover should be hardened off and planted out only when all danger of frost has passed. Because they are pollinated by wind rather than insects or birds, plant them closely in blocks rather than in long rows. Water regularly, particularly when the cobs are fattening up.

Harvesting
Check the cobs for ripeness when the tassels or silks have turned brown. Peel back the husk and prick one of the kernels. If the juice is milky, the cob is ripe.

Troubleshooting
- PESTS aphids, birds, mice, squirrels.
- DISEASES corn smut.

Supersweet and tendersweet varieties have a higher concentration of sugar than traditional cultivars and taste wonderful.

Okra

Okra are slim, tapering pods sometimes called "ladies' fingers" or "gumbo." Usually green, although occasionally white or red, they contain lots of small, white, rounded seeds. The pods are cooked and eaten whole. Thought to have originated in East Africa, the plants need the warmth and humidity of a hot summer. In cool, temperate climates okra may need to be grown under cover.

	spring			summer			autumn			winter		
	E	M	L	E	M	L	E	M	L	E	M	L
sow indoors	■	■										
plant out			■	■								
harvest					■	■	■					

(right) **Okra** like its relative cotton, needs moist heat. Pick the pods at their most tender—no longer than 3 in (8 cm).

Where to grow
A warm, sunny, sheltered site and rich, fertile, moisture-retentive soil.

Sowing and planting
■ WHEN TO SOW Seeds need a minimum temperature of 60°F (16°C) to germinate, so sow indoors in March and April, and plant out only when thoroughly warm, in late May and June.
■ SOWING DEPTH Just below the surface.
■ PLANTING DISTANCE 16–24 in (40–60 cm) apart.
■ ROW SPACING 24–30 in (60–75 cm) apart.

Tips on growing
Soak seeds in warm water before sowing in order to soften them, and if necessary use a propagator to encourage germination and the growth of young seedlings. In warm regions, harden off and transplant when seedlings are about 3–4 in (8–10 cm) high. As plants grow, tie them in to canes for support. In cool regions—or in a poor summer—fruits may not ripen outdoors.

Harvesting
Cut pods regularly when they are no bigger than 3 in (8 cm) long, or they become tough and woody.

Troubleshooting
■ PESTS outdoors: aphids; under cover: red spider mite, whitefly.
■ DISEASES botrytis.

WHICH OKRA TO GROW
■ 'Clemson's Spineless'
■ 'Pure Luck'

Squashes, pumpkins, and cucumbers

Strictly speaking, these vegetables are all fruits because they contain seeds. But, with the exception perhaps of pumpkin pie, we usually eat them as an ingredient in savory dishes or salads. They vary astonishingly in scale—from tiny, bite-sized gherkins to huge, record-breaking pumpkins that can reach 13 ft (4.5 m) in circumference and that can weigh more than 1,000 lbs (450 kg). However large or small, provided that you feed and water them generously, they are all remarkably easy to grow.

The cucurbit family includes plants that grow swiftly in favorable conditions, covering a large amount of ground. Their huge, slightly prickly leaves suppress most weeds and the large yellow flowers may be harvested as well as the fruits.

(above left to right) **Summer squashes, pumpkin, cucumbers**

(far left) **Winter squashes**
(left) **Zucchinis**

Vegetable marrows

It's hard not to feel that growing marrows is more about size than flavor. To many of us, they look and taste like overgrown zucchinis—bland and watery. But their fans are fiercely loyal, cosseting them on rich beds of compost and manure, feeding them day and night, and raising prize-winning giants.

	spring			summer			autumn			winter		
	E	M	L	E	M	L	E	M	L	E	M	L
sow indoors		■	■									
sow outdoors				■								
plant out			■	■								
harvest					■	■	■	■				

Where to grow
A sunny, sheltered site and a fertile soil that has had lots of rich organic material added to it.

Sowing and planting
■ WHEN TO SOW In April or May, sow indoors or under cover at a minimum temperature of 68°F (20°C). Harden off and transplant from May. Sow direct outdoors in June.
■ SOWING DEPTH 1 in (2.5 cm) deep.
■ SOWING/PLANTING DISTANCE 36 in (90 cm).
■ ROW SPACING 4 ft (1.2 m) apart.

Tips on growing
Water regularly and feed with a liquid fertilizer once baby marrows form. Raise large marrows off the soil to reduce the risk of rotting, and turn them occasionally so that they harden evenly in the sun.

Harvesting
Pick and eat when the fruits are about 6 in (15 cm) long, or leave them to grow on into giants.

Troubleshooting
■ PESTS aphids, slugs and snails.
■ DISEASES cucumber mosaic virus, foot and root rots, powdery mildew.

WHICH VEGETABLE MARROWS TO GROW
■ 'Emerald Cross'
■ 'Long Green Bush'
■ 'Long Green Trailing'
■ 'Tiger Cross'

Large marrows may be stored for use over winter; let them grow to full size, ripen evenly, and develop a hard skin. A brick or tile under each fruit will keep it dry and prevent rot.

Zucchinis and summer squashes

The key to growing zucchinis and summer squashes is not to plant too many of them. At the height of summer, they produce fruits uncannily quickly, and you will have trouble eating enough to keep up with them. For an average family, two or three green zucchini plants, a couple of yellow or round ones, and perhaps an unusual-shaped summer squash should be plenty over one season.

	spring			summer			autumn			winter		
	E	M	L	E	M	L	E	M	L	E	M	L
sow indoors		■	■									
sow outdoors				■								
plant out				■	■							
harvest					■	■	■	■				

Zucchinis grow so fast that they are very hungry and thirsty plants. Plant them in a rich soil, kept moist with a mulch. You can even plant one in a layer of soil on top of a compost heap.

Where to grow
A sunny, sheltered site, and in fertile soil that has had lots of rich organic material added to it.

Sowing and planting
■ WHEN TO SOW In April or May, sow indoors or under cover at a minimum temperature of 68°F (20°C). Harden off and transplant from May. Sow direct outdoors only in June.
■ SOWING DEPTH 1 in (2.5 cm) deep.
■ SOWING/PLANTING DISTANCE 36 in (90 cm) apart.
■ ROW SPACING 36 in (90 cm) apart.

Tips on growing
Zucchinis are very susceptible to frost, so don't sow or plant too early. If you raise plants under cover, insects may not be able to get to the flowers and pollinate them, in which case you'll have to do it yourself (see p.62).

Harvesting
Pick young fruits often. They become watery and tasteless if they are allowed to grow too large.

Troubleshooting
■ PESTS outdoors: aphids, slugs and snails; under cover: aphids, red spider mite, whitefly.
■ DISEASES cucumber mosaic virus, foot and root rots, powdery mildew.

Pumpkins and winter squashes

Whereas zucchinis and summer squashes are generally picked when small and eaten immediately, pumpkins and winter squashes can also be stored, making them a valuable source of food during the winter. The key to ensuring that they keep for as long as possible without rotting is to allow them to ripen fully and then "cure" them in the sun so that their skins harden.

Harvest pumpkins and squashes when the stems begin to crack: cut each off with a short stalk and leave in the sun for about 10 days to "cure" the skin and seal in the moisture.

	spring E	M	L	summer E	M	L	autumn E	M	L	winter E	M	L
sow indoors		■	■									
sow outdoors				■								
plant out			■	■								
harvest							■	■				

Where to grow
All squashes like a sunny site with plenty of space to spread and a fertile soil.

Sowing and planting
■ WHEN TO SOW In April or May, sow indoors or under cover. Harden off young plants and transplant them from May onward when the risk of frosts is past. Sow direct outdoors in June.
■ SOWING DEPTH 1 in (2.5 cm) deep.
■ SOWING/PLANTING DISTANCE 3–5 ft (1–1.5 m) apart.
■ ROW SPACING 3–5 ft (1–1.5 m) apart.

Tips on growing
Before planting, enrich the soil by adding lots of rich, well-rotted organic material. Watering is crucial, especially for pumpkins that grow very large. Mulch to help the soil retain moisture. Small varieties may be trained up canes and other supports.

Harvesting
Leave fruits that you plan to store to grow for as long as possible. After cutting, let them ripen in the sun: the harder their skins, the longer they'll keep.

Troubleshooting
■ PESTS aphids, slugs and snails.
■ DISEASES cucumber mosaic virus, foot and root rots, powdery mildew.

WHICH PUMPKINS AND WINTER SQUASHES TO GROW

Pumpkins
■ 'Atlantic Giant'
■ 'Becky'
■ 'Jack o'Lantern'
■ 'Rouge Vif d'Etampes'

Winter squashes
■ 'Butternut'

■ 'Crown Prince'
■ 'Golden Hubbard'
■ 'Queensland Blue'
■ 'Spaghetti Squash'
■ 'Sweet Dumpling'
■ 'Turk's Turban'
■ 'Uchiki Kuri'

Must-try squashes and pumpkins

Mention pumpkins and most people think of Halloween: large, spherical, bright orange fruits carved out to make lanterns. But there is far more to this versatile vegetable than that. Summer and winter squashes come in an extraordinary variety of shapes, sizes, textures, and colors, and the flavors vary widely too. They can be big or small, elongated or round, smooth or knobbly, and some are happy to climb, while others sprawl over the ground. Here is a selection to try.

1 Patty Pan 'Sunburst'
This small summer squash, also known as a custard squash, is best harvested when immature, at a diameter of 2–3 in (5–8 cm).

2 'Queensland Blue'
A large winter squash, this swells to 11–20 lb (5–9 kg) when mature, has tasty, semi-sweet, dense, golden flesh, and keeps well.

3 'Little Gem Rolet'
This variety produces a good number of softball-sized summer squashes. They are very sweet and young fruits may be cooked without peeling.

4 'Turk's Turban'
The "cap" at its top gives this winter squash its name. It is often used as an ornamental squash in displays and lasts a long time if not bruised.

5 'Tromboncino'
Left to trail on the ground, this summer squash curves dramatically; grown upward on supports, it straightens out and can grow up to 36 in (90 cm).

6 'Uchiki Kuri'
Also called 'Red Kuri' or 'Onion Squash', this winter squash produces small fruits with a smooth flesh and nutty flavor. It keeps well.

7 'Butternut'
There are several different butternut varieties, some bred specially for temperate climates. They all share the same long, bulbous, pear shape and have bright orange, sweet-tasting flesh.

8 'Sweet Dumpling'
These pretty, little winter squashes are often cooked whole and stuffed; the orange flesh is very sweet and tender.

9 'Crown Prince'
Inside the steely blue-gray skin of this distinctive winter squash you'll find dense, orange flesh with a sweet, nutty flavor. It keeps well and tastes superb roasted or made into pumpkin soup.

YOU COULD ALSO TRY:

'Golden Hubbard'
A large, onion-shaped winter squash with slightly ridged, wrinkled skin, it has sweet-tasting, deep-orange skin and will store well.

'Summer Crookneck'
Long, yellow summer squashes with curved necks are produced abundantly by this variety. They are most edible if picked when about 6 in (15 cm) long, before the skins mature and become warty.

'Tennessee Sweet Potato'
A descendent of the American potato pumpkin, this plant bears large, pear-shaped whitish pumpkins, with pale green stripes and cream-colored flesh, and is very decorative.

'Spaghetti Squash'
Also known as 'Vegetable Spaghetti', this squash has flesh that separates into strands when cooked and is delicious when topped with a pasta sauce. The fruits start off a pale, ivory color then turn yellow as they ripen. Spaghetti squash is another good one to store for the winter.

Cucumbers

Choosing the correct variety of cucumber to grow is important. Outdoor or "ridge" cucumbers—traditionally rough-skinned or even slightly spiny—are specially selected for their ability to tolerate cooler temperatures. Greenhouse cucumbers are smoother and longer but need warmth, and in temperate climates may be grown only under cover. Increasingly, today's modern varieties may be grown either outdoors or in polytunnels and greenhouses.

	spring			summer			autumn			winter		
	E	M	L	E	M	L	E	M	L	E	M	L
sow indoors	■	■										
sow under cover	■	■	■									
sow outdoors				■								
plant out			■	■								
harvest					■	■	■					

Where to grow
Outdoor cucumbers need a sunny, sheltered site with rich, fertile soil. Add lime only if the soil is very acid; that is, with a pH of 5.5 or lower.

Sowing and planting
■ WHEN TO SOW From March onward, sow in pots or modules indoors, or outdoors under cover if the temperature is a minimum 68°F (20°C). Harden off and transplant them from May. Attempt to sow direct outdoors only in June.
■ SOWING DEPTH 1 in (2.5 cm) deep.
■ SOWING/PLANTING DISTANCE Climbing 18 in (45 cm) apart; sprawling 36 in (90 cm) apart.
■ ROW SPACING 30 in (75 cm) apart.

Tips on growing
If necessary, dig in well-rotted compost or manure to soil well before planting. Train climbing varieties up a cane wigwam, trellis, or framework of strings and wires. Once stems reach the top, remove their growing tips. Start feeding every two weeks with a general-purpose, liquid fertilizer as soon as fruits start to form. Water regularly—don't ever let cucumbers dry out.

GROWING GHERKINS
Gherkins are really no more than small, immature cucumbers, although a number of cultivars have been developed specifically for growing as gherkins.

They are usually picked when they are about 1 in (2.5 cm) long (in which case, they are known as cornichons) or when they reach up to 3 in (8 cm) in length (for dill pickles, perhaps). Either way, they are usually preserved by being pickled in flavored vinegar or brine.

Gherkins grow very quickly and should be picked while still young, so harvest them regularly.

Harvesting

Cucumbers taste best and have smaller seeds if picked while still young, before they grow to the size of the vegetables that you buy in the stores. And the more you pick, the more will grow, so there's no reason to hold back.

Remove any cucumbers that turn yellow to avoid their diverting energy from the plant, and finish harvesting before the first frost.

Troubleshooting

■ PESTS outdoors: aphids, slugs and snails; under cover: aphids, red spider mite, whitefly.
■ DISEASES cucumber mosaic virus, foot and root rots, powdery mildew.

(above, left) **Outdoor cucumbers** are prone to attack by slugs if left to trail over the ground.

(above, right) **'Crystal Apple'** (shown here) and 'Crystal Lemon' cucumbers are unusual—small, rounded, and bright yellow in color. They taste wonderful and are reputed to be easier to digest.

WHICH CUCUMBERS TO GROW

- ■ 'Burpless Tasty Green'
- ■ 'Carmen'
- ■ 'Crystal Apple'
- ■ 'La Diva'
- ■ 'Marketmore'
- ■ 'Tanja'

Perennial vegetables

Asparagus, globe artichokes, Jerusalem artichokes, and rhubarb are unlike the other vegetables in this book in that they are all perennials—which means that, once established, they simply go on and on from one year to the next. In other words, you don't have to raise them from seed and then plant them out at the start of each new year. Of course, they are not quite everlasting—in time they'll become exhausted and will need renewing. Even then, globe artichokes and rhubarb can be dug up, divided into so-called "sets" or "offsets," and then replanted to produce reenergized new plants.

Perennial vegetables are an attractive and diverse group, and their edible parts range from stems to flower buds. Robust and hardy, they require less care and attention than many annual vegetables.

(above, left to right) **Globe artichoke, Jerusalem artichokes, asparagus**
(left) **Rhubarb**

Asparagus

An asparagus bed is a long-term investment since plants can last for as long as 20 years. Each spring, they produce delicious, edible spurs, followed by tall, fernlike foliage that is cut down in the autumn. Asparagus can be grown from seed, but it is easier to buy ready-to-plant rootstocks or "crowns."

	spring			summer			autumn			winter		
	E	M	L	E	M	L	E	M	L	E	M	L
plant crowns			■	■								
harvest				■	■							

Cut spears with a very sharp knife and at the last possible moment before you plan to eat them.

Where to grow

A sheltered site with light, well-drained, fertile soil that has a pH of 6.5–7.5. Sandy soil is ideal; on heavy, clay soils, grow asparagus in ridges or raised beds.

Sowing and planting

■ WHEN TO PLANT Plant new crowns or divide existing ones in March or April.
■ PLANTING DEPTH 4 in (10 cm) down in trenches 8 in (20 cm) deep.
■ PLANTING DISTANCE 12–18 in (30–40 cm) apart.
■ ROW SPACING 18 in (40 cm) apart.

Tips on growing

Plant crowns in prepared trenches (see p.56). Keep well watered and weedfree. Feed twice a year—once in March and again after cropping has finished. Cut down yellowing foliage in autumn (see p.159), and spread a mulch of well-rotted compost or manure over the beds.

Harvesting

Don't harvest newly planted asparagus in its first year. In following years, cut the spears just below ground level, when they are about 5–7 in (13–18 cm) long.

Troubleshooting

■ PESTS asparagus beetle, slugs and snails.
■ DISEASES foot and root rots, violet root rot.

WHICH ASPARAGUS TO GROW

■ 'Ariane'
■ 'Connover's Colossal'
■ 'Gijnlim'
■ 'Jersey Knight'
■ 'Purple Pacific'

Globe artichokes

Globe artichokes can be raised from seed, but it's easier and quicker to grow new plants from side shoots or "offsets" cut from existing plants (see p.75). Plants should last for three or four years before they begin to tire and themselves become candidates for dividing and propagating.

(right) **Harvest** the top "king" bud first.

(opposite) **Purple varieties** stand out well against fresh architectural foliage.

	spring			summer			autumn			winter		
	E	M	L	E	M	L	E	M	L	E	M	L
sow indoors	■											■
plant out		■	■									
plant offsets		■	■									
harvest					■	■	■	■	■			

Where to grow
A sunny, sheltered spot and fertile soil with a slightly acid pH of 6.5.

Sowing and planting
■ WHEN TO SOW/PLANT Raise seeds indoors in February or March. Plant out seedlings or "offsets" in April or May.
■ PLANTING DEPTH 2 in (5 cm) deep.
■ PLANTING DISTANCE 36 in (90 cm) apart.
■ ROW SPACING 36 in (90 cm) apart.

Tips on growing
In a new plant's first year, cut off its main flowerhead as soon as it appears. Harsh perhaps, but doing so will stimulate growth and produce a stronger plant in following years. In autumn, cut out any dead foliage and cover with straw or bracken for the winter. Mulch or feed in spring.

Harvesting
Cut the topmost globe (the "king") first, after it has fattened up but before its scales begin to open, then work your way down the plant.

Troubleshooting
■ PESTS earwigs, slugs and snails.
■ DISEASES petal blight fungus.

(left) **Fat, round globes** must be picked promptly or the scales will open to reveal huge blue or purple thistle heads.

WHICH GLOBE ARTICHOKES TO GROW
■ 'Green Globe'
■ 'Gros Vert de Laon'
■ 'Purple Globe'
■ 'Violetto di Chioggia'

Jerusalem artichokes

Jerusalem artichokes are grown for their edible tubers, which form underground among their roots, like potatoes. The plants themselves are members of the sunflower family and grow very tall—up to 10 ft (3 m) in height. Because they are perennials, any tubers inadvertently left behind in the ground after harvesting will produce new plants the next year.

	spring			summer			autumn			winter		
	E	M	L	E	M	L	E	M	L	E	M	L
plant tubers outdoors	■	■										■
harvest							■		■	■		■

(above) **Vigorous plants** can yield up to ten tubers each.

(left) **Harvest tubers** as you need them, from mid-autumn, but not when the soil is frozen.

Where to grow
They should grow anywhere, in sun or shade, as long as the soil is not waterlogged or too acid—add lime if the pH is below 5.

Sowing and planting
■ WHEN TO PLANT Plant new tubers as soon as the soil is workable, in February or March.
■ PLANTING DEPTH 4–6 in (10–15 cm) deep.
■ PLANTING DISTANCE 12–18 in (30–40 cm) apart.
■ ROW SPACING 12–18 in (30–40 cm) apart.

Tips on growing
Growing plants need support: earth them up initially, then stake them. In July or August, cut them down to 5 ft (1.5 m) and remove any flowers. This concentrates the plants' energy on fattening up the tubers. Cut yellowed foliage down to the ground in autumn.

Harvesting
Leave tubers in the ground until you need them, then lift them like potatoes.

Troubleshooting
■ PESTS slugs and snails.
■ DISEASES sclerotinia (a white fungus).

WHICH JERUSALEM ARTICHOKES TO GROW
■ 'Fuseau'
■ Chinese artichokes are from a different plant family. They are smaller, ridged, and have a subtle, nutty taste.

Rhubarb

Full-grown rhubarb plants can easily spread to 6 ft (2 m) across in summer. They need a lot of space. But if you have a plot large enough to accommodate them, they're worth growing. Once established, they need very little attention and should crop continuously through the spring and most of the summer. A word of warning: the leaves are poisonous, so don't eat them.

	spring			summer			autumn			winter		
	E	M	L	E	M	L	E	M	L	E	M	L
sow indoors												■
transplant			■									
plant sets outdoors	■							■	■	■	■	■
harvest	■	■	■	■	■							

WHICH RHUBARB TO GROW
- 'Timperley Early'
- 'Victoria'

Where to grow
An open, sunny site in fertile soil that doesn't get waterlogged in winter.

Sowing and planting
- WHEN TO SOW/PLANT Sow seeds indoors in February and plant out in May. Plant new sets when dormant in winter, any time between October and March unless the ground is frozen.
- PLANTING DEPTH Bud just above soil surface.
- PLANTING DISTANCE 36 in (90 cm) apart.
- ROW SPACING 12–18 in (30–40 cm) apart.

Tips on growing
Rhubarb can be grown from seed, but it's fussy. If you can, it's simpler to divide established plants by splitting off new "sets" from their rootstocks (see p.192).

In summer, remove any stalks that have flowered. In autumn, clear away all dead foliage and mulch around the plants with well-rotted manure or compost. Leave the crowns exposed over winter.

Harvesting
You can start to "force" rhubarb to produce tender, blanched stalks as early as January (see p.38). From early March, break off stems as and when you need them.

Troubleshooting
- PESTS aphids, slugs and snails.
- DISEASES crown rot, honey fungus.

Once established, rhubarb prefers to stay put. Keep plants moist in summer, well fed, and let the frost get to them in winter, and they will carry on producing.

Herbs

A selection of different herbs is an important component of any kitchen garden—arguably, almost as important as your vegetables and fruit themselves. For cooking, herbs are essential, but they also have countless medicinal, cosmetic, and household uses. And, if you grow them yourself, you'll not only be able to use them more liberally but also take the opportunity to experiment with unusual herbs that may be difficult to buy in the store—for example, most people are familiar with parsley and basil, but why not try chervil, lovage, or savory.

Adding freshly picked herbs to your homegrown produce when cooking will add flavor to your dishes and fill your kitchen with wonderful, mouth-watering aromas.

(above left to right) **Purple basil, golden marjoram, Chinese chives**

(far left) **Sage 'Tricolor'**
(left) **Basil mint**

Must-grow essential herbs

Potted, ready-to-plant herbs are inexpensive and widely available in garden centers and nurseries. However, there's something satisfying about raising herbs from seed or propagating them from established plants. Here is a selection of reliable herbs for your plot.

1 Basil
A native of tropical Asia, basil needs warmth and sunshine. It can be tricky to grow outdoors in cool, temperate climates. Grow from seed sown under cover each year. Pick leaves regularly, and pinch out growing tips to encourage bushy growth.

2 Tarragon
Of the two varieties (French and Russian) French has the best flavor—a mild, peppery, aniseed taste. It is unavailable as seed, so buy potted plants or propagate from an existing one. Mulch plants with straw over winter.

3 Chervil
An annual with tiny, feathery, aniseed-tasting leaves. Grow chervil in partial shade, sowing seeds direct into the ground at any time between spring and autumn. Water plants regularly in summer.

4 Chives
A grasslike perennial that is a member of the onion family. Both leaves and flowers can be eaten. Grow from seed sown in spring, or propagate from established clumps by dividing them in autumn.

5 Cilantro
Known in Britain as coriander, cilantro has distinctive-tasting lower leaves and its seeds are used as a spice. Sow seeds direct between spring and late summer each year. Harvest leaves and water regularly to stop the plant from bolting.

6 Thyme
The many varieties of thyme have subtly different flavors and are best bought as plants rather than as seeds. Once established, they can be propagated by division, from cuttings, or by layering. Prune quite hard after flowering to stimulate the growth of new leaves.

7 Lovage
Lovage is a perennial that looks like parsley but can grow to a giant height of 6 ft (2 m). Its leaves taste of celery and yeast. Grow from seed sown direct in spring or by lifting and dividing an existing rootball. Prune hard in early summer before flowering to stimulate a second flush of leaves.

8 Fennel
Related to dill—and with a similar taste—fennel is actually a different species; the two shouldn't be grown nearby or they may cross-pollinate. Sow direct from April onward, and in autumn cut all the foliage down to ground level. You can save the ripe seedheads and dry them.

9 Marjoram
Of the different varieties, sweet and pot marjoram are usually used fresh, while Greek and wild marjoram (also known as oregano) may also be dried. Marjoram needs warmth and sunshine. It can be tricky to germinate, so buy potted plants or propagate from cuttings or by division.

10 Savory
Both summer and winter savory have small evergreen leaves that look and taste a little like thyme. Summer savory is an annual, and winter savory a perennial. Sow seeds of either in spring or summer. The leaves taste best if they are harvested when still young.

11 Mint
Mint has scores of different-flavored varieties, from pineapple to ginger. It is almost impossible to fail with it, and it is so notoriously invasive that it comes close to being considered a weed. Prevent it from spreading by constraining it in a raised bed or a container sunk into the ground.

12 Sage

An evergreen with gray-green, purple, or variegated leaves. Grow from seed sown in spring, from softwood cuttings taken in summer, or heel cuttings taken in autumn. Cut back established plants in spring and pinch out growing shoots in summer to keep bushes compact.

13 Rosemary

An aromatic, evergreen shrub that likes warmth and sunshine and will tolerate dry conditions. Rosemary is difficult to grow from seed but easily established from cuttings taken in late summer. Prune in spring to keep bushes in shape.

14 Dill

An annual with feathery, fernlike leaves that have a delicate aniseed flavor. The seeds have a stronger taste. Dill dislikes being disturbed so sow directly into the ground in batches between about April and July. Pick leaves shortly before you need them, and water regularly to prevent bolting.

15 Parsley

Grow both curly-leaved and flat-leaved varieties afresh each year, even though the plant is actually a biennial—it's the leaves you want, not the flowers that appear in the second year. Sow seeds in pots or modules indoors or under cover, or directly outdoors from May onward. You need to be patient: parsley can be slow to germinate.

ALSO TRY

Bay

An evergreen shrub that's perhaps not as hardy as it looks and may not survive harsh winters. Bays are difficult to grow from seed, and are best bought as young, potted plants or propagated from cuttings. Harvest at any time throughout the year.

Lemon balm

With mintlike leaves and a lemon flavor, lemon balm is used primarily for herbal teas. It's a hardy perennial that is easy to grow—so easy that unchecked it can reach heights of up to 5 ft (1.5 m). Sow seeds direct in spring, or propagate by division.

Fruit

Most fruit falls into one of two categories: tree fruit or soft fruit. Tree fruits (sometimes called top fruit) contain seeds in the form of either small seeds (apples and pears) or larger stones (plums, cherries, apricots, peaches, and so on). Not all can be grown outdoors in temperate zones—tender tree fruits will thrive only in favorable conditions, and those that require subtropical temperatures (citrus and pomegranates, for example) are unlikely to ripen at all unless grown under glass or in a polytunnel.

Soft fruits include those that grow on bushes (currants and gooseberries); those that grow on canes (raspberries, blackberries, and hybrid berries); and so-called heathland berries (blueberries and cranberries). Strawberries, grapes, cape gooseberries, and melons are soft fruits in subcategories of their own.

Not all gooseberries are green. 'Whinham's Industry' is a variety that ripens to a deep red and produces berries so plump, juicy, and sweet that they can be eaten straight from the bush.

Fruit families

- **Tree fruits** include both hardy apples, pears, plums, and cherries, and tender apricots, peaches, nectarines, and figs. Tender tree fruits need sheltered sites and long, hot summers for fruit to ripen reliably.
- **Soft fruits** include all the various berries and currants that grow on bushes or canes, as well as strawberries—which are low-growing herbaceous perennials—and melons, which are in fact closely related to pumpkins and squash, although much more tender.
- **Grapes** are sometimes classified separately as vine fruits.

Apples

A maze of terminology surrounds the cultivation of apples and navigating your way through can be daunting, but it's not as complex as it looks. The fruits themselves are classified according to their sweetness (whether they are dessert apples or "eaters" or culinary varieties, called "cookers"), and also whether they are ready for picking early, in midseason, or late. Trees are categorized according to size (dictated largely by their rootstocks) and shape (determined by how they are pruned and trained). In addition, they are grouped according to when their blossom appears.

	spring			summer			autumn			winter		
	E	M	L	E	M	L	E	M	L	E	M	L
plant	■								■	■	■	■
winter-prune									■	■	■	■
summer-prune wire-trained trees				■	■							
harvest					■	■	■					

Where to grow

Apples like a sheltered site in full sun with fertile, well-drained soil that has a slightly acid pH of about 6.5. Don't plant trees in frost pockets.

Planting

■ WHEN TO PLANT The best time for bare-root trees is between November and March while they are dormant; this is the best time for container-grown trees, too, although they can be planted at other times of the year if conditions permit.
■ PLANTING DEPTH To the level of the soil mark on the stem.
■ PLANTING DISTANCE Depends on the rootstock and its vigor: it may vary from just 30 in (75 cm) apart for dwarf cordons to 21 ft (6.5 m) or more for vigorous, stand-alone trees.

(left, top to bottom) **'Ellison's Orange'** has an aniseed flavor and is resistant to scab and frost but prone to canker. **'Winston'** is a firm apple and makes a strong-growing tree. **'Egremont Russet'** is a reliable grower with a lovely nutty taste.

WHICH APPLES TO GROW

Cooking apples
- 'Arthur Turner'
- 'Bramley's Seedling'
- 'Grenadier'

Dessert apples: early
- 'Discovery'
- 'Katy'

Dessert apples: mid-season
- 'Ellison's Orange'
- 'Egremont Russet'

- 'James Grieve'
- 'Kidd's Orange Red'
- 'Queen Cox'

Dessert apples: late
- 'Claygate Pearmain'
- 'Fiesta'
- 'Howgate Wonder'
- 'Laxton's Superb'
- 'Tydeman's Late Orange'
- 'Winston'

Tips on growing

Most apples need to be cross-pollinated from other, compatible trees—that is, ones that flower at the same time—and are grouped accordingly. If the trees in your yard are not from the same group, they tend to produce small crops, or none at all, so it's best to plant two compatible trees. Insects such as bees will carry the pollen from one tree to another as long as they are in reasonably close proximity.

Ripe apples should come away easily from the tree. Hold each one firmly and give it a gentle twist: if it will not come free, it is not fully ripe.

(below, left) **'Howgate Wonder'** and (right) **'Bramley's Seedling'** are both classic cookers. Late croppers, they store well and have a good acid flavor.

(above) **Insect pollinators** carry pollen from one tree to another, so you need at least one other compatible apple cultivar growing nearby, and no late frosts, for a good fruit set.

(opposite) **'Kidd's Orange Red'** is a descendant of 'Cox's Orange Pippin', but has much sweeter apples. It produces a regular, but not huge, crop late in the season.

In spring, sprinkle a general fertilizer in a circle around the trees and spread a mulch of well-rotted manure or compost.

In early summer, most trees allow a number of their young, acorn-sized fruits to fall to the ground. This is called the June drop and is the tree's way of ensuring that it is not overloaded. Even so, it's worth removing any diseased fruit and then thinning still further, to one dessert apple every 4–6 in (10–15 cm) and one cooking apple every 6–9 in (15–23 cm).

Pruning and training

Winter-prune trees from November to February, while they're dormant. Cut out any dead, damaged, or diseased wood, reduce congested growth, and maintain the overall shape. Summer-prune trained trees such as espaliers and fans to remove any unwanted growth and encourage new fruiting spurs.

Harvesting

Early varieties don't keep, so eat them right away. Late varieties can be stored (see p.174).

Troubleshooting

■ PESTS aphids, apple sawfly, apple sucker (like aphids), birds, capsid bug, caterpillars, codling moth.
■ DISEASES bitter pit, blossom wilt, brown rot, canker, fireblight, powdery mildew, scab.

BUYING APPLE TREES

When buying trees, there are two things to consider: the rootstock, and the form or shape of the tree. The rootstock provides the root system and base of the trunk, and it is the foundation onto which the bud or shoot ("scion") of a particular cultivar is grafted when the tree is propagated. Dwarf rootstocks produce short trees; vigorous ones give tall trees. One- to three-year-old trees will establish well; anything older may struggle.

In terms of form or shape, bush trees have open, goblet-shaped centers. Spindlebush and pyramid trees are smaller and conical. Trained trees (right) include cordons, with single, or multiple straight stems. Minarettes are miniature cordons. Espaliers have several symmetrical, horizontal arms in one plane, and fans are...fan-shaped.

Pears

Growing pears is in many ways very similar to growing apples because they are propagated, raised, trained, and pruned in the same way. But there are a few important differences: pears flower earlier than apples, so they may need more protection from frost damage; they require more warmth and sunshine for their fruits to ripen, which is why they are often grown as cordons or espaliers against south-facing walls and fences; and to control their size they are often grafted onto quince rootstocks.

WHICH PEARS TO GROW

- 'Beth'
- 'Beurré Superfin'
- 'Concorde'
- 'Conference'
- 'Doyenné du Comice'
- 'Williams' Bon Chrétien'

(below, left to right) **Blossom** is prone to frost damage. **Thin fruitlets** to two per cluster to gain full-sized pears.

	spring			summer			autumn			winter		
	E	M	L	E	M	L	E	M	L	E	M	L
plant	■								■	■	■	■
winter-prune									■	■	■	■
summer-prune wire-trained trees					■	■						
harvest						■	■	■				

Where to grow

Pears thrive in a warm, sheltered position in deep, well-drained soil that has a slightly acid pH of about 6.5. Avoid frost pockets.

Planting

- WHEN TO PLANT For bare-root trees, plant between November and March while they are dormant; this is the best time for container-grown

trees, too, although they can be planted at other times of the year, if conditions are suitable.

■ PLANTING DEPTH To the level of the soil mark on the stem.

■ PLANTING DISTANCE Depends on the rootstock and its vigor—from just 30 in (75 cm) apart for dwarf cordons to 18 ft (5.5 m) or more for vigorous stand-alone trees.

Tips on growing

Like apples, each pear tree needs to be pollinated by one or more compatible trees that flower at the same time and are members of the same pollination group. Once pollination takes place, the fruit will set and young fruitlets start to develop. Around June, some will fall naturally as the trees unload excess fruitlets, but it's wise to thin them further. Remove any weak or misshapen fruits to allow space for the remainder to grow to full size.

In spring, feed and mulch the pear trees in the same way as for apples (see p.292).

Pruning and training

Pears can be grown as stand-alone trees or trained as cordons, espaliers, or fans. Winter-prune stand-alone trees between November and February, while they are dormant. Cut out any damaged, diseased, or dead wood, open up any overcrowding, and maintain the tree's overall shape. Summer-prune wire-trained trees to remove any unwanted growth and stimulate new fruiting spurs.

Harvesting

There's a knack to gauging when pears are ready to pick. If in doubt, err on the side of picking early varieties when under-ripe. Try this test: lift a pear in the palm of your hand and give it a gentle twist to see if it comes away easily with its stalk intact. If it does, it's probably ready. Eat early pears within a couple of weeks. Later varieties can be stored until fully ripe. (see p.174).

Troubleshooting

■ PESTS aphids, birds, capsid bug, caterpillars, codling moth, pear leaf blister mite, pear midge, pear and cherry slugworm (small black larvae that "skeletonize" leaves).

■ DISEASES blossom wilt, brown rot, canker, fireblight, scab.

(below) **The pear crop** is influenced by many factors, from the vigor of the cultivar and rootstock, to the soil, seasonal weather patterns, and the way the tree is trained. This pear, 'Gorham', usually has a reliable crop of juicy, musk-flavored fruits.

Plums

Plums vary widely in size and color—from deep purple to pale yellow—and in taste from lusciously sweet dessert fruits to sharp, tangy cooking varieties. The plum family also includes the less familiar gages, mirabelles, cherry plums, damsons, and even "wild" cousins such as bullaces and sloes. Like cherries (see p.298), some trees are self-fertile and may be grown on their own. Other plums are not; they need to be cross-pollinated and must be planted near compatible trees if they are to bear any fruit.

	spring			summer			autumn			winter		
	E	M	L	E	M	L	E	M	L	E	M	L
plant									■	■	■	■
prune		■	■	■	■	■						
harvest					■	■	■	■				

Where to grow
Plums are happy in any reasonably fertile, well-drained soil, but they need a warm, sheltered position with as much frost protection as possible.

Planting
■ WHEN TO PLANT Between November and February, while the trees are dormant.
■ PLANTING DEPTH To level of soil mark on stem.
■ PLANTING DISTANCE Semidwarf 8–12 ft (2.5–3.6 m); semivigorous 12–16 ft (3.6–5 m); vigorous 18–21 ft (5.5–6.5 m) or more apart.

Tips on growing
Semidwarfing rootstocks such as 'Pixy' produce trees not much more than 7 ft (2.1 m) tall, making frost-prone varieties that flower early easier to protect with fleece. Some plum varieties are self-fertile, but even these will produce a better crop if they are cross-pollinated with other trees. In June or July, when fruits are about half-grown, thin them out to prevent the tree from becoming overloaded.

Pruning and training
Never prune in winter—the risk of silver leaf disease is too high. Prune young trees in spring, once growth has started. Established trees should be pruned only to remove damaged, diseased, or overcrowded branches, or maintain the shape of trained trees.

Harvesting
Pick dessert plums when they are as ripe as possible; they should pull away easily. Pick cooking types when they are not quite so ripe.

Troubleshooting
■ PESTS aphids, birds, caterpillars, plum fruit moth, wasps.
■ DISEASES bacterial canker, brown rot, silver leaf.

(clockwise, from top left) **'Reine Claude de Bavay'** is a sweet late-cropping greengage of French origin. **'Giant Prune'** plums are large and sweet. **'Warwickshire Drooper'** makes an attractive tree with a weeping habit. **'Laxton's Cropper'** is a century-old, purple-blue heritage variety.

WHICH PLUMS TO GROW
Dessert plums
■ 'Cambridge Gage'
■ 'Opal'
■ 'Oullins Golden Gage'
■ 'Victoria'

Culinary plums
■ 'Marjorie's Seedling'

Damsons
■ 'Farleigh'
■ 'Merryweather'

Cherries

Sweet cherries can be eaten raw, while acid cherries need cooking, and duke cherries are between the two. None are hard to grow, but it is difficult is prevent birds from eating the fruit. In the past, netting tall trees was impractical for gardeners, but dwarfing rootstocks now produce smaller, more manageable trees, ideal for kitchen gardens.

WHICH CHERRIES TO GROW

Sweet cherries
- 'Merton Glory'
- 'Stella'
- 'Sunburst'
- 'Sweetheart'

Acid cherries
- 'Morello'
- 'Nabella'

	spring			summer			autumn			winter		
	E	M	L	E	M	L	E	M	L	E	M	L
plant									■	■	■	■
prune	■	■			■	■	■					
harvest				■	■	■	■					

Where to grow
A warm, sheltered frost-free position; in deep, well-drained, slightly acid soil with a pH of 6.5.

Planting
- WHEN TO PLANT Between November and February while the trees are dormant.
- PLANTING DEPTH To level of soil mark on stem.
- PLANTING DISTANCE Dwarf 8–9 ft (2.5–2.7 m); semivigorous 12–16 ft (3.6–5 m); vigorous 20–23 ft (6–7 m) or more apart.

Tips on growing
Cherries flower early so the blossom is always likely to be at risk from frost. Sweet and some duke cherries need a compatible tree nearby for pollination, but acid cherries can be planted singly.

Pruning and training
Never prune in winter; risk of silver leaf disease or canker is too high. Prune young trees in spring once growth starts, and established trees only if needed in summer. Cut out damaged or diseased wood.

Harvesting
Snip off cherries with their stalks intact; tearing the bark or leaving the stalks in place encourages disease. They are best eaten within a few days.

Troubleshooting
- PESTS cherry blackfly, birds, caterpillars.
- DISEASES bacterial canker, blossom wilt, brown rot, silver leaf.

(below, left to right) **Sweet cherries** need a compatible tree nearby for pollination. **Harvest fruit** with scissors or clippers.

Peaches and nectarines

These crops are grown in exactly the same way. Both are hardy and can survive cold winters, yet are still difficult to grow in cool climates because they flower very early when frosts are rife and before pollinating insects are about. They also need a long, hot summer with plenty of warm sunshine to ripen the fruits.

	spring			summer			autumn			winter		
	E	M	L	E	M	L	E	M	L	E	M	L
plant							■	■	■	■		
prune		■	■	■	■	■	■					
harvest					■	■	■					

Peaches (top) do not need as warm conditions as **nectarines** (bottom) so may be a better bet for growing outdoors.

Where to grow
In a warm, sunny, sheltered position—with as much frost protection as possible—in deep, fertile, slightly acidic soil with a pH of about 6.5.

Planting
■ WHEN TO PLANT Between September and December when trees are dormant; November is best for bare-root trees.
■ PLANTING DEPTH To the level of the soil mark on the stem.
■ PLANTING DISTANCE Bush forms 15–18 ft (4.5–5.5 m) apart; fan-trained trees 12–15 ft (3.5–4.5 m) apart.

Tips on growing
Fan-shaped trees trained against a wall or fence are most likely to succeed in temperate climates. They are easier to protect from frost, rain, and birds. Peaches and nectarines are self-fertile but may still need hand-pollinating (see p.62) because the blossom is so early.

Pruning and training
Never prune in winter: the risk of silver leaf disease or canker is too high. Prune established fans in spring and in late summer or autumn, after harvesting. Thin out fruits to leave one every 6–9 in (15–23 cm).

Harvesting
Fruits are ripe when slightly soft to the touch around the stalk. They should come away easily with a gentle twist.

Troubleshooting
■ PESTS aphids, birds, brown scale, red spider mite, wasps.
■ DISEASES bacterial canker, brown rot, peach leaf curl, silver leaf.

WHICH PEACHES AND NECTARINES TO GROW
Peaches
■ 'Duke of York'
■ 'Peregrine'
■ 'Rochester'
Nectarines
■ 'Lord Napier'

Apricots

These fruit trees are grown in much the same way as peaches and nectarines. They are slightly easier since they are less prone to disease and the fruit ripens more readily, but in cool temperate climates they're still challenging. The start of the year is the most critical time. Apricots may flower even earlier than peaches, so they need to be protected from frost and probably to be hand-pollinated.

	spring			summer			autumn			winter		
	E	M	L	E	M	L	E	M	L	E	M	L
plant									■	■	■	
prune		■	■	■	■	■	■					
harvest					■	■	■					

Where to grow
Apricots like a warm, sunny, sheltered position—with as much frost protection as possible—in deep, reasonably fertile soil that is slightly acid to slightly alkaline, with a pH of 6.5–7.5.

Planting
■ WHEN TO PLANT Between October and December, when trees are dormant; November is best for bare-root trees.
■ PLANTING DEPTH To level of soil mark on stem.
■ PLANTING DISTANCE Bush forms 11–18 ft (3.5–5.5 m); fans 15 ft (4.6 m) apart.

Tips on growing
Fan-train a tree against a wall or fence or grow it as an open-centered bush form. Trees on the semi-dwarfing rootstock 'Pixy' remain manageably small. In February or March, apply some fertilizer around the tree; mulch with compost. Keep well watered.

Pruning and training
Never prune in winter; the risk of silver leaf disease or canker is too high. Prune established fans in spring and again in late summer or autumn after fruit harvesting. Prune bush trees only if necessary.

Harvesting
Fruits are ripe when they are slightly soft, deeply colored, and pull away easily without bruising.

Troubleshooting
■ PESTS aphids, birds, brown scale, red spider mite.
■ DISEASES apricot dieback (cut out all infected wood), bacterial canker, silver leaf.

WHICH APRICOTS TO GROW
■ 'Flavorcot'
■ 'Moorpark'
■ 'New Large Early'
■ 'Tomcot'

A good crop can be achieved in cool climates if you protect outdoor plants from frost with fleece. Once flowers open, roll up the fleece during the day to allow in pollinating insects.

Figs

Figs are not hard to grow, but outdoors fruit will ripen only if you can offer the plants a warm, sheltered, relatively frost-free site, such as the south-facing side of a shed. They also need long, hot summers. In other words, they need similar conditions to those in the Mediterranean, where they thrive. Figs may be grown under cover, but beware—unless they're in containers they can grow very large.

	spring			summer			autumn			winter		
	E	M	L	E	M	L	E	M	L	E	M	L
plant	■								■	■	■	■
prune		■		■	■							
harvest						■	■					

Where to grow
Figs require a warm, sunny, sheltered position, ideally frost-free, in any well-drained soil. To control the size of the tree, restrict its roots within a lined planting pit or in a container.

Planting
- WHEN TO PLANT Between November and March; ideally, in March.
- PLANTING DEPTH To level of soil mark on stem.
- PLANTING DISTANCE 12–16 ft (4–5 m) apart.

Tips on growing
In cool regions, figs produced in spring won't ripen by autumn. In early November, remove and discard any that have reached cherry size (see p.184). Leave the smaller, pea-sized, baby figs nearer the stem tips to overwinter and ripen next summer.

Pruning and training
In April, prune out damaged, diseased, and over-long branches, as well as a proportion of the older wood. In June or July, cut new growth back to four or five leaves to encourage new, embryo fruits to form so they can overwinter and crop next year.

Harvesting
Pick figs when fully colored and slightly soft. A bead of nectar may appear in the open eye at the base of the fig when it is perfectly ripe.

Troubleshooting
- PESTS birds.
- DISEASES coral spot.

For ripe figs in temperate climates, protect the embryonic fruits over winter. Trees trained against the side of sheds can be covered with fleece or straw under netting, and small trees in containers can be moved under cover.

WHICH FIGS TO GROW
- 'Brown Turkey'
- 'Brunswick'
- 'White Marseilles'

Strawberries

Most strawberries produce a single crop each year between late May and the end of July, depending on whether they are early, late, or midseason varieties. So-called perpetual varieties crop more than once and keep on producing right into October—or at least until the first frosts. Although strawberries are perennials, they are not everlasting; replace them after three or four years.

	spring			summer			autumn			winter		
	E	M	L	E	M	L	E	M	L	E	M	L
Summer strawberries												
plant	■	■	■	■	■	■	■	■				
harvest					■	■	■					
Perpetual strawberries												
plant	■	■	■	■	■	■	■	■				
harvest					■	■	■	■	■			

WHICH STRAWBERRIES TO GROW

Summer-fruiting
- ■ 'Cambridge Favorite'
- ■ 'Honeoye'
- ■ 'Mae'
- ■ 'Florence'

Perpetual
- ■ 'Flamenco'
- ■ 'Mara des Bois'
- ■ 'Aromel'

ALPINE STRAWBERRIES

These miniature versions of regular strawberries are easy to grow. Buy them as small container plants or raise them from certified virus-free seed. Sow the seed indoors or under cover in early spring and plant out in May. You may get a few berries in the first year, but a lot more in the second. Established plants will readily spread and are often used as ground cover in potager gardens.

Alpine strawberries are tiny—not much larger than peas. They fruit throughout the summer and, although not as sweet as cultivated strawberries, they are fragrant and intensely flavored, and much prized.

Where to grow

Strawberries grow best in full sun, on light, well-drained, fertile soil with a slightly acid pH of 6–6.5. They can be grown through plastic sheet mulches that are stretched over mounded or raised beds.

Planting

- ■ WHEN TO PLANT Pot-grown and bare-root runners any time between March and October, although July–September is best. Do not allow March–June plantings to crop in the year of planting; allow October plantings to fruit only lightly in the following year. Cold-stored runners that are planted March–July should crop within two months.
- ■ PLANTING DEPTH Keep the plant crown level with or just above the surface of the soil.
- ■ PLANTING DISTANCE 18 in (45 cm) apart.
- ■ ROW SPACING 3 ft (1 m) apart.

Tips on growing

Plant strawberries where they haven't been grown for at least three years and choose a fresh site to grow them after three seasons.

Water strawberries regularly, especially just after planting and while the berries are developing, but be careful not to splash the fruits or to let plants get

waterlogged. Snip off any runners that you don't want to use for the propagation of new plants. Cover the plants with fine netting to keep off pigeons and other birds.

In spring, and again after cropping, remove any dead, diseased, or damaged leaves and runners from established plants.

Harvesting
Pick the berries when they become dark-colored and completely ripe, and before they start to soften. Choose a warm day for the juiciest fruits. Eat them as soon as possible after picking; strawberries do not freeze well.

Troubleshooting
■ PESTS aphids, beetles, birds, slugs and snails.
■ DISEASES botrytis, powdery mildew, viruses.

(above and below) **A straw mulch** will prevent the fruits from becoming muddy, as well as keeping down weeds and protecting the fruits from slugs. You could also use special strawberry mats or plastic and fabric sheet mulches.

Raspberries

Raspberries fall into one of two categories: summer-fruiting and autumn-fruiting. The former are truly seductive—who can resist the first berries of summer? But their season is very short and since birds are equally anxious to get at them, you'll have to grow them under nets or in a cage. However, fruits borne in autumn last for several months and, surprisingly, birds seem to lose interest in them.

	spring			summer			autumn			winter		
	E	M	L	E	M	L	E	M	L	E	M	L
summer raspberries												
plant		■							■	■	■	■
prune					■	■						■
harvest					■	■						
autumn raspberries												
plant		■							■	■	■	■
prune		■										■
harvest						■	■	■	■			

Raspberries can be picked for almost six months of the year, if you grow both summer-fruiting (left) and autumn-fruiting (right) varieties.

WHICH RASPBERRIES TO GROW

Summer-fruiting	**Autumn-fruiting**
■ 'Glen Ample'	■ 'Autumn Bliss'
■ 'Tulameen'	■ 'Joan J'

Where to grow

Raspberries prefer a sheltered site with fertile, slightly acid, well-drained soil that won't become waterlogged.

Planting

■ WHEN TO PLANT Bare-root canes between November and March—although not if the ground is frozen.
■ PLANTING DEPTH 2–3 in (5–8 cm) deep.
■ PLANTING DISTANCE 14–18 in (35–45 cm) apart.
■ ROW SPACING 4–6 ft (1.2–2 m) apart.

Tips on growing

Tie canes into a simple, sturdy, post-and-wire fence for support. Mulch in spring to keep down weeds and cover with fine-mesh nets to protect fruit against birds.

Pruning and training

■ SUMMER-FRUITING PLANTS Cut all canes that bore fruit this year down to the ground as soon as harvesting has finished. Tie in new canes—those that didn't bear fruit. In the following February, trim the tops of the canes to just above a bud, if necessary.
■ AUTUMN-FRUITING PLANTS Cut all last year's canes down to the ground in February or March. New canes will grow up and bear fruit in the autumn.

Harvesting

Pick summer-fruiting raspberries in July and August, and autumn-fruiting ones from August until the first frosts.

Troubleshooting

■ PESTS aphids, birds, leaf and bud mite, raspberry beetle.
■ DISEASES cane blight, cane spot, fungal leaf spot, raspberry spur blight, viruses.

Blackberries and hybrid berries

Wild blackberries (or brambles) are not quite the same thing as cultivated varieties. Commercial cultivars are specially bred to produce reliably large, sweet fruits. Some canes are even thornless. Hybrid berries are usually crossbred from blackberries and raspberries, and they include tayberries, boysenberries, loganberries, and many more.

	spring			summer			autumn			winter		
	E	M	L	E	M	L	E	M	L	E	M	L
plant	■								■	■		
train				■	■	■	■	■	■			
prune							■	■	■			
harvest				■	■	■						

WHICH BLACKBERRIES TO GROW

- 'Black Butte'
- 'Loch Tay'
- 'Oregon Thornless'
- 'Sylvan'

Where to grow

Blackberries are not fussy about soil but they do require plenty of space. Hybrid berries are more particular and need full sun to thrive.

Planting

- WHEN TO PLANT Bare-root canes in November or December; otherwise, wait until March.
- PLANTING DEPTH Top of rootball 3 in (8 cm) deep.
- PLANTING DISTANCE 8–12 ft (2.5–4 m) apart.

Tips on growing

Tie canes into a simple, sturdy, post-and-wire fence to keep them tidy. Weed regularly and mulch in spring.

Pruning and training

Fruit forms on one-year-old canes, so those that grew last year will fruit this year. Train any new canes upward or tie them to one side to keep them separate. In the autumn, cut out all the old canes that have borne fruit and retrain the new ones into place in preparation for the following year.

Harvesting

Depending on the variety, pick berries on a dry day when they are ripe, plump, and juicy.

Troubleshooting

Potentially, these plants could suffer from the same pests and diseases as raspberries, although problems are rare.

Hybrid berries such as tayberries (above) tend to look more like raspberries in color than blackberries (top). Thankfully, some are thornless and are not as rampant as blackberries.

Gooseberries

It's sometimes said that anyone can grow gooseberries. This is partly true in that they will put up with indifferent soils and a certain amount of neglect, but they won't produce a bumper harvest unless you look after them. Weed, water, mulch, feed, prune, and net them—and they'll repay your efforts. Dessert varieties tend to be larger and sweeter and when fully ripe can be eaten fresh.

	spring			summer			autumn			winter		
	E	M	L	E	M	L	E	M	L	E	M	L
plant	■							■	■	■	■	■
winter-prune	■								■	■	■	■
summer-prune				■	■							
harvest				■	■							

Where to grow
In a sheltered position on fertile, well-drained soil. Gooseberries will tolerate partial shade.

Planting
■ WHEN TO PLANT Plant bare-root bushes between October and March and container-grown plants at any suitable time.

■ PLANTING DEPTH To level of soil mark on stem.
■ PLANTING DISTANCE Single bushes 4–5 ft (1.2–1.5 m) apart; cordons 12–18 in (30–45 cm) apart.
■ ROW SPACING 5 ft (1.5 m) apart.

Tips on growing
Mulch in spring to keep down weeds, and water regularly as soon as the berries start to swell. Cover with nets to protect against birds.

Pruning and training
In winter, cut out any old or diseased wood and prune back new growth by about half. Keep the center open and airy. Cut sideshoots back to 2–3 in (5–8 cm). In summer, prune new sideshoots to leave about five leaves.

Harvesting
Pick berries when they are plump and slightly soft.

Troubleshooting
■ PESTS aphids, birds, capsid bug, caterpillars, gooseberry sawfly.
■ DISEASES American gooseberry mildew, botrytis, fungal leaf spot.

(left) **Pick fruits** with a bit of stalk attached; otherwise, the skins of the berries may tear.

(opposite) **Berries are borne** on one-year-old and older wood so cutting back sideshoots regularly encourages fruiting spurs.

WHICH GOOSEBERRIES TO GROW
■ 'Hinnonmaki Red'   ■ 'Langley Gage'
■ 'Invicta'   ■ 'Pax'

Black currants

Black currants are generally easy to grow, although they need generous feeding and careful pruning to get a good crop. Modern 'Ben' varieties, bred in Scotland, flower later and so are less susceptible to frost damage. Their trusses or "strigs" of berries also are more likely to ripen all at once, making picking easier.

	spring			summer			autumn			winter		
	E	M	L	E	M	L	E	M	L	E	M	L
plant	■							■	■	■	■	■
winter-prune	■								■	■	■	■
summer-prune					■							
harvest					■	■						

Where to grow
Black currants like a sheltered site in full sun or partial shade with rich, fertile, well-drained soil.

Planting
■ WHEN TO PLANT Plant bare-root bushes that are certified disease-free between October and March, and container-grown plants at any suitable time.
■ PLANTING DEPTH 2 in (5 cm) deeper than the level of the soil mark on the stem.
■ PLANTING DISTANCE 5 ft (1.5 m) apart.
■ ROW SPACING 5 ft (1.5 m) apart.

Tips on growing
Apply general fertilizer in February; mulch with well-rotted compost or manure in March. Net to protect against birds.

Pruning and training
Prune new, bare-root bushes to 2 in (5 cm) above the ground immediately after planting. After two years, in winter, remove up to one-third of the oldest stems; their almost black bark looks different from new pale shoots.

Harvesting
Snip off entire strigs when berries are plump and shiny.

Troubleshooting
■ PESTS aphids, big bud mite, birds, capsid bug, caterpillars, gall midge (tiny white maggots that feed on leaves).
■ DISEASES American gooseberry mildew, botrytis, fungal leaf spot, reversion.

Fruits ripen on older varieties in sequence, so you need to pick ripe berries individually from strigs. You can snip off entire strigs of ripe berries on 'Ben' varieties.

WHICH BLACK CURRANTS TO GROW
■ 'Ben Connan'
■ 'Ben Lomond'
■ 'Ben Sarek'

Red currants and white currants

Red and white currants are, unsurprisingly, very closely related. If there's a difference, it's that white currants are perhaps a little sweeter and red currants are more often used for cooking and for jams and jellies. What is odd is that they are both grown like gooseberries rather than black currants.

Red currants (top) are ready to pick when plump and bright scarlet. **White currants** (above) make delicious jellies and are good mixed with red varieties in desserts.

	spring			summer			autumn			winter		
	E	M	L	E	M	L	E	M	L	E	M	L
plant	■								■	■	■	■
winter-prune									■	■	■	■
summer-prune				■	■							
harvest					■	■							

Where to grow
These currants grow on almost any well-drained soil. They tolerate partial shade, but do not like being waterlogged.

Planting
■ WHEN TO PLANT Bare-root bushes are planted between October and March; container-grown plants can be planted at any time, if conditions are suitable.
■ PLANTING DEPTH To the level of the soil mark on stem.
■ PLANTING DISTANCE Single bushes 4–5 ft (1.2–1.5 m) apart; cordons 12–18 in (30–45 cm) apart.
■ ROW SPACING 5 ft (1.5 m) apart.

Tips on growing
Mulch in spring to keep down weeds and water regularly as soon as the berries start to swell. Cover with nets to protect against birds.

Pruning and training
Grow as stand-alone bushes or in rows as cordons. Prune and train in the same way as gooseberries (see p.306), cutting out old growth and pruning new growth in winter.

Harvesting
Snip off entire strigs, or trusses, when the berries are plump, but before they go soft.

Troubleshooting
■ PESTS aphids, birds, capsid bug, caterpillars, gooseberry sawfly.
■ DISEASES botrytis, coral spot, fungal leaf spot.

WHICH CURRANTS TO GROW

Red currants
■ 'Jonkheer van Tets'
■ 'Red Lake'
■ 'Redstart'
■ 'Stanza'

White currants
■ 'Blanka'
■ 'White Versailles'

Blueberries

The bottom line is that blueberries will grow only in acid soils. But all is not lost if your soil is alkaline with a high pH since you can grow the plants in large tubs and containers of specialized, ericaceous (lime-free) compost. Another option is to put them in raised beds with lots of acidic organic material, such as composted sawdust, pine bark, and pine-needle leafmold worked into the soil.

The cultivated blueberry is the American highbush blueberry—a taller cousin of the bilberry, a low plant that grows wild on mountain slopes and in woodlands.

WHICH BLUEBERRIES TO GROW
- 'Bluecrop'
- 'Earliblue'
- 'Herbert'
- 'Patriot'

	spring			summer			autumn			winter		
	E	M	L	E	M	L	E	M	L	E	M	L
plant	■								■	■	■	■
trim	■									■	■	■
harvest						■	■	■				

Where to grow
Blueberries thrive in a sheltered site in sun or partial shade and need very acid soil with a pH of 4–5.5.

Planting
- WHEN TO PLANT Between November and March unless the ground is frozen.
- PLANTING DEPTH To level of soil mark on stem.
- PLANTING DISTANCE 5 ft (1.5 m) apart.

Tips on growing
A single bush will produce some fruit, but two or three other blueberry varieties planted close by will cross-pollinate and yield a bigger crop. Feed with specialized ericaceous fertilizer. If your tap water is "hard" (alkaline), use rainwater whenever possible. Cover with nets to protect the fruit from birds.

Pruning and training
In winter, cut out any diseased, damaged, or any low-lying stems, as well as a few of the older or unproductive branches.

Harvesting
Pick berries singly when they're plump, slightly soft, have a distinct surface bloom, and pull away easily.

Troubleshooting
- PESTS birds.
- DISEASES botrytis (occasionally).

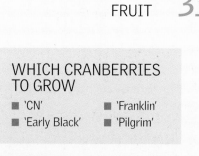

Cranberries should only be watered with rainwater—water from the faucet is likely to have too much lime in it.

Cranberries

Like blueberries, cranberries need acid soils with a low pH and may be best grown in containers or raised beds. In North America, cranberries are harvested commercially by flooding entire fields; the berries float and are collected by machine—not a method recommended for the average kitchen gardener.

	spring			summer			autumn			winter		
	E	M	L	E	M	L	E	M	L	E	M	L
plant	■	■	■				■	■	■			
trim	■								■			
harvest							■	■	■			

Where to grow
A damp, boggy site or in containers kept very well watered, and very acid soil, with a pH of 4–5.5.

Planting
- WHEN TO PLANT Anytime, but ideally in spring or autumn.
- PLANTING DEPTH To level of soil mark on stem.
- PLANTING DISTANCE 2 ft (60 cm) apart or in pots with a minimum diameter of 18 in (45 cm).

Tips on growing
Cranberries are low-growing, straggly, spreading evergreens. They need a lot of water—almost boggy conditions, in fact. If you grow them in containers, stand the pots in trays that are continually topped up with rainwater.

Pruning and training
All that's needed is a trim to keep them tidy in spring and autumn.

Harvesting
Pick the berries from September onward; they should last on the bush until you need them.

Troubleshooting
Problems are very rare.

LINGONBERRIES
Like cranberries, lingonberries grow on low, spreading bushes that need acid soil. The bright red berries, which ripen in summer and early autumn, are rich in vitamins and have antioxidant properties. However, they are far too sharp-tasting to be eaten raw and are best cooked or made into jams and jellies.

Melons

In cool regions, growing melons is a challenge. In these areas they are best grown in a greenhouse or polytunnel, but if you start them off indoors and plant them outside in June under cloches or in a cold frame, and if it's a hot summer, they may well ripen. Otherwise, try cantaloupes, which are more reliable.

	spring			summer			autumn			winter		
	E	M	L	E	M	L	E	M	L	E	M	L
sow indoors	■											
sow under cover		■										
plant outdoors			■									
harvest				■	■	■	■					

WHICH MELONS TO GROW

- ■ 'Edonis'
- ■ 'Galia'
- ■ 'Ogen'
- ■ 'Sweetheart'

Harvest ripe melons by cutting through the stalks with clippers or sturdy scissors. Support fruits on climbing plants— if they fall and get bruised, they won't keep for long.

Where to grow
Melons outdoors need a very warm, sunny, sheltered site, in soil that has had lots of rich, well-rotted organic material dug into it.

Sowing and planting
■ WHEN TO SOW Indoors in April at a minimum temperature of 61°F (16°C). Grow on seedlings at 70°F (21°C) or above. Harden them off carefully and plant out in June, under cover if necessary.
■ SOWING DEPTH ½ in (1 cm).
■ PLANTING DISTANCE 3 ft (1 m) apart.
■ ROW SPACING 3 ft (1 m) apart.

Tips on growing
Hand-pollinate the flowers if you are growing the plants under cover. Water them regularly and feed with a liquid fertilizer. Thin the melon fruitlets to no more than four per plant, and pinch out the growing tips on the stems to leave two or three leaves beyond each fruit.

Pruning and training
Support climbing plants with canes, wires, or nets. Pinch out the growing point at the fifth leaf to encourage side shoots. Lift melons that are growing in cold frames off the ground.

Harvesting
Check the ripening fruits regularly for "perfect" ripeness. A cracked stalk, slight softness at one end, and a wonderful scent are the tell-tale clues.

Troubleshooting
■ PESTS aphids, red spider mite, slugs and snails, whitefly.
■ DISEASES cucumber mosaic virus, downy mildew, foot and root rots, powdery mildew.

Cape gooseberry is related to the ornamental perennial, Chinese lantern, but don't confuse the two—the ornamental fruits are not edible.

Cape gooseberries

Also known as physalis (from their botanical name), cape gooseberries are small, round, orange fruits that grow inside a papery shell, or husk. The plant is originally from South America and needs a warm climate. But if you have successfully grown tomatoes outdoors, it is worth a try. You will get a more reliable result under cover, but take note that the bushes can grow large.

	spring			summer			autumn			winter		
	E	M	L	E	M	L	E	M	L	E	M	L
sow indoors	■											
transplant under cover		■	■									
plant out			■	■								
harvest							■	■				

Where to grow
Cape gooseberries prefer fertile, well-drained soil, in a warm, sunny, sheltered position.

Sowing and planting
■ WHEN TO SOW Indoors in March, in a heated propagator if necessary to maintain a minimum temperature of about 65°F (18°C). Harden off and plant out from late April, initially under cover.
■ SOWING DEPTH ¼ in (½ cm) deep.
■ PLANTING DISTANCE 30 in (75 cm) apart.
■ ROW SPACING 3–4 ft (1–1.2m) apart.

Tips on growing
Use stakes or canes to support the plants. Pinch out the growing tips to encourage production of flowers. Water regularly (but not over-generously) and feed with tomato fertilizer when fruits begin to form.

Harvesting
Pick the berries in September and October, when the husks have dried and turned brown and the fruits are bright orange. They get sweeter as they ripen, but still have a sharp tang. Plants won't survive the winter, so after harvesting cut down the top-growth and compost it. Don't grow cape gooseberries in the same place the following year.

Troubleshooting
■ PESTS outdoors: aphids; under cover: aphids, whitefly.

Grapes

The key to growing grapes outdoors on an kitchen garden is to choose the right varieties. Unless you have a polytunnel or greenhouse many cultivars will be disappointing. There are, however, plenty of modern varieties that are appropriate for cool, temperate regions; in a good summer, they can produce grapes suitable for both eating and wine-making.

	spring			summer			autumn			winter		
	E	M	L	E	M	L	E	M	L	E	M	L
plant	■	■						■	■			■
winter-prune									■	■	■	
summer-prune			■	■	■							
harvest							■	■				

Where to grow
On a warm, sunny, sheltered site in well-drained soil that has had some organic material dug into it.

Planting
- WHEN TO PLANT In October or November or from February to April, but the best time is March.
- PLANTING DEPTH To level of soil mark on stem.
- PLANTING DISTANCE 3–5 ft (1–1.5 m) apart.
- ROW SPACING 6 ft (2 m) apart.

Tips on growing
A support system is essential: provide a pergola, trellis, or arch for vines that will be allowed to climb somewhat informally; use stakes and horizontal wires for vines grown as cordons or trained with the Guyot system (often employed in vineyards).

Pruning and training
Major pruning is done in winter when the vines are dormant. Vines fruit on the current season's growth, so wood that has just borne fruit is pruned back each winter to make way for new growth. In summer, new lateral shoots are tied in, cut back, and any sideshoots on them are pinched back to one leaf.

Harvesting
Leave grapes on the vine for as long as possible—the riper they are, the sweeter they'll be.

Troubleshooting
- PESTS birds, vine weevil, wasps.
- DISEASES botrytis, downy mildew, powdery mildew.

(far left) **Tie-in the main stem** to the support as it grows,.

(left) **Pinch out any sideshoots** that form on new lateral shoots in summer, to leave one leaf.

WHICH GRAPES TO GROW
- 'Boskoop Glory'
- 'Brant'
- 'Müller-Thurgau'
- 'Regent'
- 'Siegerrebe'

(opposite) **Harvest grapes** when the skins are almost translucent. If you want to preserve the bloom, don't touch the fruit and sever the bunch along with a short "handle" of stem.

Troubleshooter

It's an unfortunate fact that most kitchen gardens are a battleground. The healthier your plants and the more abundant your crops, the more they will prove as irresistible to hungry birds, animals, and insects as they are to you. Inevitably, much of your time and effort will therefore be spent in tirelessly defending your plants against attack.

That's not all. Even if you do succeed in repelling pests and parasites, your fruit and vegetables are also vulnerable to a daunting array of fungal diseases, bacterial infections, viruses, and nutritional disorders. The plants can never be immune to them all, of course, but it pays to become familiar with the various early warning signs, to understand what might be wrong, and to learn how to prevent and to treat the most damaging diseases and disorders.

Growing healthy fruit and vegetables entails vigilance in providing them with the optimum conditions. Lack of water at an early stage followed by a sudden growth spurt has caused the skin on this pear to split and dry out.

What's wrong?

Plant problems fall into three categories. The first is pests and parasites: any animals, birds, or insects that actively damage plants. The second is diseases: pathological conditions caused by microorganisms such as fungi, viruses, or bacteria. And the third is cultural disorders, usually the effect of nutritional deficiencies. Learning to distinguish and diagnose the problem is the first step toward treating it—or at least preventing its reoccurrence.

Early warning signs

Plants that are in distress have only a limited number of ways of displaying the fact, so the visible symptoms often look very similar, whether the plants are under attack by pests or suffering from a disease or disorder. Don't rush into making a diagnosis. And, most importantly, don't resort to chemicals unless you're sure you have no other alternative.

Poor growing conditions

Lack of water, unusually high or low temperatures, exposure to strong winds, insufficient light, damp, waterlogged soil, and mineral deficiencies are common causes of plant disorders. They all produce symptoms that may look like the result of disease, but aren't. The good news is that usually they can be fairly easily resolved. The bad news is that, if allowed to persist, they will weaken plants' natural defenses and make them prone to more serious problems.

Controlling pests

Sometimes it's a fine line between friend and foe. Birds can be valuable allies; they keep down the insect population by eating grubs and larvae.

But they can be one of your worst enemies too: pigeons will strip brassicas, fruit bushes, and strawberry beds given half a chance. Insects are the same. Some are positively beneficial—bees, hoverflies, lacewings, and ladybugs, for example. Others are extremely destructive, tunneling into crops and feeding voraciously on plant tissue and on ripening fruit.

Interestingly, it is possible to use insect against insect. Biological controls involve deliberately introducing predatory mites or parasitic wasps to kill specific pests such as whitefly or red spider mites. The same can be done with nematodes (microscopic worms), which target slugs, and with bacteria that infect certain caterpillars.

Controlling disease
Hygiene is the key here. It's true that many plant diseases are transmitted in the air, by rainwater splash, and by animals and insects, but they are often spread by humans too. They travel on the soles of boots and on tools, pots, seed trays, and other pieces of equipment that

have not been properly cleaned. Clearing away plant debris and destroying any diseased material, rather than composting it, will also help prevent the spread of infection.

Pesticides and fungicides
The use of these controls is a controversial issue. Organic gardeners employ them as a last resort, and then only those derived from natural sources—pyrethrum and insecticidal soaps to control insects, and sulfur or potassium bicarbonate as fungicides, for example. Synthetic, nonorganic products are available and are strictly regulated. Often they are selective rather than wide-ranging: they target specific species and do not harm others. However, only you can decide if you wish to use them on crops that you grow and eat.

(far left to right) **Underwatering** makes plants like spinach wilt and starve, since they can't absorb soil nutrients. **Overwatering** results in plants drowning: the roots can't breathe and rot, leaves wilt, and fruits split. **Frost damage** is another cause of plants wilting, as seen in these runner beans: stem tips, buds, and leaves look scorched and die back. **Bolting** or running to seed of lettuces and other vegetables often occurs in hot, dry conditions.

Common plant diseases

1 Powdery mildew
A fungal disease that produces a white powdery growth on foliage, shown here on the leaves of an apple. See p.327.

2 Blossom end rot
Lack of water makes tomatoes unable to absorb sufficient calcium from the soil. This in turn causes rot to set in at the bottom or flowering end of the fruits. See p.323.

3 Potato blight
This serious fungal disease also afflicts tomatoes. It takes hold and spreads rapidly in warm, wet conditions. See p.326.

4 Botrytis (gray mold)
An off-white mold triggered by this common fungal infection grows on a wide variety of vegetables and fruits. It is shown here on grapes. See p.323.

5 Brown rot
Tree fruits such as apples (shown here), pears, and plums develop brown patches on which paler fungal spots or pustules appear. The rot can spread to the whole crop. See p.323.

6 Peach leaf curl
The first leaves to open on peaches and nectarines are puckered and distorted. Leaves that develop later may escape unaffected. See p.326.

7 Clubroot
A very serious fungal disease, it can attack all brassicas, causing swollen, distorted roots. Once present in the soil, it may persist for years. See p.324.

8 Scab
Dark brown or black fungal patches appear on the skin of pears (shown here) or apples. Fruit may split and rot. See p.327.

3

7

8

1

12

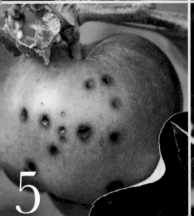

5

16

9 Downy mildew
Thriving in damp, humid conditions, this fungal disease attacks many vegetables, including cabbages and other brassicas. See p.324.

10 Onion white rot
White, fluffy mold and blue-black fungal growths build up on the base of onion, shallot, and garlic bulbs. See p.326.

11 Rust
Brightly colored orange or brown patches containing rustlike fungal spores appear on leaves. It is shown here on leeks. See p.327.

12 Canker
Fungal cankers cause the bark on fruit trees to split, shrink back, and inhibit further new growth. See p.323.

13 Tomato blight
Leaves curl up, wither, and die, and fruits turn brown and rot. The culprit is the same fungus as the one that causes potato blight. See p.328.

14 Potato common scab
Brown corky patches form on the skins of potatoes. The flesh beneath may also be discolored. The cause is a bacteria in the soil. See p.326.

15 Bitter pit
Dark, sunken spots appear on the skin of apples, owing to the tree's inability to absorb enough calcium from the soil, perhaps because it is too dry. See p.322.

16 American gooseberry mildew
White, powdery patches appear on the leaves and then fruits turn brown and leathery. See p.322.

A–Z of plant diseases

Fungi, viruses, and bacteria are responsible for almost all plant diseases. In each case, the plant is invaded by microorganisms that disrupt or interfere with its normal, healthy growth. Symptoms may be minor and treatable, or so severe that the plant dies. In addition, plants may suffer from nutritional disorders caused by a lack of the essential minerals that they need in order to thrive (see pp.329–31). Confusingly, such disorders can look very like diseases.

Apple and pear canker
See Canker (opposite).

Apple scab
See Scab (p.327).

American gooseberry mildew
The mildew is actually caused by a fungus that thrives in still, stale air. The disorder tends to be worse on fruit bushes that have been fed with too much nitrogenous fertilizer.
■ **Crops affected** Black currants, gooseberries.
■ **Symptoms** Initially, powdery, white patches appear on leaves, branches, and fruits. New shoots may become misshapen and fail to grow properly. Eventually, the skins of the fruits may turn brown and leathery and, although the mildew can be cleaned off and the fruits eaten, they are frankly less than appetizing.
■ **Action** Cut out and destroy affected areas. Prune to open up the centers of bushes, in order to allow air to circulate more freely. If necessary, spray with a fungicide. In future, grow resistant varieties and use a general-purpose, rather than a high-nitrogen, fertilizer.

Bacterial canker
See Canker (opposite).

Bacterial leaf spot
The leaf tissue is attacked by bacteria, which often enter through damaged areas. They spread by means of rain, or water from a watering can or hose, splashing from one leaf to the next. See also Fungal leaf spot (p.325).
■ **Crops affected** Various—particularly cabbages and other brassicas, and cucumbers.
■ **Symptoms** Leaves develop gray or brown spots or patches of dead leaf tissue, often with bright yellow "haloes" around them. As these spread, the leaves die.
■ **Action** If you catch it early, the disease is unlikely to be fatal. Remove and destroy all infected leaves, and water the soil around the plant, rather than its foliage.

Bacterial soft rot
Soft rots may be caused by a variety of different bacteria, although the one that is also responsible for potato black leg (see p.326) is among the most common. Bacteria usually attack through wounds and are spread by insects or contaminated tools.
■ **Crops affected** Brassicas (particularly rutabagas and turnips), celery, zucchini, lettuces, the onion family, parsnips, potatoes, squashes, tomatoes.
■ **Symptoms** Beneath the skin, brown, slimy rots develop and can spread rapidly. They may ooze out of the plant, releasing an extremely unpleasant smell.
■ **Action** There is no cure. Remove and destroy all infected material. Rotate crops the next year and clean tools carefully.

Bitter pit
This is a calcium-deficiency disorder similar to blossom end rot (see opposite). It occurs when apple trees—particularly large, heavy-cropping varieties—are unable to absorb sufficient calcium from the soil, often because the soil is too dry. As a result, clusters of cells in the fruits die and rot.
■ **Crops affected** Apples.
■ **Symptoms** Small, round, dark spots or sunken pits appear on the skin of apples, and sometimes in the flesh too. The fruits may taste slightly bitter.
■ **Action** Mulch around trees and, if needed, water to keep soil moist. Use a general-purpose, not high-nitrogen, fertilizer.

Black currant reversion virus
See Reversion (p.327).

Blight
See Potato blight (p.326), Tomato blight (p.328).

Blossom end rot
Like bitter pit in apples (see opposite), blossom end rot is a calcium-deficiency disorder. It is caused by the soil drying out to such an extent that roots are no longer able to take up sufficient essential calcium from the soil, with the result that plant cells turn brown and die. Unsurprisingly, the problem is worse in acid soils that contain low levels of calcium. See also Calcium deficiency (p.329).
■ **Crops affected** Peppers, tomatoes.
■ **Symptoms** The skin at the base of the tomato or the pepper sinks, turns leathery, and goes dark brown or black. The rot then spreads through the fruit.
■ **Action** Remove and destroy all damaged fruits immediately, to avoid the rot affecting other ones. Begin watering the plant more often and more regularly.

Blossom wilt
This disease is caused by the same fungus that is responsible for brown rot (see below) in plums and is closely related to the one that causes brown rot in apples.
■ **Crops affected** Apples, apricots, cherries, peaches, pears, plums.
■ **Symptoms** New blossom turns brown, withers, and dies. So too do new leaves.
■ **Action** Remove and destroy infected blossom before the fungus spreads to leaves and stems.

Botrytis
Also known as gray mold, *Botrytis cinerea* is a fungus. The spores are spread in the air or by rain or water splash, and usually get into plants through wounds or damaged areas. Infections are worse in wet summers.
■ **Crops affected** A wide range of vegetables, particularly soft-leaved ones such as zucchini, lettuces, peas and beans, and tomatoes. Fruits worst affected include apples, blackberries, figs, gooseberries, grapes, raspberries, and strawberries.
■ **Symptoms** As its common name suggests, fluffy, off-white, gray, or grayish brown mold appears on the stems, leaves, fruits, and flowers. On vegetables such as tomatoes, brown patches may turn into rot. Plants with badly infected stems may yellow, wilt, and die.
■ **Action** Remove and destroy any affected parts of the plant. Don't leave any infected plant material lying around because the spores will survive if they transfer to the soil. Ensure surviving plants have sufficient space for air to circulate freely around them.

Brown rot
This particular form of rot is caused by a fungus. The spores often find their way into fruits through damaged areas in the skins, where birds and insects have been feeding. Spores can also be spread by rainwater.
■ **Crops affected** Apples, pears, plums, and other tree fruits.

■ **Symptoms** Initially, the fruit develops soft brown rotten patches. As these spread, white crusty spots or pustules appear, often in circular patterns. The fruit eventually shrivels up and either falls to the ground or remains on the tree in a desiccated state.
■ **Action** Pick off and destroy all infected fruit, including windfalls. Prune out any stems or branches that have become infected; otherwise, the fungus will be able to overwinter and survive from one year to the next.

Cane blight
See Raspberry cane blight (p.327).

Cane spot
See Raspberry cane spot (p.327).

Canker
Cankers may be either bacterial or fungal, and different types affect different tree fruits. Most enter through wounds in leaves, stems, or branches and become very destructive if not treated.
■ **Crops affected** Tree fruits.
■ **Symptoms** Bacterial canker causes dark spots in leaves that then turn into holes. The leaves subsequently yellow, wither, and die. Buds do not open, and areas of bark flatten and then become sunken and may ooze resin. Fungal canker causes areas of bark to shrink and crack. The infected site swells up, growth ceases above it, and fruit may rot.
■ **Action** Prune out and destroy all infected wood, removing whole branches if necessary and treating the cuts with special wound paint. Spray with copper-based fungicide such as Bordeaux mixture.

Chocolate spot

A fungus that targets broad beans, at best reducing crops and at worst killing the plants. It thrives in damp, humid weather.

- **Crops affected** Broad beans.
- **Symptoms** Chocolate-brown spots on the stems, leaves, and pods gradually darkening and spreading.
- **Action** Weed thoroughly and space plants far enough apart to allow air to circulate freely. If winters are usually wet, sow in spring rather than in autumn.

Clubroot

This fungus can attack all crops in the brassica family. It is extremely serious, not just because in severe cases it kills the plants, but also because the spores can survive in the soil for up to twenty years. There is no cure.

- **Crops affected** All brassicas, including radishes, rutabagas, and turnips.
- **Symptoms** Plants wilt during the day and grow poorly. Leaves turn pale and may have a pinkish red tinge. Affected roots swell and become distorted as fungal spores build up inside them.
- **Action** Dig up and destroy all diseased plants. Rotate crops (see pp.18–19); avoid waterlogged sites; add lime to the soil if it is acid; and delay planting seedlings until they are large enough for their roots to develop some resistance to infection.

Coral spot

This is a waterborne fungus that grows on woody stems and branches. If it is allowed to spread, it can be lethal to crops.

- **Crops affected** Currants, figs, and other trees and bushes.
- **Symptoms** Pink or orange spots or pustules appear on the bark, often around a wound or ragged pruning cut.
- **Action** Prune out and burn all infected wood.

Cucumber mosaic virus

The virus is transmitted by aphids and can be widespread. In severe cases, it can kill plants.

- **Crops affected** Eggplant, zucchini, cucumbers, gherkins, marrows, pumpkins, squashes.
- **Symptoms** Leaves become misshapen and stunted, and develop yellow mosaic patterning. Flowers may not appear, and even if they do, the ensuing fruits are small, hard, and inedible. Plants may die.
- **Action** There is no cure. Dig up and destroy infected crops. Try growing resistant varieties.

Damping off

The disease is caused by a fungus that lives in the soil. It spreads rapidly in damp, poorly ventilated conditions, and can quickly destroy whole seed trays of young plants.

- **Crops affected** All young seedlings.
- **Symptoms** Roots and the bases of stems darken and rot, causing the seedlings to collapse.
- **Action** Once the disease has taken hold, there is no remedy. Try to avoid it by not sowing seeds too densely, by using fresh potting soil, and by scrupulously cleaning seed trays or pots. Ensure good ventilation and avoid overwatering. Spraying with a copper-based fungicide may also help.

Downy mildew

The mildew is caused by a range of different fungi that thrive in damp, humid conditions.

- **Crops affected** A wide range of plants—particularly cabbages and other brassicas, grapes, lettuces, onions, peas, as well as root vegetables.
- **Symptoms** Yellow or brown patches develop on the upper surfaces of leaves, with off-white, fluffy mold on the undersides. As the patches spread, the leaves die. Once the disease takes hold and the plant is weakened, botrytis (see p.323) may follow.
- **Action** Remove and destroy infected leaves. Spray with a fungicide. Discourage the onset of the disease by sowing seeds thinly, ensuring good air circulation, and avoiding overwatering.

Fireblight

This is a serious bacterial disease that infects trees through their flowers. It is transmitted by rain splash, and may in time be lethal.

- **Crops affected** Apples, pears.
- **Symptoms** Flowers turn brown, wither, and die. Then the leaves do the same. As the disease spreads, stems and branches are affected too. Peeling back a strip of bark may reveal fiery, orange-red markings on the wood.
- **Action** Prune out and destroy all infected wood—or dig up and burn the entire tree.

Foot and root rots

These rots are caused by a range of different fungi, including the one responsible for damping off (see above). The fungi live in the soil and in standing water.

■ **Crops affected** Asparagus, beans, celery, zucchini, cucumbers, melons, peas, tomatoes, soft fruits.
■ **Symptoms** If the base of the plant stem is infected, it will darken and the tissues will start to shrink and die. Leaves and stems above the rot will wilt, turn yellow or brown, and die. Infected roots may turn black or brown and break up or rot.
■ **Action** Once the disease has taken hold there is no remedy. Immediately remove and destroy infected plants—and the soil in which they are growing. In the future, use fresh, sterile potting soil and thoroughly clean the seed trays or pots. Practice crop rotation (see pp.18–19) to avoid repeated attacks.

Fungal leaf spot
A range of different fungi attack the leaf tissues of infected plants. Some of the fungi target only specific types of crop. See also Bacterial leaf spot (p.322).
■ **Crops affected** Beets, blackberries, celeriac, celery, currants, gooseberries, raspberries, Swiss chard.
■ **Symptoms** Leaves develop spots of dead tissue that may be made up of concentric gray or brown rings, that sometimes look similar to bacterial leaf spots. The spots may spread and join up. Tiny, pinprick-sized, black or brown growths are the tell-tale signs that the disease is fungal, rather than bacterial leaf spot.
■ **Action** If you catch it early, the disease is unlikely to be fatal. Remove and destroy all infected leaves. Don't leave any lying around at the end of the year,

because the spores may survive the winter to reinfect plants in the following year.

Gray mold
See Botrytis (p.323).

Halo blight
The disease is caused by bacteria that may have lain dormant in the seeds. It spreads by means of rain, or in water from a watering can or hose, splashing from one leaf to the next.
■ **Crops affected** Dwarf French beans, runner beans.
■ **Symptoms** Leaves develop dark spots, each with a bright yellow "halo" around it. They then go yellow between the veins. As the yellow areas spread, the leaves die. Infected bean pods develop gray patches.
■ **Action** Remove and destroy infected plants, including seeds. Water the soil around any plants that appear unaffected, instead of splashing the foliage from above.

Honey fungus
The term covers a range of fungi; they can attack all fruits and some vegetables.
■ **Crops affected** All tree and bush fruits, globe artichokes, rhubarb, and strawberries.
■ **Symptoms** A warning sign may be wilting leaves or stunted foliage, but in some cases a plant may die surprisingly quickly and unexpectedly. Peel back the bark at the base of the trunk or stem, or inspect the roots, and you may find white fungal patches that smell of mushrooms. Sometimes, honey-colored toadstools grow around the base of infected trees.

Another sign is the presence of rhizomorphs (dark bootlace- or root-like extensions) that grow in the soil around roots or under the bark at the base of tree fruits.
■ **Action** Dig up and destroy all infected plants, including their root systems. Healthy plants have more resistance.

Leaf spot
See Bacterial leaf spot (p.322), Fungal leaf spot (see above).

Leek rust
The disease that causes rust on leeks and other members of the onion family is a fungus and, although common, it is rarely destructive.
■ **Crops affected** Chives, garlic, leeks, onions, shallots.
■ **Symptoms** Tiny, orange blisters appear on the outer leaves. When they burst, they spread orange, powdery spores, like rust.
■ **Action** Cut off and destroy affected leaves. Crops should still be edible. Rotate crops next year.

Onion neck rot
A fungus that causes onion bulbs to rot, usually after they have been lifted and are in storage. The disease can survive in the soil or may already be present in infected seeds and onion sets.
■ **Crops affected** Garlic, onions, shallots.
■ **Symptoms** Bulbs become soft and slightly transparent. A fluffy gray mold appears, particularly around the necks.
■ **Action** Check stored crops regularly and remove any that are infected. Rotate crops next year.

Onion white rot

In contrast to onion neck rot (see p.325), this fungal disease affects the bases and roots of bulbs while they're still in the soil. It is much more serious since it can survive in the soil for seven years or more, and there is no known cure.
- **Crops affected** Garlic, leeks, onions, shallots.
- **Symptoms** Leaves turn yellow and wilt. Fluffy, white mold and small, black growths appear around the bases of the bulbs.
- **Action** Dig up and destroy all infected crops, together with the surrounding soil. Be scrupulous about hygiene, and rotate crops (see pp.18–19) in following years.

Parsnip canker

The cankers, which damage roots, are caused by a fungus and are worse in wet, poorly drained soils.
- **Crops affected** Parsnips.
- **Symptoms** Orange-brown, purple, or black lesions, or cankers, appear on the roots.
- **Action** Rotate crops (see pp.18–19), improve soil drainage, and grow resistant varieties.

Pea leaf and pod spot

Various fungi may be responsible. They can survive from one year to the next in saved seeds and plant debris left in or on the ground.
- **Crops affected** Peas.
- **Symptoms** Small, yellow or brown spots appear on leaves, pods, and stems.
- **Action** Remove and destroy infected plants. Rotate crops.

Peach leaf curl

This fungus is the bane of any gardener who grows peaches and nectarines. However, although unsightly, it is not usually fatal.
- **Crops affected** Nectarines, peaches.
- **Symptoms** Leaves curl, blister, and turn yellow or orange-red. If left in place, they develop an off-white, powdery mold, turn brown, and drop. New leaves that open subsequently are unaffected, but the tree may be weakened by the initial loss of foliage.
- **Action** Remove and destroy infected leaves immediately. Spray with copper fungicide in winter—but not when the buds open—and cover with a temporary, rainproof sheet to prevent spores from spreading the disease.

Pear rust and Plum rust

See Rust (opposite).

Pear scab

See Scab (opposite).

Potato black leg

Black leg, so-called because of the discolored stems or haulms, is a bacterial disease; it is worse in damp conditions.
- **Crops affected** Potatoes.
- **Symptoms** Stems turn black and rot just above soil level. Leaves are smaller than normal, go yellow, and curl inward at the edges. Potato tubers themselves may rot.
- **Action** Remove and destroy diseased plants. The next year, rotate crops and buy certified disease-free seed potatoes.

Potato blight

This is the disease that all potato-growers dread, especially if the summer is warm and wet. Blight is a fungus, spread by wind and rain.
See also Tomato blight (p.328).
- **Crops affected** Potatoes.
- **Symptoms** The first signs are brown patches on the tips and edges of leaves, sometimes with white, fluffy mold underneath. As the leaves wither, stems or haulms develop dark patches and collapse. Underground, the potatoes also have dark patches, beneath which the flesh turns reddish brown, slimy, and smelly as it rots.
- **Action** Spray with a copper fungicide such as Bordeaux mixture as soon as conditions are warm and humid. Remove and destroy infected foliage if any symptoms appear. Next year, rotate crops and buy certified disease-free seed potatoes.

Potato common scab

Common scab is caused by a bacteria found in most soils, although it is less prevalent in acid soils that contain plenty of organic matter. The disease tends to be worst in hot, dry years.
- **Crops affected** Potatoes, beets, radishes, rutabagas, turnips.
- **Symptoms** Rough, brown, corky patches appear on the skins. They're unsightly, but can still be eaten if scraped or peeled well.
- **Action** To prevent attacks, water regularly, do not add lime, and grow resistant varieties.

Potato powdery scab

Powdery scab looks similar to common scab (see above), but is fungal rather than bacterial.
- **Crops affected** Potatoes, tomatoes.
- **Symptoms** Circular, brown patches on the skins of potatoes contain powdery spores that

spread into the soil. They may also appear on tomato roots.

■ **Action** Remove and destroy affected plants. In the next year, rotate crops (see pp.18–19); buy certified disease-free seed potatoes; grow resistant varieties.

Powdery mildew

This mildew is caused by a range of different fungi that thrive in dry soils. The spores spread in the air and by rain or water splash.

■ **Crops affected** A wide range of vegetables, as well as apples, gooseberries, grapes, peaches, plums, and strawberries.

■ **Symptoms** A white, powdery coating of mildew appears on affected leaves—usually on the upper surfaces, but sometimes on the undersides as well. The mildew may turn slightly purple. Leaves yellow and fall off; fruits may split. The plant's growth is impaired, and it may even die.

■ **Action** Remove and destroy infected leaves. Spray with a fungicide. Try preventing onset of the disease by sowing seeds thinly, ensuring good air circulation, and watering regularly.

Raspberry cane blight

Cane blight is caused by a soil-borne fungal infection that gets into the stems through wounds made by insects, pruning, or frost.

■ **Crops affected** Raspberries.

■ **Symptoms** Bark splits and peels just above soil level, and canes become brittle and may die.

■ **Action** Cut down and destroy all the infected canes. Spray the remaining canes with a copper-based fungicide, for example Bordeaux mixture.

Raspberry cane spot

This fungus targets many cane fruits. It is not uncommon.

■ **Symptoms** Purple spots with white centers appear on canes, as well as leaves, flowers, and sometimes fruit. In severe cases, the leaves may fall and canes may split and die.

■ **Crops affected** Blackberries, hybrid berries, and raspberries.

■ **Action** Cut down and destroy all infected canes.

Raspberry spur blight

Like cane blight (see above), raspberry spur blight is a fungal disease, but a less common and less serious one.

■ **Crops affected** Blackberries, hybrid berries, and raspberries.

■ **Symptoms** Leaves develop brown blotches and purple patches appear around new buds. Toward autumn, they turn from purple to dark brown, then silvery-gray with visible black spores. The following year's crop will be poor.

■ **Action** Cut down and destroy all infected canes. Thin out any overcrowded growth.

Raspberry viruses

A number of different viruses can attack raspberry canes. Once established, they are extremely difficult to eradicate.

■ **Crops affected** Blackberries, hybrid berries, and raspberries.

■ **Symptoms** Yellow mosaic patterns appear on leaves, which may curl downward at the edges and become smaller than normal. Plants grow and crop poorly.

■ **Action** Remove and destroy all infected plants. Do not grow cane fruit in the same position again.

Reversion

Also known as black currant reversion virus, this disease is widespread and results in lower-than-normal yields of berries. It is thought to be transmitted by big bud mite (see p.334).

■ **Crops affected** Black currants.

■ **Symptoms** Diagnosis is difficult since the only symptom may be smaller leaves and fewer flowers than uninfected plants.

■ **Action** Dig up and destroy diseased plants. Inspect bushes regularly; remove any swollen buds in order to control big bud mites.

Rust

Rusts, which vary in color from yellow and orange to brown, are all caused by fungi. They thrive in damp conditions. See also Leek rust (p.325).

■ **Crops affected** Vegetables such as asparagus, beans, leaf beets, lettuces, leeks and other members of the onion family, and fruit such as blackberries, gooseberries, pears, plums, and raspberries.

■ **Symptoms** Brightly colored, rustlike patches of spores, or pustules, on leaves and stems.

■ **Action** Cut off and destroy infected foliage. If necessary, spray with an appropriate fungicide. The following year, rotate crops (see pp.18–19), leave plenty of space for air to circulate easily, and grow resistant varieties.

Scab

These fungal growths may spread rapidly in damp, humid conditions.

■ **Crops affected** Apples, pears.

■ **Symptoms** Dark brown scabs appear on the skins of the fruits and may spread to cover almost the entire surface. Badly infected apples and pears are small and distorted, and may crack and rot. The leaves and stems may be affected too.

■ **Action** Cut out infected wood, remove all infected fruits, and collect up and destroy fallen leaves. If necessary, spray with an appropriate fungicide. In winter, prune to open out the tree and improve air circulation.

Sclerotinia

A pernicious fungus that causes numerous plants to wilt, become moldy, and then rot. It is worse in cool, damp conditions.

■ **Crops affected** A range of vegetable crops, including beans, cauliflowers, celery, chicory, cucumbers, Jerusalem artichokes, lettuces, peas, potatoes, and tomatoes. It also infects stored carrots and parsnips.

■ **Symptoms** Leaves yellow and wilt. Stems rot, often near their bases, and become covered with white, fluffy mold, inside which may be found black fungal bodies called sclerotia—these are the resting stage of the fungi. If left in the ground, they will generate spores in subsequent years.

■ **Action** There is no cure. Remove and destroy all infected plant material. Rotate crops (see pp.18–19) the next year.

Silver leaf

This fungal disease takes its name from the silvery sheen that develops on affected leaves. The fungus enters through fresh wounds in bark and pruning cuts.

■ **Crops affected** Cherries and plums; also apples, nectarines, peaches, and pears.

■ **Symptoms** Infected leaf tissues have a silvery sheen, and the leaves may brown at the edges. Infected wood is stained brown inside and branches and stems may die back. Purple, white, or brown fungus may colonize the dead wood.

■ **Action** Remove badly infected trees. Otherwise, prune out affected (stained) wood. In subsequent years, prune only in summer and be scrupulous about sterilizing tools.

Sooty mold

See Aphids (p.334).

Tomato blight

Blight in tomatoes is caused by the same fungus as blight in potatoes (see p.326).

■ **Crops affected** Tomatoes.

■ **Symptoms** Leaves develop brown patches, curl up, dry out, and die. Stems may also show patches and darken, and fruits turn brown, shrink, and rot.

■ **Action** Prevent attack by spraying with a copper fungicide, such as Bordeaux mixture, at the first indication of warm, wet, humid weather. Remove and destroy infected foliage as soon as symptoms appear. The next year, grow tomatoes elsewhere.

Tomato ghost spot

Ghost spot is a botrytis fungus (see p.323).

■ **Crops affected** Tomatoes.

■ **Symptoms** Tomatoes that have not yet ripened develop pale rings on their skins; the rings may turn yellow or orange.

■ **Action** Ghost spot is not fatal. Unaffected parts of the fruit are fine to eat.

Violet root rot

A fungus is the culprit. It thrives in warm, wet, acid soils, where it can survive for years.

■ **Crops affected** Asparagus, celery, and root vegetables such as beets, carrots, parsnips, and potatoes.

■ **Symptoms** Beneath ground, tubers and roots are covered in a dense mass of purple strands or threads to which the soil sticks. Velvety black fungal growths appear, and the roots themselves tend to rot. Above ground, infected plants discolor and grow poorly.

■ **Action** Violet root rot is a serious disease. There is no cure for it, and it can be very difficult to eradicate. Immediately remove and destroy infected plants—and the soil in which they grew. Rotate crops (see pp.18–19) to discourage any recurrence.

White blister

White blister is caused by a fungus that thrives in damp, humid air.

■ **Crops affected** Cabbages and other brassicas.

■ **Symptoms** Chalky or shiny, white spots or blisters appear on the undersides of leaves, and yellowish brown patches develop on the upper surfaces. The leaves and flowerheads may become badly distorted.

■ **Action** Remove and destroy infected leaves or plants. In future, choose resistant varieties, rotate crops (see pp.18–19), space out plants to encourage good air circulation and minimize humidity.

Malnutrition

Just like humans, plants need a well-balanced diet for healthy growth. If their diet is poor, they may suffer from all kinds of disorders that are associated with malnutrition. These can be serious, although they are notoriously hard to diagnose. Usually, plants are able to absorb all the nutrients they need from the soil. The three key elements are nitrogen (N), phosphorus (P), and potassium (K). They also need calcium (Ca), magnesium (Mg) and sulfur (S), although in smaller quantities. Together, these six make up the major soil-borne nutrients. In addition, further micronutrients, or trace elements, are required. They include boron, copper, iron, manganese, and molybdenum. These are as important as the major ones; but they are not needed in such large quantities.

Boron deficiency

Boron is easily washed out of light soils by heavy rain. Low levels may also be found in recently limed soils that are very alkaline or that have been allowed to dry out.
- **Crops affected** See below.
- **Symptoms** Different plants are affected in different ways.
Beets Rough, dead patches appear on the skins, and the hearts may rot.
Cabbages Leaves are distorted, and stems become hollow.
Carrots Roots split and cores become gray; the leaves turn yellow or pink.
Cauliflowers Brown patches appear on the heads, and stems and stalks become rough.
Celery Stems start to crack and turn red or brown inside.
Corn Kernels may not develop properly.
Lettuces Hearts fail to form.
Pears Distorted fruits.
Radishes Skins split and the radishes become woody.
Rutabagas and turnips Roots develop "brown heart," going brown or gray inside, sometimes in concentric rings.
Strawberries The berries are small and pale, and leaves are distorted with yellowed tips.
- **Action** Mix borax with horticultural sand and rake it into the soil before you sow or plant any new crops.

Calcium deficiency

In acid soils, calcium levels will most likely be low. Even where there is sufficient calcium, plants may be unable to absorb it if the ground is very dry.
- **Crops affected** See below.
- **Symptoms** Different plants are affected in different ways.
Brassicas The inner leaves turn brown.
Carrots Discolored spots, cracks, and craters in the roots.
Celery Central leaves turn black.
Lettuces Tips of leaves become brown and scorched-looking.
Potatoes Leaves roll up and shoots are spindly.
Tomatoes and sweet peppers See Blossom end rot (p.323).
Apples See Bitter pit (p.322).
- **Action** Add lime to the soil in order to increase the pH level (see p.47). Prevent soil from drying out by watering regularly when needed and apply a surface mulch to encourage moisture retention.

Copper deficiency

Copper deficiency is rare. It's most likely on peaty and other acid soils.
- **Crops affected** All vegetables and fruit.
- **Symptoms** Copper deficiency is hard to diagnose. Leaves may turn yellow or blue-green, and the plant may die back.
- **Action** Try applying a general-purpose fertilizer.

Iron deficiency

Iron deficiency often goes hand-in-hand with manganese deficiency, and is also known as lime-induced chlorosis. In fact, it's rare to find soil that is truly short of iron. What tends to happen is that the high levels of calcium in recently limed or very alkaline soils prevent plants from absorbing the iron that is available.

■ **Crops affected** All vegetables and particularly fruit such as apples, blackberries, blueberries, pears, and raspberries.

■ **Symptoms** Leaves yellow or go brown, starting at the edges, then spreading in between the veins. New leaves are worst affected.

■ **Action** Try to increase the acidity of the soil: apply some sulfur or aluminum sulfate and ferrous sulfate well before before you sow or plant, or spread an acid mulch of pine needles or chopped conifer bark. It is also possible to buy specialized, chelated or sequestered iron mixtures, which provide plants with iron in a readily available form when added to soil.

Magnesium deficiency

Heavy rain will readily wash magnesium out of light soils. Levels may also be low in acid soils or when potash or high-potassium fertilizers have been used to increase the amount of potassium in the soil.

■ **Crops affected** Vegetables such as cabbages and other brassicas, lettuces, potatoes, and tomatoes. Fruit such as apples, cherries, and grapes.

■ **Symptoms** Leaves turn yellow between the veins and around the edges, because there is insufficient magnesium to enable the plant to produce green chlorophyll. The yellowed areas may then turn red, purple, or brown.

■ **Action** Apply Epsom salts (magnesium sulfate), either as a foliar spray or spread over the soil.

Manganese deficiency

Insufficient manganese is most common on peaty soils or poorly drained, sandy soils with a pH of 6 or higher, and on alkaline soils.

■ **Crops affected** A wide range of vegetables, particularly beets, onions, parsnips, peas and beans, potatoes, spinach, and also fruit.

■ **Symptoms** Similar to those of iron deficiency, with which it is often associated. Leaves yellow in between the veins, and brown spots or patches may appear. New leaves are worst affected.

■ **Action** Avoid adding too much lime to soils where the problem has been identified. Spray any affected plants with a solution of manganese sulfate.

Molybdenum deficiency

Acid soils may prevent plants from absorbing molybdenum. This in turn interferes with the way they process nitrogen, and as a result growth is affected.

■ **Crops affected** Cauliflowers, sprouting broccoli, and other brassicas.

■ **Symptoms** Leaves turn yellow and are thin, narrow, and stringy, giving rise to the terms brassica "whiptail" and "wire stem." Heads may be very small or may fail to develop completely.

■ **Action** Add lime to acid soils in order to increase their pH—or avoid growing brassicas there. Spray affected plants or the soil

around them with ammonium or sodium molybdate solution.

Nitrogen deficiency

Heavily cropped, light soils—whether acid or alkaline—that do not contain much organic matter are most likely to have insufficient nitrogen. So too are soils in containers. Periods of heavy rain, which wash out nutrients, make the problem worse.

■ **Crops affected** All vegetables and fruit are vulnerable, except peas and beans, which absorb their own nitrogen from the air.

■ **Symptoms** Leaves are pale green or yellow, due to insufficient chlorophyll. Some may even turn pink, red, or purple. Older leaves near the base of the plant are the worst affected. The plants will be generally smaller than they should be, and may even be spindly or stunted.

■ **Action** Add lots of well-rotted compost, manure, or other organic material, or some high-nitrogen fertilizer. Plant green manures (see p.143) that take nitrogen from the air and "fix" it in their roots and for the soil. Grow peas and beans that don't need nitrogen-rich soils.

Phosphorus deficiency

Insufficient phosphorus is rare. It's most likely on acid soils, heavy clay, or deep peat after periods of prolonged heavy rain.

■ **Crops affected** All vegetables and fruit.

■ **Symptoms** Phosphorus stimulates fast-growing shoots and roots and without it plants grow poorly and may be slow to flower and fruit. Leaves may turn yellow, blue-green, or purple, and may drop prematurely.

■ **Action** Add a superphosphate fertilizer or organic bone meal.

Potassium deficiency

Potassium deficiency is most likely on light, sandy soils that do not contain much clay.

■ **Crops affected** A wide range of crops—particularly potatoes and tomatoes.

■ **Symptoms** Potassium is essential to the process by which plants absorb water and photosynthesize (manufacture food in green leaves). Without enough potassium, leaves curl, turn yellow, scorch at the edges, and may have purplish brown spots on the undersides. Flowering is poor; fruits are small, and plants may be more vulnerable to disease. Tomatoes may not ripen evenly.

■ **Action** Apply sulfate of potash fertilizer. Composted bracken or comfrey will also help restore potassium levels.

(far left to right) **Boron deficiency** in corn. **Iron deficiency** in a raspberry leaf. **Calcium deficiency** causes blossom end rot on tomatoes. **Magnesium deficiency** in potato foliage. **Nitrogen deficiency** has induced chlorosis in a tomato leaf. **Potassium deficiency** in raspberry foliage.

Common pests and parasites

1 Apple sawfly
Ribbonlike scars show where a sawfly maggot has tunneled just below the surface of the skin before eating its way into the core. See p.334.

2 Whitefly
Tiny flies with white, wedge-shaped wings lay eggs on leaves and feed on the sap. Shown here on a cabbage leaf. See p.339.

3 Carrot fly
Small white maggots tunnel into carrots (shown here), parsnips, and celery, and may ruin the whole crop. See p.335.

4 Slugs
Regulars in the top ten of many gardeners' most hated pests, both slugs and snails can decimate crops very quickly. See p.339.

5 Aphids
The wide range of different blackfly and greenfly includes species that target specific plant types, feeding on the sap and multiplying at alarming rates. See p.334.

6 Capsid bugs
Raised scabs on the skin of apples show where sap-sucking insects have fed on the young fruit. See p.335.

7 Red spider mite
Mites hatch and start to feed on the undersides of leaves, mottling the surface with a silvery-bronze sheen. See p.338.

8 Codling moth
The telltale exit hole in an apple or pear betrays where the caterpillar has departed after eating its way out from the core. See p.336.